WOMEN WRITING AND WRITING ABOUT WOMEN

THE OXFORD WOMEN'S SERIES

This volume, the third in the series, derives from papers presented at a seminar convened under the auspices of the Oxford University Women's Studies Committee, during the summer of 1978.

Other volumes

DEFINING FEMALES: The Nature of Women in Society
Edited by Shirley Ardener

FIT WORK FOR WOMEN
Edited by Sandra Burman

CONTROLLING WOMEN: The Normal and the Deviant
Edited by Bridget Hutter and Gillian Williams

WOMEN AND SPACE: Ground Rules and Social Maps
Edited by Shirley Ardener

WOMEN'S RELIGIOUS EXPERIENCE
Edited by Pat Holden

WOMEN AND PROPERTY — WOMEN AS PROPERTY
Edited by Renée Hirschon

WOMEN WRITING AND WRITING ABOUT WOMEN

EDITED BY MARY JACOBUS

CROOM HELM
London & Sydney
in association with the
OXFORD UNIVERSITY WOMEN'S STUDIES COMMITTEE

© 1979 Gillian Beer, Inga-Stina Ewbank, Elaine Feinstein,
John Goode, Mary Jacobus, Cora Kaplan, Laura Mulvey,
Elaine Showalter, Anne Stevenson

Croom Helm Ltd, Provident House, Burrell Row,
Beckenham, Kent, BR3 1AT

Croom Helm Australia Pty Ltd, Suite 4, 6th Floor,
64-76 Kippax Street, Surry Hills, NSW 2010, Australia

Reprinted 1984 and 1986

British Library Cataloguing in Publication Data

Women writing and writing about women.
   — (The Oxford women's series; 3).
   1. Women authors
   2. Literature, modern — 19th century —
History and criticism
   3. Literature, modern — 20th century —
History and criticism 4. Women in literature
   1. Jacobus, Mary II. Oxford University
Women's Studies Committee III. Series
809′.89287   PN471

ISBN 0-85664-745-4
ISBN 0-85664-979-1 Pbk

Printed and bound in Great Britain
by Billing & Sons Limited, Worcester.

CONTENTS

PREFACE AND ACKNOWLEDGEMENTS

The essays included in this book, with the exception of Elaine Feinstein's and my own, were originally delivered as lectures at Oxford
during the summer of 1978 under the general heading 'Women and
Literature', and formed part of a continuing interdisciplinary series on
women organised by the Oxford Women's Studies Committee. The
volume based on the first term's seminars was published as *Defining
Females*, edited by Shirley Ardener (Croom Helm, London, 1978);
the volume based on the second term as *Fit Work for Women*, edited
by Sandra Burman (Croom Helm, London, 1979). Royalties from all
three books are to be used to continue the seminar series and to
encourage Women's Studies at Oxford.

The aim of the essays included in this volume is not to present a
unified manifesto, but rather to bring together a spectrum of approaches
and positions within their common focus on writing by and about
women. Contributions differ widely, not only in critical method and
in the material they draw on — novels, poetry, drama, film — but also
in their theoretical and political stance. In addition, they include the
work of poets, translators, and a film-maker alongside that of critics,
attempting to bridge theory and practice. This book, therefore, contains many feminisms, many definitions of the relationship between
women and literature, between women and representation. The hope
is that its differences of view might fruitfully play off against one
another, initiating debate within its covers as well as indicating some of
the issues which animate current feminist literary criticism and theory.
Each essay is written from the individual standpoint of its author and
speaks for itself, but each raises problems that are of common concern
to the collection as a whole — problems ranging from the nature of a
female literary tradition to assessing the decisive innovations made by
women writers; from defining the specificity of women's language and
experience to exploring the implications of that 'specificity' for both
women and literature; from the extent to which representation
oppresses women to the ways in which it may be challenged from
within and transformed by women themselves. Above all, what does
writing as a woman mean, and to what extent does it involve a new
theory and a new practice? And finally — a question explicitly or
implicitly central to many of the essays — what is the proper scope

and method for feminist literary criticism itself?

For questions like these there are no easy answers. Rather than imposing an editorial overview, a brief introductory essay opens the question of women writing and writing about women. Elaine Showalter indicates some of the routes that may be taken by the feminist critic, and some of the dangers and divisions that may beset her. My own essay points to a different division within Charlotte Brontë's writing, as Romanticism and feminism threaten to subvert the stability of Victorian realism; while Cora Kaplan scrutinises the role of obscurity and fantasy in allowing Victorian women poets like Christina Rossetti and Emily Dickinson to represent alien psychic states and censored eroticism. Gillian Beer elucidates from the novels of George Eliot and Virginia Woolf the alternative patterns by which both evade the determinants of determinism as they impinge on the woman writer. For John Goode, the New Women herself opens up the structure of reality to expose its ideological basis, confronting the reader with the radical unintelligibility which is her real challenge. Discussing Ibsen's language in a sociolinguistic context, Inga-Stina Ewbank reaches the paradoxical conclusion that the specificity of women's language became for Ibsen not only a central aspect of his style, but a means to explore the human predicament. The question of a female literary tradition is raised in an unfamiliar context, that of the twentieth-century Russian women poets who look back to Akhmatova and Tsvetayeva, and whose work is translated and discussed by Elaine Feinstein. Anne Stevenson resumes the question of the role of women's experience in shaping their writing, analysing some of the conflicts which form both the background and the subject of her own poetry while finally refusing to be constrained by them. Laura Mulvey concludes the volume by placing its questions in the context of the evolution of feminist film theory and practice in the light of the conjunction of feminism and the *avant-garde*.

It remains to thank our audience, whose discussion often helped to clarify the issues as well as to argue them. I am also grateful to the contributors themselves, and to a number of other women who have been generous with their time and help: especially, to Ann Brandom for typing the manuscript, to Penny Boumelha for checking it, and to Jacqueline Simms for her thoughtful and energetic editorial comments; to Jo Garcia and other members of the Oxford Women's Studies Committee as well as to the convenors of the two preceding series of seminars, Shirley Ardener and Sandra Burman; and, last of all, to Keith

Hope, without whose generosity in making over funds to the University for Women's Studies the series could not have taken place.

Mary Jacobus
Lady Margaret Hall, Oxford

THE DIFFERENCE OF VIEW

Mary Jacobus

For George Eliot, as for her heroines (wrote Virginia Woolf),

> the burden and the complexity of womanhood were not enough; she must reach beyond the sanctuary and pluck for herself the strange bright fruits of art and knowledge. Clasping them as few women have ever clasped them, she would not renounce her own inheritance — *the difference of view, the difference of standard* . . .[1]

The terms here are worth lingering on; they bring to light a hidden problem as well as articulating an obvious one. The problem explicitly located is, in one way or another, the theme of many of the essays included in this book — or rather, their question: that is, the nature of women's access to culture and their entry into literary discourse. The demand for education ('the strange bright fruits of art and knowledge') provides the emancipatory thrust of much nineteenth- and twentieth-century feminism, and goes back to Mary Wollstonecraft's attempt to appropriate the language of Enlightenment Reason for her own sex in *The Rights of Woman*. But this access to a male-dominated culture may equally be felt to bring with it alienation, repression, division — a silencing of the 'feminine', a loss of women's inheritance. The problem, then, is not George Eliot's alone; it is that of women's writing (and of feminist literary criticism) itself. To propose a difference of view, a difference of standard — to begin to ask what the difference might be — is to call in question the very terms which constitute that difference.

The terms used by Virginia Woolf, therefore, also uncover something of the rift experienced by women writers in a patriarchal society, where language itself may re-inscribe the structures by which they are oppressed. Reaching beyond the sanctuary, transgressing the boundaries of womanhood (*womanhood*: the sacred hearth, at once home, womb and tomb; something is being stilled into silence, for the burden of womanhood is also the burden of the mystery) — the movement becomes an exit from the sacred into the profane. In this scheme, woman as silent bearer of ideology (virgin, wife, mother) is the necessary sacrifice to male secularity, worldliness, and tampering with forbidden knowledge. She is the term by which patriarchy creates a reserve of

10

purity and silence in the materiality of its traffic with the world and its noisy discourse. Feminised, the Faustian hero becomes a militant adventuress, Eve, plucking 'the strange bright fruits' that bring both knowledge and unhappiness. The archetypal gesture installs George Eliot in a specifically Judaeo-Christian drama, that of sin and death; the fall is from innocence (mindlessness?) into mortality. It's not surprising, therefore, that Virginia Woolf should end her essay with what amounts to a funeral oration. For her, George Eliot was literally worn into the grave by the battle with 'sex and health and convention' which attended her quest for 'more knowledge and more freedom'.

In this traditional drama, a lively sense of sin is matched with a weighty sense of ancient female suffering and hopeless desire; but George Eliot's heroines, Virginia Woolf tells us, no longer suffer in silence:

> The ancient consciousness of woman, charged with suffering and sensibility, and for so many ages dumb, seems in them to have brimmed and overflowed and uttered a demand for something — they scarcely know what — for something that is perhaps incompatible with the facts of human existence.[2]

(That notion of dumbness and utterance, of demand for an impossible desire, forms a recurrent motif in both women's writing and feminist literary criticism.) What is striking here is the association of ancient suffering and modern desire with women's inheritance, as if they were almost synonymous. This is elegy, not affirmation. Elegy which, in Virginia Woolf's case, one might justifiably link with the death of a mother or mothering step-sister. Our mothers were killed by the burden and the complexity of womanhood; or, like George Eliot, died in giving birth to their writing (as Dorothea rests in an unvisited tomb in order that 'George Eliot' may write her epitaph). Such, at any rate, seems to be the melancholy inference. It's surely significant that for at least one woman looking back at another, the price of combining womanhood and writing seemed so high — that the transgression of writing seemed to bring with it mortal consequences; the sacrifice not only of happiness, but of life itself.

Contemporary feminist criticism is more likely to stress pleasure than suffering — the freeing of repressed female desire; *jouissance* and *'la mère qui jouit'* (no longer barred from sexual pleasure) as against the burden of womanhood. Recent French writing about women and literature, marked as it is by the conjunction of neo-Freudian psychoanalysis and structuralism, has particularly tended to diagnose the repression of women's desire by representation itself, and by the order of language as instated by the Law of the Father: the Symbolic order, predicated on lack and castration.[3] In this theoretical scheme, femininity itself — heterogeneity, Otherness — becomes the repressed term by which discourse is made possible. The feminine takes its place with the absence, silence, or incoherence that discourse represses; in what Julia Kristeva would call the *semiotic*, the pre-Oedipal phase of rhythmic, onomatopoeic babble which precedes the Symbolic but remains inscribed in those pleasurable and rupturing aspects of language identified particularly with *avant-garde* literary practice. But here again, there's a problem for feminist criticism. Women's access to discourse involves submission to phallocentricity, to the masculine and the Symbolic: refusal, on the other hand, risks re-inscribing the feminine as a yet more marginal madness or nonsense. When we speak (as feminist writers and theorists often do) of the need for a special language for women, what then do we mean?

Not, surely, a refusal of language itself; nor a return to a specifically feminine linguistic domain which in fact marks the place of women's oppression and confinement. Rather, a process that is played out within language, across boundaries. The dream of a language freed from the Freudian notion of castration, by which female difference is defined as lack rather than Otherness, is at first sight essentially theoretical, millennial and Utopian. Its usefulness lies in allying feminism and the *avant-garde* in a common political challenge to the very discourse which makes them possible; the terms of language itself, as well as the terms of psychoanalysis and of literary criticism, are called in question — subverted from within. Woman and artist, the feminine and the *avant-garde*, are elided in the privileged zone of contemporary intellectual and aesthetic concern: writing. Such a move has the advantage of freeing off the 'feminine' from the religion-bound, ultimately conservative and doom-ridden concept of difference-as-opposition which underlies Virginia Woolf's reading of the 'case' of George Eliot. *Difference* is redefined, not as male *versus* female — not as biologically constituted — but as a multiplicity, joyousness and heterogeneity which is that of textuality itself. Writing, the production of meaning, becomes the site both of challenge and Otherness; rather than (as in more traditional approaches) simply yielding the themes and representation of female oppression. *Difference*, in fact, becomes a traversal of the boundaries inscribed in Virginia Woolf's terms, but a traversal that exposes these very boundaries for what they are — the product of phallocentric discourse and of women's relation to patriarchal culture. Though necessarily working within 'male' discourse, women's writing (in this scheme) would work ceaselessly to deconstruct it: to write what cannot be written.

So much for one formulation of the question: what is the nature (the difference) of women's writing? Another way to pose the question is to explore the extent to which patriarchal representation, by contrast, 'silences' women — the extent to which *woman* or *womanhood*, considered not as an image but as a sign, becomes the site of both contradiction and repression. For D.H. Lawrence, woman is 'the unutterable which man must forever continue to try to utter'; she achieves womanhood at the point where she is silenced (like Sue Bridehead) and installed within the sanctuary.[4] If writing is a transgression punishable by death, being written about, by however loving a Father, can also prove fatal. Take the disquieting way in which Hardy, in a famous scene from *Tess of the D'Urbervilles*, reveals the sign *woman* to be a rich source of mythic confusion, ideological contradiction, and erotic fascination:

> She was yawning, and he saw the red interior of her mouth as if it had been a snake's. She had stretched one arm so high above her coiled-up cable of hair that he could see its satin delicacy above the sunburn; her face was flushed with sleep, and her eyelids hung heavy over their pupils. The brim-fulness of her nature breathed from her. It was a moment when a woman's soul is more incarnate than at any other time; when the most spiritual beauty bespeaks itself flesh; and sex takes the outside place in the presentation. (XXVII)

Sex having taken the outside place in the presentation, it's not surprising that within a short space Tess should become, first feline, and then Eve. The language of incarnation (body and soul, presence and absence) signals an underlying structure which comes near to collapse before the threat of female sexuality. Though Hardy seems to be salvaging Tess's body for spirituality (the vessel is brim-full), the yawning mouth opens up a split in the very terms he uses. The incarnate state of Tess's soul appears to be as close to sleep — to unconsciousness — as is compatible with going about her work. At the same time, the snake-mouth marks the point of (desired) entry to an interior which is offered to us as simply yet more body (she is all red inside, *not* all soul). Fascination with this unknown, unrepresentable, interiorised sexuality is surely at the centre of male fantasies of seduction and engulfment. No wonder that Hardy goes on to make Tess, not the object of male gaze, but the mirror in which the male is reflected (*'she* regarded *him* as Eve at her second waking might have regarded Adam'; my italics): Otherness is domesticated, made safe, through narcissism — the female mouth can't utter, only receive and confirm the male.

Tess's silence, like her purity, makes female desire dumb; places her on the side of unconsciousness and, finally, death. 'Shut up already' might be the hidden message which a feminist critique uncovers. But to stop at such readings (or at exposing the reproduction of sexist ideology by male critics) is to take only the first step towards uttering an alternative. Utterance, though, brings the problem home for women writers (as for feminist critics). The options polarise along familiar lines: appropriation or separatism. Can women adapt traditionally male-dominated modes of writing and analysis to the articulation of female oppression and desire? Or should we rather reject tools that may simply re-inscribe our marginality and deny the specificity of our experience, instead forging others of our own? — reverting, perhaps, to the traditionally feminine in order to revalidate its forms (formlessness?) and preoccupations — rediscovering subjectivity; the language of feeling; ourselves. The risks on either side are illuminatingly played out in the writing of feminism's founding mother herself: Mary Wollstonecraft. *The Rights of Woman*, in claiming sense for women rather than sensibility, pays a price that is reflected in its own prose. Putting herself outside the confines of a despised femininity, aligning herself with 'sense', Mary Wollstonecraft also eschews 'pretty feminine phrases' as a male conspiracy designed to soften female slavery. Linguistic pleasure (literary language) is placed on the side of the feminine; banned, like female desire:

> I shall disdain to cull my phrases or polish my style. I aim at being useful, and sincerity will render me unaffected; for, wishing rather to persuade by the force of my arguments than dazzle by the elegance of my language, I shall not waste my time in rounding periods, or in fabricating the turgid bombast of artificial feelings, which, coming from the head, never reach the heart. I shall be employed about things, not words! and, anxious to render my sex more respectable members of society, I shall try to avoid that flowery diction which has slided from essays into novels, and from novels into familiar letters and conversations. ('Author's Introduction')

A swagger of busy self-presentation makes this as much the creation of an alienated persona as it is a feminist preface to *Lyrical Ballads*. A plain-speaking utilitarian speaks not so much *for* women, or *as* a woman, but *against* them — over their dead bodies, and over (having attempted to cast it out) the body of the text too: 'I shall be employed about things, not words!'

Speaking both for and as a woman (rather than 'like' a woman): this is the problem of women's writing. For the feminist critic, the problem may resolve itself as one of style. For Mary Wollstonecraft, the solution lay in fiction that gave her access not only (paradoxically) to her own situation as a woman, but to literarity. *The Wrongs of Woman* inverts both the title and the assumptions of her earlier essay in order to show how, if 'sense' excludes women, 'sensibility' confines them — yet offers a radical challenge to patriarchy; a challenge which it must repress. (When the heroine pleads her own case in a court of law, the judge alludes to 'the fallacy of letting women plead their feelings . . . What virtuous woman thought of her feelings?', thereby exposing the double-bind.) The prison of sensibility is created by patriarchy to contain women; thus they experience desire without Law, language without power. Marginalised, the language of feeling can only ally itself with insanity — an insanity which, displaced into writing, produces a moment of imaginative and linguistic excess over-brimming the container of fiction, and swamping the distinction between author and character:

> What is the view of the fallen column, the mouldering arch, of the most exquisite workmanship, when compared with this living memento of the fragility, the instability, of reason, and the wild luxuriancy of noxious passions? Enthusiasm turned adrift, like some rich stream overflowing its banks, rushes forward with destructive velocity, inspiring a sublime concentration of thought. *Thus thought Maria* — These are the ravages over which humanity must ever mournfully ponder . . . It is not over the decaying productions of the mind, embodied with the happiest art, we grieve most bitterly. The view of what has been done by man, produces a melancholy, yet aggrandizing, sense of what remains to be achieved by human intellect; but a mental convulsion, which, like the devastation of an earthquake, throws all the elements of thought and imagination into confusion, makes contemplation giddy, and we fearfully ask on what ground we ourselves stand.[5]

This is what it means for women to be on the side of madness as well as silence. Like the rich stream overflowing its banks, a wash of desire throws all the elements of thought and imagination into confusion. By contrast with the ruins of (male) cultural imperialism, the earthquake is feminised; demands 'on what ground we ourselves stand'; opens on to a feminist sublime where all foundations are called in question.

Mary Wollstonecraft's concern in this passage for 'words', not 'things', makes it a crucial moment for both women's writing and feminist literary criticism. A mental convulsion breaches the impasse between undifferentiated disappearance into a 'male' text and the prison of sensibility. Rejecting the essentialism that keeps women subjected as well as subjective, it also rejects mastery and dominance. Madness imagined as revolution, or the articulation of Utopian desire ('a demand for something − they scarcely know what'), represent gestures past the impasse played out in Mary Wollstonecraft's prose. In writing, such gestures may release possibilities repressed by a dominant ideology or its discourse. The transgression of literary boundaries − moments when structures are shaken, when language refuses to lie down meekly, or the marginal is brought into sudden focus, or intelligibility itself refused − reveal not only the conditions of possibility within which women's writing exists, but what it would be like to revolutionise them. In the same way, the moment of desire (the moment when the writer most clearly installs herself in her writing) becomes a refusal of mastery, an opting for openness and possibility, which can in itself make women's writing a challenge to the literary structures it must necessarily inhabit.

'Thus thought Maria' − the container overflowed by authorial Enthusiasm − has its analogue in a famous 'awkward break' noticed by Virginia Woolf. Her example is Charlotte Brontë's intrusion into *Jane Eyre* with what *A Room of One's Own* rightly identifies as a protest against the confinement of the nineteenth-century woman writer:

It is in vain to say human beings ought to be satisfied with tranquillity: they must have action; and they will make it if they cannot find it . . . Women are supposed to be very calm generally: but women feel just as men feel; they need exercise for their faculties, and a field for their efforts as much as their brothers do; they suffer from too rigid a restraint, too absolute a stagnation, precisely as men would suffer . . . It is thoughtless to condemn them, or laugh at them, if they seek to do more or learn more than custom has pronounced necessary for their sex.

When thus alone, I not unfrequently heard Grace Poole's laugh
. . . [6]

('That is an awkward break, I thought', comments Virginia Woolf.) The author herself has burst the bounds of 'too rigid a restraint' — making action if she cannot find it. By a breach of fictional decorum, writing enacts protest as well as articulating it. It is not simply that the excess of energy disrupts the text; it is that the disruption reveals what the novel cannot say within its legitimate confines, and hence reveals its fictionality. The unacceptable text gets the blue pencil from Virginia Woolf ('the woman who wrote those pages . . . will write in a rage where she should write calmly . . . She will write of herself where she should write of her characters. She is at war with her lot'); but it also opens up a rift in her own seamless web. What she herself cannot say without loss of calmness (rage has been banned in the interests of literature) is uttered instead by another woman writer. The overflow in *Jane Eyre* washes into *A Room of One's Own*. This oblique recuperation of feminist energy has implications for feminist criticism as well as for fiction; might, in fact, be said to characterise the practice of the feminist critic, for whom the relation between author and text (her own text) is equally charged. Editing into her writing the outburst edited out of Charlotte Brontë's, Virginia Woolf creates a point of instability which unsettles her own urbane and polished decorum. The rift exposes the fiction of authorial control and objectivity, revealing other possible fictions, other kinds of writing; exposes, for a moment, its own terms.

The slippage here is both seductive and threatening. Seductive, because passion is involved; threatening, because the structures on which both fiction and criticism depend are seen to be built on words alone. And perhaps the correction of authorial transgression — the domestication of authorial desire — may be necessary in the interests of writing itself. Take a significant moment of self-censorship like that which closes the 'Finale' of *Middlemarch*. George Eliot's compassionately magisterial verdict on the 'determining acts' of Dorothea's life ('the mixed result of young and noble impulse struggling amidst the conditions of an imperfect social state, in which great feelings will often take the aspect of error, and great faith the aspect of illusion') cancels what had originally been 'an awkward break' in the final pages of the first edition:

> They were the mixed results of young and noble impulse struggling under prosaic conditions. Among the many remarks passed on her mistakes, it was never said in the neighbourhood of Middlemarch that such mistakes could not have happened if the society into

which she was born had not smiled on . . . modes of education which make a woman's knowledge another name for motley ignorance – on rules of conduct which are in flat contradiction with its own loudly-asserted beliefs. While this is the social air in which mortals begin to breathe, there will be collisions such as those in Dorothea's life, where great feelings will take the aspect of error, and great faith the aspect of illusion.[7]

Authorial indignation risks turning the neighbourhood of Middlemarch into 'social air', uncovering fiction as polemic. Whether the cancellation springs from loss of nerve or aesthetic judgement, it makes George Eliot (so to speak) the heir of Virginia Woolf as well as Charlotte Brontë. In doing so, it opens up the possibility of the author's dissolution into her own text; the closing sentences of the novel point beyond the 'Finale' to their own writing – to the full nature that has its strength broken by being diverted into channels whose effect is incalculably diffusive:

> Her finely-touched spirit had still its fine issues, though they were not widely visible. Her full nature, like that river of which Cyrus broke the strength, spent itself in channels which had no great name on the earth. But the effect of her being on those around her was incalculably diffusive: for the growing good of the world is partly dependent on unhistoric acts; and that things are not so ill with you and me as they might have been, is half owing to the number who lived faithfully a hidden life, and rest in unvisited tombs. ('Finale')

Earlier, George Eliot has referred to Casaubon's turgid scholarship as 'minor monumental productions'; monuments to dead languages. By contrast with this sterile imperialism (Casaubon *versus* the world), we have the unhistoric acts that make for growing good. Though a new St Theresa will find no conventual life to reform, a new Antigone no Creon to oppose with self-immolation ('the medium in which their ardent deeds took shape is forever gone'), still, the writer may find another 'medium' of her own for ardent deeds. Dorothea's hidden life and entombment make her a silent reformer, an unremembered protester; but her silence and anonymity are the sacrifice which allows 'George Eliot' speech and name.

If the gain seems marginal, this may be because writing is itself marginal, unhistoric; if diffusive, incalculably so. But the possibility glimpsed at the end of *Middlemarch* – that of Enthusiasm overflowing into ink – points to the quietly subversive power of writing, its power to destabilise the ground on which we stand. In *A Room of One's Own*, Virginia Woolf dissolves 'truth' (the withheld 'nugget of truth') into 'the lies that flow from my pen'; the subject of women and writing becomes a fiction: 'I propose, making use of all the liberties and licences of a novelist, to tell you the story . . .'[8] As hard fact dissolves into fluid fiction, so the authorial 'I' becomes 'only a convenient term for somebody who has no real being'; many 'I's', many Marys, ('Mary Beton, Mary Seton, Mary Carmichael' and I) — a plurality contrasted to the unified 'I' which falls as a dominating phallic shadow across the male page, like Casaubon's monumental egotism. And as the subject ('I') is dissolved into writing, so boundaries themselves are called into question; rendered, not *terra firma*, but fiction too. Once returned to its proper medium (the Cam), the thought-fish which swims through *A Room of One's Own* 'as it darted and sank, and flashed hither and thither, set up such a wash and tumult of ideas that it was impossible to sit still'. The story becomes the narrative of its own inception, then of the arrest of verbal energy — this darting, flashing, linguistic play — by the figure of a man, representative of the Law, of the phallic 'I' that bars and bounds:

> It was thus that I found myself walking with extreme rapidity across a grass plot. Instantly a man's figure rose to intercept me. Nor did I at first understand that the gesticulations of a curious-looking object, in a cut-away coat and evening shirt, were aimed at me. His face expressed horror and indignation. Instinct rather than reason came to my help; he was a Beadle; I was a woman. This was the turf; there was the path. Only the Fellows and Scholars are allowed here; the gravel is the place for me. Such thoughts were the work of a moment. As I regained the path the arms of the Beadle sank, his face assumed its usual repose . . .[9]

The protest against male exclusiveness is obvious enough; so is the comical reduction of an educational institution to a grass plot and a clockwork beadle. Acquiescing in the terms of her trespass, Virginia Woolf yet shows, with pleasurable obliqueness (via her short cut), that these terms are arbitrary — a matter of cut-away coats and gravel paths.

Virginia Woolf's satire, in delineating the confines within which women must walk ('This was the turf; there was the path') traverses and exposes them. The story she tells is in fact that of her own oblique relation, as a woman writer, to the dominant culture and to patriarchal institutions (she labels them Oxbridge, the educational system which inscribes her marginality). At once within this culture and outside it, the woman writer experiences not only exclusion, but an internalised split. Elsewhere in *A Room of One's Own* she puts it like this:

> if one is a woman one is often surprised by a sudden splitting off of consciousness, say in walking down Whitehall, when from being the natural inheritor of that civilisation, she becomes, on the contrary, outside of it, alien and critical.[10]

'Alien and critical' — the stance glimpsed behind the urbane and playful style of *A Room of One's Own*. Though Virginia Woolf never fails to remind us that the matter of inheritance is absolutely a matter of access to power, property and education, an experienced division forms part of that inheritance too. To recognise both the split and the means by which it is constituted, to challenge its terms while necessarily working within them — that is the hidden narrative of the trespass on the grass. But what about that elusive thought-fish? For Virginia Woolf, rage drove it into hiding; the rage that for her distorts Charlotte Brontë's fiction ('She will write in a rage where she should write calmly'). It is in this light, perhaps, that we should re-read her famous remarks about androgyny — not as a naïve attempt to transcend the determinants of gender and culture (though it is that), not as a Romantic enshrining of Shakespearian creativity (though it is that too), but rather as a harmonising gesture, a simultaneous enactment of desire and repression by which the split is closed with an essentially Utopian vision of undivided consciousness. The repressive male/female opposition which 'interferes with the unity of the mind' gives way to a mind paradoxically conceived of not as one, but as heterogeneous, open to the play of difference: 'resonant and porous . . . it transmits emotion without impediment . . . it is naturally creative, incandescent, and undivided.'[11] That's as good a description as one could wish, not of the mind, but of Virginia Woolf's own prose — and of the play of difference perpetually enacted within writing.

The gesture towards androgyny is millennial, like all dreams of another language or mode of being; but its effect is to remove the area of debate (and the trespass) from biological determination to the field of signs; from gender to representation ('words' not 'things'). And in holding open other possibilities — Otherness itself — such writing posits 'the difference of view' as a matter of rewriting. 'A woman writing thinks back through her mothers'; thinking back through the mother becomes at once recuperation and revision. The rediscovery of a female literary tradition need not mean a return to specifically 'female' (that is, potentially confining) domains, any more than the feminist colonising of Marxist, psychoanalytic, or post-structuralist modes of thought necessarily means a loss of that alien and critical relation which is one aspect of women's inheritance. Rather, they involve a recognition that all attempts to inscribe female difference within writing are a matter of inscribing women within fictions of one kind or another (whether literary, critical, or psychoanalytic); and hence, that what is at stake for both women writing and writing about women is the rewriting of these fictions — the work of revision which makes 'the difference of view' a question rather than an answer, and a question to be asked not simply of women, but of writing too.

Notes

1. *Collected Essays*, vol. i (London, 1966), p. 204; my italics.
2. Ibid., p. 204.
3. See Elaine Marks, 'Women and Literature in France', *Signs: Journal of Women in Culture and Society*, vol. iii (1978), pp. 833-42 for a discussion of the work of recent French feminist literary and psychoanalytic theorists, especially Hélène Cixous, *La Jeune Née* (Paris, 1975) and 'Le Rire da la Méduse', translated as 'The Laugh of the Medusa' by Keith and Paula Cohen, *Signs:*, vol. i (1976), pp. 875-93; Luce Irigaray, *Speculum de l'autre femme* (Paris, 1974) and *Ce Sexe qui n'en est pas un* (Paris, 1977); Julia Kristeva, *La Révolution du language poétique* (Paris, 1974), *Polylogue* (Paris, 1977) and, from *La Révolution du language poétique*, 'Phonétique, phonologie et bases pulsionelles', translated as 'Phonetics, Phonology and Impulsional Bases' by Caren Greenberg, *Diacritics*, vol. iv (Fall 1974), pp. 33-7. See also Michèle Montrelay, 'Inquiry into Femininity', translated by Parveen Adams, *m/f*, vol. i (1978), pp. 83-101, from *L'Ombre et le nom: sur la féminité* (Paris, 1977). The work of Luce Irigaray and Julia Kristeva is reviewed and compared by Josette Feral, 'Antigone or *The Irony of the Tribe*', *Diacritics*, vol. viii (Fall 1978), pp. 2-14. See also Stephen Heath, 'Difference', *Screen*, vol. xix (1978), pp. 51-112, esp. pp. 78-83 for a discussion of the theoretical implications raised by these writers.
4. See 'Study of Thomas Hardy' in E.D. Macdonald (ed.), *Phoenix: The Posthumous Papers of D.H. Lawrence* (London, 1967), p. 496.
5. Gary Kelly (ed.), *Mary, A Fiction and The Wrongs of Woman* (London, 1976), pp. 83-4; my italics.
6. *A Room of One's Own* (London, 1929), p. 104 (*Jane Eyre*, XII); my italics.
7. *Middlemarch* (4 vols., Edinburgh and London, 1871-2), vol. iv, pp. 369-70.
8. *A Room of One's Own*, p. 7.
9. Ibid., p. 9.
10. Ibid., p. 146.
11. Ibid., p. 148.

1 TOWARDS A FEMINIST POETICS

Elaine Showalter

In 1977, Leon Edel, the distinguished biographer of Henry James, contributed to a London symposium of essays by six male critics called
Contemporary Approaches to English Studies. Professor Edel presented
his essay as a dramatised discussion between three literary scholars who
stand arguing about art on the steps of the British Museum:

> There was Criticus, a short, thick-bodied intellectual with spectacles,
> who clung to a pipe in his right hand. There was Poeticus, who
> cultivated a Yeatsian forelock, but without the eyeglasses and the
> ribbon. He made his living by reviewing and had come to the B.M. to
> look up something or other. Then there was Plutarchus, a lean and
> lanky biographer wearing a corduroy jacket.

As these three gentlemen are warming to their important subject, a taxi
pulls up in front of them and releases 'an auburn-haired young woman,
obviously American, who wore ear-rings and carried an armful of
folders and an attaché case'. Into the Museum she dashes, leaving the
trio momentarily wondering why femininity requires brainwork. They
are still arguing when she comes out, twenty-one pages later.[1]

I suppose we should be grateful that at least one woman — let us call
her Critica — makes an appearance in this gathering, even if she is not
invited to join the debate. I imagine that she is a feminist critic — in
fact if I could afford to take taxis to the British Museum, I would think
they had perhaps seen me — and it is pleasing to think that while the
men stand gossiping in the sun, she is inside hard at work. But these are
scant satisfactions when we realise that of all the approaches to English
studies current in the 1970s, feminist criticism is the most isolated and
the least understood. Members of English departments who can
remember what Harold Bloom means by *clinamen*, and who know the
difference betweeen Tartu and Barthian semiotics, will remark that they
are against feminist criticism and consequently have never read any.
Those who have read it, often seem to have read through a glass darkly,
superimposing their stereotypes on the critical texts. In his introduction
to Nina Auerbach's subtle feminist analysis of *Dombey and Son* in the
Dickens Studies Annual, for example, Robert Partlow discusses the

deplorable but non-existent essay of his own imagining:

> At first glance, Nina Auerbach's essay . . . might seem to be a
> case of special pleading, another piece of women's lib propaganda
> masquerading as literary criticism, but it is not quite that . . . such
> an essay could have been . . . ludicrous . . . it could have seen dark
> phallic significance in curving railroad tracks and upright church
> pews — but it does not.[2]

In contrast to Partlow's caricature (feminist criticism will naturally
be obsessed with the phallus), there are the belligerent assumptions of
Robert Boyers, in the Winter 1977 issue of the influential American
quarterly *Partisan Review*, that it will be obsessed with destroying great
male artists. In 'A Case Against Feminist Criticism', Boyers used a single
work, Joan Mellen's *Women and Their Sexuality in the New Film*
(1973), as an example of feminist deficiency in 'intellectual honesty'
and 'rigour'. He defines feminist criticism as the 'insistence on asking
the same questions of every work and demanding ideologically satisfactory answers to those questions as a means of evaluating it', and
concludes his diatribe thus:

> Though I do not think anyone has made a credible case for feminist
> criticism as a viable alternative to any other mode, no one can
> seriously object to feminists continuing to try. We ought to demand
> that such efforts be minimally distinguished by intellectual candour
> and some degree of precision. This I have failed to discover in most
> feminist criticism.[3]

Since his article makes its 'case' so recklessly that Joan Mellen brought
charges for libel, and the *Partisan Review* was obliged to print a retrac-
tion in the following issue, Boyers hardly seems the ideal champion to
enter the critical lists under the twin banners of honesty and rigour.
Indeed, his terminology is best understood as a form of intimidation,
intended to force women into using a discourse more acceptable to
the academy, characterised by the 'rigour' which my dictionary defines
as strictness, a severe or cruel act, or 'state of rigidity in living tissues or
organs that prevents response to stimuli'. In formulating a feminist
literary theory, one ought never to expect to appease a Robert Boyers.
And yet these 'cases' cannot continue to be settled, one by one, out of
court. The absence of a clearly articulated theory makes feminist
criticism perpetually vulnerable to such attacks, and not even feminist

critics seem to agree what it is that they mean to profess and defend.

A second obstacle to the articulation of a feminist critical practice is the activist's suspicion of theory, especially when the demand for clarification comes from sources as patently sexist as the egregiously named Boyers and Mailers of the literary quarterlies. Too many literary abstractions which claim to be universal have in fact described only male perceptions, experiences and options, and have falsified the social and personal contexts in which literature is produced and consumed. In women's fiction, the complacently precise and systematising male has often been the target of satire, especially when his subject is Woman. George Eliot's impotent structuralist Casaubon is a classic instance, as is Mr Ramsay, the self-pitying philosopher in Virginia Woolf's *To the Lighthouse*. More recently Doris Lessing's Professor Bloodrot in *The Golden Notebook* lectures confidently on orgasm in the female swan; as Bloodrot proceeds, the women in the audience rise one by one and leave. What women have found hard to take in such male characters is their self-deception, their pretence to objectivity, their emotion parading as reason. As Adrienne Rich comments in *Of Woman Born*, 'the term "rational" relegates to its opposite term all that it refuses to deal with, and thus ends by assuming itself to be purified of the nonrational, rather than searching to identify and assimilate its own surreal or non-linear elements'.[4] For some radical feminists, methodology itself is an intellectual instrument of patriarchy, a tyrannical Methodolatry which sets implicit limits to what can be questioned and discussed. 'The God Method', writes Mary Daly,

> is in fact a subordinate deity, serving higher powers. These are social and cultural institutions whose survival depends upon the classification of disruptive and disturbing information as nondata. Under patriarchy, Method has wiped out women's questions so totally that even women have not been able to hear and formulate our own questions, to meet our own experiences.[5]

From this perspective, the academic demand for theory can only be heard as a threat to the feminist need for authenticity, and the visitor looking for a formula he or she can take away without personal encounter is not welcome. In the United States, where Women's Studies programmes offer degree options in nearly 300 colleges and universities, there are fears that feminist analysis has been co-opted by academia, and counter-demands that we resist the pressure to assimilate. Some believe that the activism and empiricism of feminist criticism is its greatest strength, and point to the flourishing international women's press, to new feminist publishing houses, and to writing collectives and manifestoes. They are afraid that if the theory is perfected, the movement will be dead. But these defensive responses may also be rationalisations of the psychic barriers to women's participation in theoretical discourse. Traditionally women have been cast in the supporting rather than the starring roles of literary scholarship. Whereas male critics in the twentieth century have moved to centre-stage, openly contesting for primacy with writers, establishing coteries and schools, speaking unabashedly (to quote Geoffrey Hartman) of their 'pen-envy',[6] women are still too often translators, editors, hostesses at the conference and the Festschrift, interpreters; to congratulate ourselves for working patiently and anonymously for the coming of Shakespeare's sister, as Virginia Woolf exhorted us to do in 1928, is in a sense to make a virtue of necessity. In this essay, therefore, I would like to outline a brief taxonomy, if not a poetics, of feminist criticism, in the hope that it will serve as an introduction to a body of work which needs to be considered both as a major contribution to English studies and as part of an interdisciplinary effort to reconstruct the social, political and cultural experience of women.

Feminist criticism can be divided into two distinct varieties. The first type is concerned with *woman as reader* – with woman as the consumer of male-produced literature, and with the way in which the hypothesis of a female reader changes our apprehension of a given text, awakening us to the significance of its sexual codes. I shall call this kind of analysis the *feminist critique*, and like other kinds of critique it is a historically grounded inquiry which probes the ideological assumptions of literary phenomena. Its subjects include the images and stereotypes of women in literature, the omissions and misconceptions about women in criticism, and the fissures in male-constructed literary history. It is also concerned with the exploitation and manipulation of the female audience, especially in popular culture and film; and with the analysis of woman-as-sign in semiotic systems. The second type of feminist criticism is concerned with *woman as writer* – with woman as the producer of textual meaning, with the history, themes, genres and structures of literature by women. Its subjects include the psychodynamics of female creativity; linguistics and the problem of a female language; the trajectory of the individual or collective female literary career; literary history; and, of course, studies of particular writers and works. No term exists in English for such a specialised discourse, and so I have adapted the French term *la gynocritique*: *'gynocritics'* (although the significance of the male pseudonym in the history of women's writing also suggested the term 'georgics').

The feminist critique is essentially political and polemical, with theoretical affiliations to Marxist sociology and aesthetics; gynocritics is more self-contained and experimental, with connections to other modes of new feminist research. In a dialogue between these two positions, Carolyn Heilbrun, the writer, and Catherine Stimpson, editor of the American journal *Signs: Women in Culture and Society*, compare the feminist critique to the Old Testament, 'looking for the sins and errors of the past', and gynocritics to the New Testament, seeking 'the grace of imagination'. Both kinds are necessary, they explain, for only the Jeremiahs of the feminist critique can lead us out of the 'Egypt of female servitude' to the promised land of the feminist vision. That the discussion makes use of these Biblical metaphors points to the connections between feminist consciousness and conversion narratives which often appear in women's literature; Carolyn Heilbrun comments on her own text, 'when I talk about feminist criticism, I am amazed at how high a moral tone I take'.[7]

The Feminist Critique: Hardy

Let us take briefly as an example of the way a feminist critique might proceed, Thomas Hardy's *The Mayor of Casterbridge*, which begins with the famous scene of the drunken Michael Henchard selling his wife and infant daughter for five guineas at a country fair. In his study of Hardy, Irving Howe has praised the brilliance and power of this opening scene:

> To shake loose from one's wife; to discard that drooping rag of a woman, with her mute complaints and maddening passivity; to escape not by a slinking abandonment but through the public sale of her body to a stranger, as horses are sold at a fair; and thus to wrest, through sheer amoral wilfulness, a second chance out of life — it is with this stroke, so insidiously attractive to male fantasy, that *The Mayor of Casterbridge* begins.[8]

It is obvious that a woman, unless she has been indoctrinated into being very deeply identified indeed with male culture, will have a different experience of this scene. I quote Howe first to indicate how the fantasies of the male critic distort the text; for Hardy tells us very little about the relationship of Michael and Susan Henchard, and what we see in the early scenes does not suggest that she is drooping, complaining or passive. Her role, however, is a passive one; severely constrained by her womanhood, and further burdened by her child, there is no way that *she* can wrest a second chance out of life. She cannot master events, but only accommodate herself to them.

What Howe, like other male critics of Hardy, conveniently overlooks about the novel is that Henchard sells not only his wife but his child, a child who can only be female. Patriarchal societies do not readily sell their sons, but their daughters are all for sale sooner or later. Hardy wished to make the sale of the daughter emphatic and central; in early drafts of the novel Henchard has two daughters and sells only one, but Hardy revised to make it clearer that Henchard is symbolically selling his entire share in the world of women. Having severed his bonds with this female community of love and loyalty, Henchard has chosen to live in the male community, to define his human relationships by the male code of paternity, money and legal contract. His tragedy lies in realising the inadequacy of this system, and in his inability to repossess the loving bonds he comes desperately to need.

The emotional centre of *The Mayor of Casterbridge* is neither Henchard's relationship to his wife, nor his superficial romance with Lucetta Templeman, but his slow appreciation of the strength and dignity of his wife's daughter, Elizabeth-Jane. Like the other women in the book, she is governed by her own heart — man-made laws are not important to her until she is taught by Henchard himself to value legality, paternity, external definitions, and thus in the end to reject him. A self-proclaimed 'woman-hater', a man who has felt at best a 'supercilious pity' for womankind, Henchard is humbled and 'unmanned' by the collapse of his own virile façade, the loss of his mayor's chain, his master's authority, his father's rights. But in Henchard's alleged weakness and 'womanishness', breaking through in moments of tenderness, Hardy is really showing us the man at his best. Thus Hardy's female characters in *The Mayor of Casterbridge*, as in his other novels, are somewhat idealised and melancholy projections of a repressed male self.

As we see in this analysis, one of the problems of the feminist critique is that it is male-oriented. If we study stereotypes of women, the sexism of male critics, and the limited roles women play in literary history, we are not learning what women have felt and experienced, but only what men have thought women should be. In some fields of specialisation, this may require a long apprenticeship to the male theoretician, whether he be Althusser, Barthes, Macherey or Lacan; and then an application of the theory of signs or myths or the unconscious to male texts or films. The temporal and intellectual investment one makes in such a process increases resistance to questioning it, and to seeing its historical and ideological boundaries. The critique also has a tendency to naturalise women's victimisation, by making it the inevitable and obsessive topic of discussion. One sees, moreover, in works like Elizabeth Hardwick's *Seduction and Betrayal*, the bittersweet moral distinctions the critic makes between women merely betrayed by men, like Hetty in *Adam Bede*, and the heroines who make careers out of betrayal, like Hester Prynne in *The Scarlet Letter*. This comes dangerously close to a celebration of the opportunities of victimisation, the seduction *of* betrayal.[9]

Gynocritics and Female Culture

In contrast to this angry or loving fixation on male literature, the programme of gynocritics is to construct a female framework for the analysis of women's literature, to develop new models based on the study of female experience, rather than to adapt male models and theories. Gynocritics begins at the point when we free ourselves from the linear absolutes of male literary history, stop trying to fit women between the lines of the male tradition, and focus instead on the newly visible world of female culture. This is comparable to the ethnographer's effort to render the experience of the 'muted' female half of a society, which is described in Shirley Ardener's collection, *Perceiving Women*.[10] Gynocritics is related to feminist research in history, anthropology, psychology and sociology, all of which have developed hypotheses of a female subculture including not only the ascribed status, and the internalised constructs of femininity, but also the occupations, interactions and consciousness of women. Anthropologists study the female subculture in the relationships between women, as mothers, daughters, sisters and friends; in sexuality, reproduction and ideas about the body; and in rites of initiation and passage, purification ceremonies, myths and taboos. Michelle Rosaldo writes in *Woman, Culture, and Society,*

> the very symbolic and social conceptions that appear to set women apart and to circumscribe their activities may be used by women as a basis for female solidarity and worth. When men live apart from women, they in fact cannot control them, and unwittingly they may provide them with the symbols and social resources on which to build a society of their own.[11]

Thus in some women's literature, feminine values penetrate and undermine the masculine systems which contain them; and women have imaginatively engaged the myths of the Amazons, and the fantasies of a separate female society, in genres from Victorian poetry to contemporary science fiction.

In the past two years, pioneering work by four young American feminist scholars has given us some new ways to interpret the culture of nineteenth-century American women, and the literature which was its primary expressive form. Carroll Smith-Rosenberg's essay 'The Female World of Love and Ritual' examines several archives of letters between women, and outlines the homosocial emotional world of the nineteenth century. Nancy Cott's *The Bonds of Womanhood: Woman's Sphere in New England 1780-1835* explores the paradox of a cultural bondage, a legacy of pain and submission, which none the less generates a sisterly solidarity, a bond of shared experience, loyalty and compassion. Ann Douglas's ambitious book, *The Feminization of American Culture*, boldly locates the genesis of American mass culture in the sentimental literature of women and clergymen, two allied and 'disestablished' post-industrial groups. These three are social historians; but Nina Auerbach's *Communities of Women: An Idea in Fiction* seeks the bonds of womanhood in women's literature, ranging from the matriarchal households of Louisa May Alcott and Mrs Gaskell to the women's schools and colleges of Dorothy Sayers, Sylvia Plath and Muriel Spark. Historical and literary studies like these, based on English women, are badly needed; and the manuscript and archival sources for them are both abundant and untouched.[12]

Gynocritics: Elizabeth Barrett Browning and Muriel Spark

Gynocritics must also take into account the different velocities and curves of political, social and personal histories in determining women's literary choices and careers. 'In dealing with women as writers,' Virginia Woolf wrote in her 1929 essay, 'Women and Fiction', 'as much elasticity as possible is desirable; it is necessary to leave oneself room to deal with other things besides their work, so much has that work been influenced by conditions that have nothing whatever to do with art.'[13] We might illustrate the need for this completeness by looking at Elizabeth Barrett Browning, whose verse-novel *Aurora Leigh* (1856) has recently been handsomely reprinted by the Women's Press. In her excellent introduction Cora Kaplan defines Barrett Browning's feminism as romantic and bourgeois, placing its faith in the transforming powers of love, art and Christian charity. Kaplan reviews Barrett Browning's dialogue with the artists and radicals of her time; with Tennyson and Clough, who had also written poems on the 'woman question'; with the Christian Socialism of Fourier, Owen, Kingsley and Maurice; and with such female predecessors as Madame de Staël and George Sand. But in this exploration of Barrett Browning's intellectual milieu, Kaplan omits discussion of the male poet whose influence on her work in the 1850s would have been most pervasive: Robert Browning. When we understand how susceptible women writers have always been to the aesthetic standards and values of the male tradition, and to male approval and validation, we can appreciate the complexity of a marriage between artists. Such a union has almost invariably meant internal conflicts, self-effacement, and finally obliteration for the women, except in the rare cases — Eliot and Lewes, the Woolfs — where the husband accepted a managerial rather than a competitive role. We can see in Barrett Browning's letters of the 1850s the painful, halting, familiar struggle between her womanly love and ambition for her husband and her conflicting commitment to her own work. There is a sense in which she *wants* him to be the better artist. At the beginning of the decade she was more famous than he; then she notes with pride a review in France which praises him more; his work on *Men and Women* goes well; her work on *Aurora Leigh* goes badly (she had a young child and was recovering from the most serious of her four miscarriages). In 1854 she writes to a woman friend,

> I am behind hand with my poem . . . Robert swears he shall have his book ready in spite of everything for print when we shall be in London for the purpose, but, as for mine, it must wait for the next spring I begin to see clearly. Also it may be better not to bring out the two works together.

And she adds wryly, 'If mine were ready I might not say so perhaps.'[14]

Without an understanding of the framework of the female subculture, we can miss or misinterpret the themes and structures of women's literature, fail to make necessary connections within a tradition. In 1852, in an eloquent passage from her autobiographical essay 'Cassandra', Florence Nightingale identified the pain of feminist awakening as its essence, as the guarantee of progress and free will. Protesting against the protected unconscious lives of middle-class Victorian women, Nightingale demanded the restoration of their suffering:

> Give us back our suffering, we cry to Heaven in our hearts — suffer-

ing rather than indifferentism — for out of suffering may come the cure. Better to have pain than paralysis: A hundred struggle and drown in the breakers. One discovers a new world.[15]

It is fascinating to see how Nightingale's metaphors anticipate not only her own medical career, but also the fate of the heroines of women's novels in the nineteenth and twentieth centuries. To waken from the drugged pleasant sleep of Victorian womanhood was agonising; in fiction it is much more likely to end in drowning than in discovery. It is usually associated with what George Eliot in *Middlemarch* calls 'the chill hours of a morning twilight', and the sudden appalled confrontation with the contingencies of adulthood. Eliot's Maggie Tulliver, Edith Wharton's Lily Barth, Olive Schreiner's Lyndall, Kate Chopin's Edna Pontellier wake to worlds which offer no places for the women they wish to become; and rather than struggling they die. Female suffering thus becomes a kind of literary commodity which both men and women consume. Even in these important women's novels — *The Mill on the Floss*, *Story of an African Farm*, *The House of Mirth* — the fulfilment of the plot is a visit to the heroine's grave by a male mourner.

According to Dame Rebecca West, unhappiness is still the keynote of contemporary fiction by English women.[16] Certainly the literary landscape is strewn with dead female bodies. In Fay Weldon's *Down Among the Women* and *Female Friends*, suicide has come to be a kind of domestic accomplishment, carried out after the shopping and the washing-up. When Weldon's heroine turns on the gas, 'she feels that she has been half-dead for so long that the difference in state will not be very great'. In Muriel Spark's stunning short novel of 1970, *The Driver's Seat*, another half-dead and desperate heroine gathers all her force to hunt down a woman-hating psychopath, and persuade him to murder her. Garishly dressed in a purposely bought outfit of clashing purple, green and white — the colours of the suffragettes (and the colours of the school uniform in *The Prime of Miss Jean Brodie*) — Lise goes in search of her killer, lures him to a park, gives him the knife. But in Lise's careful selection of her death-dress, her patient pursuit of her assassin, Spark has given us the devastated postulates of feminine wisdom: that a woman creates her identity by choosing her clothes, that she creates her history by choosing her man. That, in the 1970s, Mr Right turns out to be Mr Goodbar, is not the sudden product of urban violence, but a latent truth which fiction exposes. Sparks asks whether men or women are in the driver's seat, and whether the power to choose one's destroyer is women's only form of self-assertion. To label the violence or self-destructiveness of these painful novels as neurotic expressions of a personal pathology, as many reviewers have done, is to ignore, Annette Kolodny suggests,

> the possibility that the worlds they inhabit may in fact be real, or true, and for them the only worlds available, and further, to deny the possibility that their apparently 'odd' or unusual responses may in fact be justifiable or even necessary.[17]

But women's literature must go beyond these scenarios of compromise, madness and death. Although the reclamation of suffering is the beginning, its purpose is to discover the new world. Happily, some recent women's literature, especially in the United States where novelists and poets have become vigorously involved in the women's liberation movement, has gone beyond reclaiming suffering to its re-investment. This newer writing relates the pain of transformation to history. 'If I'm lonely,' writes Adrienne Rich in 'Song',

> it must be the loneliness
> of waking first, of breathing
> dawn's first cold breath on the city
> of being the one awake
> in a house wrapped in sleep[18]

Rich is one of the spokeswomen for a new women's writing which explores the will to change. In her recent book, *Of Woman Born: Motherhood as Experience and Institution*, Rich challenges the alienation from and rejection of the mother that daughters have learned under patriarchy. Much women's literature in the past has dealt with 'matrophobia' or the fear of becoming one's mother.[19] In Sylvia Plath's *The Bell Jar*, for example, the heroine's mother is the target for the novel's most punishing contempt. When Esther announces to her therapist that she hates her mother, she is on the road to recovery. Hating one's mother was the feminist enlightenment of the fifties and sixties; but it is only a metaphor for hating oneself. Female literature of the 1970s goes beyond matrophobia to a courageously sustained quest for the mother, in such books at Margaret Atwood's *Surfacing*, and Lisa Alther's recent *Kinflicks*. As the death of the father has always been an archetypal rite of passage for the Western hero, now the death of the mother as witnessed and transcended by the daughter has become one of the most profound occasions of female literature. In analysing these purposeful awakenings, these reinvigorated mythologies of female culture, feminist criticism finds its most challenging, inspiriting and appropriate task.

Women and the Novel: the 'Precious Speciality'

The most consistent assumption of feminist reading has been the belief that women's special experience would assume and determine distinctive forms in art. In the nineteenth century, such a contribution was ambivalently valued. When Victorian reviewers like G.H. Lewes, Richard Hutton and Richard Simpson began to ask what the literature of women might mean, and what it might become, they focused on the educational, experiential and biological handicaps of the woman novelist, and this was also how most women conceptualised their situation. Some reviewers, granting women's sympathy, sentiment and powers of observation, thought that the novel would provide an appropriate, even a happy, outlet for female emotion and fantasy. In the United States, the popular novelist Fanny Fern understood that women had been granted access to the novel as a sort of repressive desublimation, a harmless channel for frustrations and drives that might otherwise threaten the family, the Church and the State. Fern recommended that women write as therapy, as a release from the stifling silence of the drawing-room, and as a rebellion against the indifference and insensitivity of the men closest to them:

> Look around, and see innumerable women, to whose barren and loveless lives this would be improvement and solace, and I say to them, write! write! It will be a safe outlet for thoughts and feelings that maybe the nearest friend you have has never dreamed had place in your heart and brain . . . it is not *safe* for the women of 1867 to shut down so much that cries out for sympathy and expression, because life is such a maelstrom of business or folly or both that those to whom they have bound themselves, body and soul, recognize only the needs of the former . . . One of these days, when that diary is found, when the hand that penned it shall be dust, with what amazement and remorse will many a husband or father exclaim, I never knew my wife or my child until this moment.[20]

Fern's scribbling woman spoke with fierce indirectness to the male audience, to the imagined husband or father; her purpose was to shock rather than to please, but the need to provoke masculine response was the controlling factor in her writing. At the turn of the century, members of the Women Writers Suffrage League, an important organisation of novelists and journalists, began to explore the psychological bondage of women's literature and its relationships to a male-dominated publishing industry. Elizabeth Robins, the first president of the League, a novelist and actress who had starred in early English productions of Ibsen, argued in 1908 that no woman writer had ever been free to explore female consciousness:

> The realization that she had access to a rich and as yet unrifled storehouse may have crossed her mind, but there were cogent reasons for concealing her knowledge. With that wariness of ages which has come to be instinct, she contented herself with echoing the old fables, presenting to a man-governed world puppets as nearly as possible like those that had from the beginning found such favour in men's sight.

> Contrary to the popular impression, to say in print what she thinks is the last thing the woman-novelist or journalist is so rash as to attempt. There even more than elsewhere (unless she is reckless) she must wear the aspect that shall have the best chance of pleasing her brothers. Her publishers are not women.[21]

It was to combat this inhibiting commercial monopoly that nineteenth-century women began to organise their own publishing houses, beginning with Emily Faithfull's Victoria Press in the 1870s, and reaching a peak with the flourishing suffrage presses at the beginning of this century. One of the most fervent beliefs of the Women Writers Suffrage League was that the 'terra incognita' of the female psyche would find unique literary expression once women had overthrown male domination. In *A Room of One's Own*, Virginia Woolf argued that economic independence was the essential precondition of an autonomous women's art. Like George Eliot before her, Woolf also believed that women's literature held the promise of a 'precious speciality', a distinctly female vision.

Feminine, Feminist, Female

All of these themes have been important to feminist literary criticism in the 1960s and 1970s but we have approached them with more historical awareness. Before we can even begin to ask how the literature of women would be different and special, we need to reconstruct

its past, to rediscover the scores of women novelists, poets and drama-
tists whose work has been obscured by time, and to establish the
continuity of the female tradition from decade to decade, rather than
from Great Woman to Great Woman. As we recreate the chain of
writers in this tradition, the patterns of influence and response from one
generation to the next, we can also begin to challenge the periodicity
of orthodox literary history, and its enshrined canons of achievement.
It is because we have studied women writers in isolation that we have
never grasped the connections between them. When we go beyond
Austen, the Brontës and Eliot, say, to look at a hundred and fifty or
more of their sister novelists, we can see patterns and phases in the
evolution of a female tradition which correspond to the developmental
phases of any subcultural art. In my book on English women writers, *A
Literature of Their Own*, I have called these the Feminine, Feminist and
Female stages.[22] During the Feminine phase, dating from about 1840
to 1880, women wrote in an effort to equal the intellectual achievements of the male culture, and internalised its assumptions about
female nature. The distinguishing sign of this period is the male pseudonym, introduced in England in the 1840s, and a national characteristic
of English women writers. In addition to the famous names we all know
— George Eliot, Currer, Ellis and Acton Bell — dozens of other women
chose male pseudonyms as a way of coping with a double literary
standard. This masculine disguise goes well beyond the title page; it
exerts an irregular pressure on the narrative, affecting tone, diction,
structure and characterisation. In contrast to the English male pseudonym, which signals such clear self-awareness of the liabilities of female
authorship, American women during the same period adopted super-
feminine, little-me pseudonyms (Fanny Fern, Grace Greenwood, Fanny
Forester), disguising behind these nominal bouquets their boundless
energy, powerful economic motives and keen professional skills. It is
pleasing to discover the occasional Englishwoman who combines both
these techniques, and creates the illusion of male authorship with a
name that contains the encoded domestic message of femininity — such
as Harriet Parr, who wrote under the pen name 'Holme Lee'. The
feminist content of feminine art is typically oblique, displaced, ironic
and subversive; one has to read it between the lines, in the missed possibilities of the text.

In the Feminist phase, from about 1880 to 1920, or the winning of
the vote, women are historically enabled to reject the accommodating
postures of femininity and to use literature to dramatise the ordeals of
wronged womanhood. The personal sense of injustice which feminine

novelists such as Elizabeth Gaskell and Frances Trollope expressed in their novels of class struggle and factory life become increasingly and explicitly feminist in the 1880s, when a generation of New Women redefined the woman artist's role in terms of responsibility to suffering sisters. The purest examples of this phase are the Amazon Utopias of the 1890s, fantasies of perfected female societies set in an England or an America of the future, which were also protests against male government, male laws and male medicine. One author of Amazon Utopias, the American Charlotte Perkins Gilman, also analysed the preoccupations of masculine literature with sex and war, and the alternative possibilities of an emancipated feminist literature. Gilman's Utopian feminism carried George Eliot's idea of the 'precious speciality' to its matriarchal extremes. Comparing her view of sisterly collectivity to the beehive, she writes that

> the bee's fiction would be rich and broad, full of the complex tasks of comb-building and filling, the care and feeding of the young . . . It would treat of the vast fecundity of motherhood, the educative and selective processes of the group-mothers, and the passion of loyalty, of social service, which holds the hives together.[23]

This is Feminist Socialist Realism with a vengeance, but women novelists of the period — even Gilman, in her short stories — could not be limited to such didactic formulas, or such maternal topics.

In the Female phase, ongoing since 1920, women reject both imitation and protest — two forms of dependency — and turn instead to female experience as the source of an autonomous art, extending the feminist analysis of culture to the forms and techniques of literature. Representatives of the formal Female Aesthetic, such as Dorothy Richardson and Virginia Woolf, begin to think in terms of male and female sentences, and divide their work into 'masculine' journalism and 'feminine' fictions, redefining and sexualising external and internal experience. Their experiments were both enriching and imprisoning retreats into the celebration of consciousness; even in Woolf's famous definition of life: 'a luminous halo, a semi-transparent envelope surrounding us from the beginning of consciousness to the end',[24] there is a submerged metaphor of uterine withdrawal and containment. In this sense, the Room of One's Own becomes a kind of Amazon Utopia, population 1.

Feminist Criticism, Marxism and Structuralism

In trying to account for these complex permutations of the female tradition, feminist criticism has tried a variety of theoretical approaches. The most natural direction for feminist criticism to take has been the revision, and even the subversion of related ideologies, especially Marxist aesthetics and structuralism, altering their vocabularies and methods to include the variable of gender. I believe, however, that this thrifty feminine making-do is ultimately unsatisfactory. Feminist criticism cannot go around forever in men's ill-fitting hand-me-downs, the Annie Hall of English studies; but must, as John Stuart Mill wrote about women's literature in 1869, 'emancipate itself from the influence of accepted models, and guide itself by its own impulses'[25] — as, I think, gynocritics is beginning to do. This is not to deny the necessity of using the terminology and techniques of our profession. But when we consider the historical conditions in which critical ideologies are produced, we see why feminist adaptations seem to have reached an impasse.

Both Marxism and structuralism see themselves as privileged critical discourse, and pre-empt the claim to superior places in the hierarchy of critical approaches. A key word in each system is 'science'; both claim to be sciences of literature, and repudiate the personal, fallible, interpretative reading. Marxist aesthetics offers a 'science of the text', in which the author becomes not the creator but the producer of a text whose components are historically and economically determined. Structuralism presents linguistically based models of textual permutations and combinations, offering a 'science of literary meaning', a grammar of genre. The assimilation of these positivist and evangelical literary criticisms by Anglo-American scholarship in the past fifteen years is not — I would argue — a spontaneous or accidental cultural phenomenon. In the Cold War atmosphere of the late 1950s, when European structuralism began to develop, the morale of the Anglo-American male academic humanist was at its nadir. This was the era of Sputnik, of scientific competition with the Soviet Union, of government money flowing to the laboratories and research centres. Northrop Frye has written about the plight of the male intellectual confronting

the dismal sexist symbology surrounding the humanities which he meets everywhere, even in the university itself, from freshman classes to the president's office. This symbology, or whatever one should call it, says that the sciences, especially the physical sciences, are rugged, aggressive, out in the world doing things, and so symbolically male, whereas the literatures are narcissistic, intuitive, fanciful, staying at home and making the home more beautiful but not doing anything serious and are therefore symbolically female.[26]

Frye's own *Anatomy of Criticism*, published in 1957, presented the first postulates of a systematic critical theory, and the 'possibility of literary study's attaining the progressive, cumulative qualities of science'.[27]

The new sciences of the text based on linguistics, computers, genetic structuralism, deconstructionism, neo-formalism and deformalism, affective stylistics and psychoaesthetics, have offered literary critics the opportunity to demonstrate that the work they do is as manly and aggressive as nuclear physics — not intuitive, expressive and feminine, but strenuous, rigorous, impersonal and virile. In a shrinking job market, these new levels of professionalisation also function as discriminators between the marketable and the marginal lecturer. Literary science, in its manic generation of difficult terminology, its establishment of seminars and institutes of post-graduate study, creates an élite corps of specialists who spend more and more time mastering the theory, less and less time reading the books. We are moving towards a two-tiered system of 'higher' and 'lower' criticism, the higher concerned with the 'scientific' problems of form and structure, the 'lower' concerned with the 'humanistic' problems of content and interpretation. And these levels, it seems to me, are now taking on subtle gender identities, and assuming a sexual polarity — hermeneutics and hismeneutics. Ironically, the existence of a new criticism practised by women has made it even more possible for structuralism and Marxism to strive, Henchard-like, for systems of formal obligation and determination. Feminists writing in these modes, such as Hélène Cixous and the women contributors to *Diacritics*, risk being allotted the symbolic ghettoes of the special issue or the back of the book for their essays.

It is not only because the exchange between feminism, Marxism and structuralism has hitherto been so one-sided, however, that I think attempts at syntheses have so far been unsuccessful. While scientific criticism struggles to purge itself of the subjective, feminist criticism is willing to assert (in the title of a recent anthology) *The Authority of Experience*.[28] The experience of women can easily disappear, become mute, invalid and invisible, lost in the diagrams of the structuralist or the class conflict of the Marxists. Experience is not emotion; we must protest now as in the nineteenth century against the equation of the feminine with the irrational. But we must also recognise that the questions we most need to ask go beyond those that science can answer. We must seek the repressed messages of women in history, in anthropology, in psychology, and in ourselves, before we can locate the feminine not-said, in the manner of Pierre Macherey, by probing the fissures of the female text.

Thus the current theoretical impasse in feminist criticism, I believe, is more than a problem of finding 'exacting definitions and a suitable terminology', or 'theorizing in the midst of a struggle'. It comes from our own divided consciousness, the split in each of us. We are both the daughters of the male tradition, of our teachers, our professors, our dissertation advisers and our publishers – a tradition which asks us to be rational, marginal and grateful; and sisters in a new women's movement which engenders another kind of awareness and commitment, which demands that we renounce the pseudo-success of token womanhood, and the ironic masks of academic debate. How much easier, how less lonely it is, not to awaken – to continue to be critics and teachers of male literature, anthropologists of male culture, and psychologists of male literary response, claiming all the while to be universal. Yet we cannot will ourselves to go back to sleep. As women scholars in the 1970s we have been given a great opportunity, a great intellectual challenge. The anatomy, the rhetoric, the poetics, the history, await our writing.

I am sure that this divided consciousness is sometimes experienced by men, but I think it unlikely that many male academics would have had the division in themselves as succinctly and publicly labelled as they were for me in 1976 when my official title at the University of Delaware was Visiting Minority Professor. I am deeply aware of the struggle in myself between the professor, who wants to study major works by major writers, and to mediate impersonally between these works and the readings of other professors – and the minority, the woman who wants connections between my life and my work, and who is committed to a revolution of consciousness that would make my concerns those of the majority. There have been times when the Minority wishes to betray the Professor, by isolating herself in a female ghetto; or when the Professor wishes to betray the Minority by denying the troubling voice of difference and dissent. What I hope is that neither will betray the other, because neither can exist by itself. The task of feminist critics is to find a new language, a new way of reading that can integrate our intelligence and our experience, our reason and our suffering, our scepticism and our vision. This enterprise should not be confined to women; I invite Criticus, Poeticus and Plutarchus to share it with us. One thing is certain: feminist criticism is not visiting. It is here to stay, and we must make it a permanent home.

Notes

I wish to thank Nina Auerbach, Kate Ellis, Mary Jacobus, Wendy Martin, Adrienne Rich, Helen Taylor, Martha Vicinus, Margaret Walters and Ruth Yeazell for sharing with me their ideas on feminist criticism.

1. Leon Edel, 'The Poetics of Biography' in Hilda Schiff (ed.), *Contemporary Approaches to English Studies* (London, 1977), p. 38. The other contributors to the symposium are George Steiner, Raymond Williams, Christopher Butler, Jonathan Culler and Terry Eagleton.

2. Robert Partlow, *Dickens Studies Annual*, vol. v (Carbondale, Southern Illinois, 1976), pp. xiv-xv. Nina Auerbach's essay is called 'Dickens and Dombey: A Daughter After All'.

3. Robert Boyers, 'A Case Against Feminist Criticism', *Partisan Review*, vol. xliv (Winter 1977), pp. 602, 610.

4. Adrienne Rich, *Of Woman Born: Motherhood as Experience and Institution* (New York, 1977), p. 62.

5. Mary Daly, *Beyond God the Father: Towards a Philosophy of Women's Liberation* (Boston, 1973), pp. 12-13.

6. Geoffrey Hartman, *The Fate of Reading* (Chicago, 1975), p. 3.

7. 'Theories of Feminist Criticism' in Josephine Donovan (ed.), *Feminist Literary Criticism: Explorations in Theory* (Lexington, 1976), pp. 64, 68, 72.

8. Irving Howe, *Thomas Hardy* (London, 1968), p. 84. For a more detailed discussion of this problem, see my essay 'The Unmanning of the Mayor of Casterbridge' in Dale Kramer (ed.), *Critical Approaches to Hardy* (London, 1979).

9. Elizabeth Hardwick, *Seduction and Betrayal* (New York, 1974).

10. Shirley Ardener (ed.), *Perceiving Women* (London, 1975).

11. 'Women, Culture, and Society: A Theoretical Overview' in Louise Lamphere and Michelle Rosaldo (eds.), *Women, Culture and Society* (Stanford, 1974), p. 39.

12. Carroll Smith-Rosenberg, 'The Female World of Love and Ritual: Relations Between Women in Nineteenth-Century America', *Signs: Journal of Women in Culture and Society*, vol. i (Autumn 1975), pp. 1-30; Nancy Cott, *The Bonds of Womanhood* (New Haven, 1977); Ann Douglas, *The Feminization of American Culture* (New York, 1977); Nina Auerbach, *Communities of Women* (Cambridge, Mass., 1978).

13. 'Women and Fiction' in Virginia Woolf, *Collected Essays*, vol. ii (London, 1967), p. 141.

14. Peter N. Heydon and Philip Kelley (eds.), *Elizabeth Barrett Browning's Letters to Mrs. David Ogilvy* (London, 1974), p. 115.

15. 'Cassandra' in Ray Strachey (ed.), *The Cause* (London, 1928), p. 398.

16. Rebecca West, 'And They All Lived Unhappily Ever After', *TLS* (26 July 1974), p. 779.

17. Annette Kolodny, 'Some Notes on Defining a "Feminist Literary Criticism" ', *Critical Inquiry*, vol. ii (1975), p. 84. For an illuminating discussion of *The Driver's Seat*, see Auerbach, *Communities of Women*, p. 181.

18. Adrienne Rich, *Diving into the Wreck* (New York, 1973), p. 20.

19. The term 'matrophobia' has been coined by Lynn Sukenick; see Rich, *Of Woman Born*, pp. 235 ff.

20. Quoted in Ann Douglas Wood, 'The "Scribbling Women" and Fanny Fern: Why Women Wrote', *American Quarterly*, vol. xxiii (1971), pp. 3-24.

21. Elizabeth Robins, *Woman's Secret*, WSPU pamphlet in the collection of the Museum of London, p. 6. Jane Marcus is preparing a full-length study of Elizabeth Robins.

22. Elaine Showalter, *A Literature of Their Own: British Women Novelists from Brontë to Lessing* (Princeton, New Jersey, 1977).

23. Charlotte Perkins Gilman, *The Man-made World* (London, 1911), pp. 101-2.

24. 'Modern Fiction', *Collected Essays*, vol. ii, p. 106.

25. J.S. Mill, *The Subjection of Women* (London, 1869), p. 133.

26. Northrop Frye, 'Expanding Eyes', *Critical Inquiry*, vol. ii (1975), pp. 201-2.

27. Robert Scholes, *Structuralism in Literature: An Introduction* (New Haven, 1974), p. 118.

28. Lee Edwards and Arlyn Diamond (eds.), *The Authority of Experience* (Amherst, Mass., 1977).

2 THE BURIED LETTER: FEMINISM AND ROMANTICISM IN *VILLETTE*

Mary Jacobus

Repression:

> Is this enough? Is it to live? . . . Does virtue lie in abnegation of self?
> I do not believe it . . . Each human being has his share of rights. I
> suspect it would conduce to the happiness and welfare of all, if each
> knew his allotment, and held to it as tenaciously as the martyr to his
> creed. Queer thoughts, these, that surge in my mind: are they right
> thoughts? I am not certain. (*Shirley* [1849], X)

Caroline Helstone's assertion of the inalienable rights of self, in *Shirley*,
I take to be the seed of *Villette* (1853) — a novel in which repression
returns vengefully on the heroine in the form of a ghostly nun. But
Villette is not simply about the perils of repression. It is a text formally
fissured by its own repressions; concealing a buried letter. Lucy Snowe
writes two letters to Graham Bretton, one 'under the dry, stinting
check of Reason', the other 'according to the full, liberal impulse
of Feeling' (XXII) — one for his benefit, censored and punishingly
rational, the other for hers, an outpouring of her innermost self. The
same doubleness informs the novel as a whole, making it secretive,
unstable and subversive. The narrative and representational conventions
of Victorian realism are constantly threatened by an incompletely
repressed Romanticism. Supernatural haunting and satanic revolt,
delusion and dream, disrupt a text which can give no formal recognition
to either Romantic or Gothic modes. The buried letter of Romanticism
becomes the discourse of the Other, as the novel's unconscious — not
just Lucy's — struggles for articulation within the confines of mid-
nineteenth-century realism. The resulting distortions and mutilations in
themselves constitute an aspect of the novel's meaning, like the distortions of a dream-text. But there is more to be found in *Villette* than the
incompatibility of realist and Romantic modes. It is haunted by the
unacknowledged phantom of feminism, and by the strangeness of
fiction itself. Its displacements and substitutions, like its silences and
dislocations, are a reminder that fiction is the peculiar reserve both of
repression and of the *Unheimliche* — the uncanny which, in Freud's

42

words, 'is in reality nothing new or alien, but something which is familiar and old-established in the mind and which has become alien-ated from it only through the process of repression'.[1] Lucy's haunted self-estrangement encodes the novel's alienation from its ghostly sub-text.

Neurosis and ex-centricity: 'Why is *Villette* disagreeable?' asked Matthew Arnold — 'Because the writer's mind contains nothing but hunger, rebellion and rage, and therefore that is all she can, in fact put into her book.'[2] The same qualities inspire Kate Millett's polemicis-ing of *Villette* as a radical feminist text ('one long meditation on a prison break').[3] Arnold and Millett are alike in proposing an unmediated relationship between author and work. It is easy to dismiss this collaps-ing of Charlotte Brontë and her fictional creation, Lucy Snowe; in her letters the novelist writes punitively of her heroine, 'I can hardly ex-press what subtlety of thought made me decide upon giving her a cold name' and 'I am not leniently disposed towards Miss *Frost* . . . I never meant to appoint her lines in pleasant places.'[4] Yet the assumption that autobiographical release fuels the novel is natural enough, and not only because the letters evince the same straining after dissociation as the novel itself. For *Villette*, belonging as it appears to do to the tradition of the *roman personnel* (the lived fiction), invites its readers to make just such a covert identification between Charlotte Brontë and her creation — and then frustrates it. The novel's real oddity lies in perversely withholding its true subject, Lucy Snowe, by an act of repression which mimics hers. Her invisibility is more than evasive; it is devious, duplicitous. Lucy lies to us. Her deliberate ruses, omissions and falsifications break the unwritten contract of first-person narrative (the confidence between reader and 'I') and unsettle our faith in the reliability of the text. 'I, Lucy Snowe, plead guiltless of that curse, an overheated and discursive imagination' (II), she tells us; but the same sentence goes on to speak of the infant Paulina's incommensurately powerful grief 'haunting' the room — as Lucy herself will later be haunted by the 'discursive' imagination she denies. 'I, Lucy Snowe, was calm,' she insists again, after a heart-rending account of Paulina's part-ing from her father (disclosing the lie): 'she dropped on her knees at a chair with a cry — "Papa!" It was low and long; a sort of "Why hast thou forsaken me?" ' (III). Riven with such contradictions, Lucy's narrative calls itself in question by forcing us to misread it. 'I seemed to hold two lives — the life of thought, and that of reality' (VIII), she tells us later; the hidden life of thought strives ceaselessly to evade her censorship in the very language she uses: that of supernatural haunting and the Christian Passion – the product of an inverted martyrdom in which Lucy renounces her share of rights instead of cleaving to them.

Displacement: at the start of the novel, Lucy observes and narrates another's drama, the diminutive Paulina's. Of her own painful circumstances we learn only that she has been shipwrecked in the metaphoric tempest which recurs at moments of crisis through the novel ('To this hour, when I have the nightmare, it repeats the rush and saltiness of briny waves in my throat, and their icy pressure on my lungs' (IV)). Paulina's grief – that of the abandoned child cast among strangers – has in any case already acted out Lucy's. Asking no pity for herself, Lucy earlier had invoked it for her surrogate: ' "How will she get through this world, or battle with this life? How will she bear the shocks and repulses, the humiliations and desolations . . .?" ' (III). So, too, Paulina's premature love for the adolescent Graham Bretton is at once a displacement and a prefiguration of Lucy's future relationship with him; just as, later, Miss Marchmont's state of erotic arrest and confinement are annexed to Lucy herself: 'Two hot, close rooms thus became my world . . . All within me became narrowed to my lot' (IV). As the novel quarries deeper into Lucy's subconsious, the displacement becomes more bizarre. Confined alone at the Rue Fossette during the long vacation, she finds herself looking after a crétin – a creature conjured from nowhere to be her 'strange, deformed companion', an image of deranged self who 'would sit for hours together moping and mowing and distorting her features with indescribable grimaces' (XV). That the heart-sick Miss Marchmont and the untamed crétin, warped in mind and body, are aspects of Lucy's repression (as Paulina had been an aspect of her loss) hardly needs emphasising. Her regression from child to invalid to crétin parodies and reverses the Romantic quest for self which is the real 'plot' (the conspiracy of silence) of *Villette*. ' "Who *are* you, Miss Snowe?" ', asks Ginevra Fanshawe inquisitively – ' "But *are* you anybody? . . . Do – *do* tell me who you are!" ' (XXVII). And again, ' "If you really are the nobody I once thought you, you must be a cool hand" ' (XXVII). A cool hand indeed; for Lucy's invisibility is a calculated deception – a blank screen on which others project their view of her. To Graham Bretton she is 'a being inoffensive as a shadow': to M. Paul, denouncing her in a melodramatic hiss, she is dangerously, sexually, insurgent – ' "vous avez l'air bien triste, soumise, rêveuse, mais vous ne l'êtes pas . . . Sauvage! la flamme à l'âme, l'éclair aux yeux!" ' (XXVII).

Actor/spectator: Lucy withholds her true identity from us as well as from the characters whose presence as actors in the novel defines her

absence. The most disconcerting of her reticences, and the least func-
tional, concerns her recognition of the medical attendant at the Rue
Fossette (Dr John) as Graham Bretton. The 'idea, new, sudden, and
startling' (X) which strikes Lucy as she observes him one day at the
Pensionnat Beck is not disclosed to the reader until her return to the
scene of her and Paulina's childhood love, the reconstituted Bretton
household: 'I first recognized him on that occasion, noted several
chapters back . . . To *say* anything on the subject, to *hint* at my discovery, had not suited my habit of thought' (XVI). Instead of declaring
herself, Lucy prefers to retain her social invisibility – at this stage she
is still employed as a nursery-governess. Her strategic silence conceals
the private life which Mme Beck's system of surveillance is at pains to
detect, while she herself sets about detecting the clandestine flirtation
between Dr John ('Isadore', in this role) and Ginevra, much as she had
earlier observed the love-game between Graham and the infant Paulina.
The novel is full of such voyeurisms (Mme Beck herself is scarcely more
on the watch than Lucy) – exhibitions in which Lucy casts herself as
an onlooker, passive yet all-powerful. Even when she takes the stage
herself, during the school play of Chapter XIV, she contrives to combine the two roles – at once spectator and participant in the sexual
drama which she enacts between 'Isadore', Ginevra, and her gallant, de
Hamal (between the 'Ours' or sincere lover, the coquette, and the fop
whose part Lucy plays). Here the divide between stage and audience,
watcher and watched, is piquantly removed in the interests of a more
complex and ambiguous drama; Lucy also crosses the sexual divide –
impersonating a man while clad as a woman from the waist down. In
the same way, the *frisson* lies in Lucy's non-subservience to her spectator role, as the game of master/slave in *Jane Eyre* is spiced by Jane's
insubordination to her master. Jane discovers a taste for sexual mastery
in preference to the more conventional role of mistress: Lucy discovers
in herself 'a keen relish for dramatic expression' and, carried away by
she knows not what, transforms her part into an unorthodox piece of
inter-sexual rivalry – 'I acted to please myself' (XIV).

Vashti: 'but it would not do for a mere looker-on at life' (XIV).
Lucy's invisibility is an aspect of her oppression: the actress, Vashti, is
an aspect of her hidden revolt. As a middle-class woman, Lucy can only
be employed within the home or its educational colony, the school; but
that 'home', since she is employee not 'mistress', must remain alien.
Though increasingly professionalised, the role of teacher retains many
of the anomalies of the governess-figure in her differing guises (mother-
substitute, educator, companion). The governess is peculiarly the victim

of middle-class sexual ideology, for the only role open to her is that of bringing up children while marriage and motherhood themselves are paradoxically tabooed to her within the family which employs her. Economically non-negotiable (non-exchangeable), she is denied both social and sexual recognition: 'No one knows exactly how to treat her.'[5] Significantly, Lucy prefers the relative independence of remaining a teacher in Mme Beck's pensionnat to Mr Home's offer of employment as Paulina's companion; while Mme Beck sees in Lucy's bid to marry M. Paul a threat to the economic and family interests on which her establishment is founded (Lucy will ultimately set up a rival school). Charlotte Brontë's letters have much to say both about the 'condition of woman' question and about being a governess; but this, finally, of the woman whose destiny is to be unmarried:

> when patience had done its utmost and industry its best, whether in the case of women or operatives, and when both are baffled, and pain and want triumph, the sufferer is free, is entitled, at last to send up to Heaven any piercing cry for relief, if by that he can hope to obtain succour.[6]

In *Villette*, that piercing cry is uttered by an actress whose release of 'hunger, rebellion and rage' sets the theatre literally alight with its revolutionary force. Vashti is a female version of the central Romantic protagonist, the satanic rebel and fallen angel whose damnation is a function of divine tyranny (Blake's Urizen, Byron's Jehovah of sacrifices, Shelley's Jupiter):

> Pain, for her, has no result in good; tears water no harvest of wisdom: on sickness, on death itself, she looks with the eye of a rebel. Wicked, perhaps, she is, but also she is strong; and her strength has conquered Beauty, has overcome Grace, and bound both at her side, captives peerlessly fair, and docile as fair. Even in the uttermost frenzy of energy is each maenad movement royally, imperially, incedingly upborne. Her hair, flying loose in revel or war, is still an angel's hair, and glorious under a halo. Fallen, insurgent, banished, she remembers the heaven where she rebelled. Heaven's light, following her exile, pierces its confines, and discloses their forlorn remoteness. (XXIII)

Villette can only be silent about the true nature and origin of Lucy's oppression; like Charlotte Brontë's letters, it never questions the enshrining of marriage within Victorian sexual ideology, nor pursues its economic and social consequences for women. But what the novel cannot say is eloquently inscribed in its sub-text — in the 'discursive' activity of Lucy's (over-) heated imagination, and in the agitated notation and heightened language which signal it. Here her mingled identification, revulsion and admiration are tellingly juxtaposed with Graham Bretton's indifference to the spectacle. We witness not only his lack of affinity 'for what belonged to storm, what was wild and intense, dangerous, sudden, and flaming' — for the Romantic mode which defines Lucy's own insurgent inner life; we witness also his sexual judgement on 'a woman, not an artist: it was a branding judgement' (XXIII). 'Branded' as a fallen woman, a rebel against conventional morality, Vashti is at once *declassée* and thereby permitted to retain her potency — a daemonic symbol of sexual energy created by a woman (actress/author) in contrast to the static, male-fabricated images of woman exhibited for Lucy's inspection in an earlier chapter: Cleopatra on one hand, the *Jeune Fille/Mariée/Jeune Mère/Veuve* (XIX) on the other (woman as sexual object or as bearer of ideology). 'Where was the artist of the Cleopatra? Let *him* come and sit down and study this different vision' (XXIII; my italics), demands Lucy — in whose scandalous pink dress M. Paul detects a latent scarlet woman.

Heimlich/unheimlich: '*heimlich* is a word the meaning of which develops in the direction of ambivalence, until it finally coincides with its opposite, *unheimlich*.' Thus Freud, for whom the uncanny in fiction provided 'a much more fertile province than the uncanny in real life, for it contains the whole of the latter and something more besides'.[7] Lucy's dream-like propulsion from one world to another — from her childhood at Bretton, to Miss Marchmont's sick-room, to the Pensionnat Beck, and back again to Bretton — makes resourceful use of this fertile province, suspending the laws of probability for those of the mind. Narrative dislocation in *Villette* insists on the irreducible otherness, the strangeness and arbitrariness, of inner experience. Lucy's return to the past (or the return of her past?) is ushered in by a nightmare of estrangement — 'Methought the well-loved dead . . . met me elsewhere, alienated' (XV) — and she recovers consciousness after her desperate visit to the confessional amidst the décor of the *unheimliche*: 'all my eye rested on struck it as spectral', 'These articles of furniture could not be real, solid arm-chairs, looking-glasses, and wash-stands — they must be the ghosts of such articles' (XVI). The real becomes spectral, the past alien, the familiar strange; the lost home (*heimlich*) and the uncanny (*unheimlich*) coincide. Like Vashti, Lucy is an exile from the paradisal world of Bretton; even when restored miraculously to it, she cannot remain there. Its true inmate is not the satanic rebel and fallen angel, but the angelic, spiritualised Paulina – whose surname, appropriately, is Home. By marrying her (it is she whom he rescues from the threatened conflagration in the theatre) Graham Bretton ensures the continuation of the *status quo*. But their conventional love-story – child-bride taken in charge by father-substitute – is upstaged by Lucy's more innovatory and disturbing inner drama. In this internalised theatre, the part that doubles Lucy's is taken by a (supposed) ghost. Freud's essay on the uncanny offers a classic formulation of Gothic strategy: 'the writer creates a kind of uncertainty in us . . . by not letting us know, no doubt purposely, whether he is taking us into the real world or into a purely fantastic one of his own creation.' The effect of this uncertainty in Charlotte Brontë's novel is to challenge the monopolistic claims of realism on 'reality' – to render its representations no less fictive and arbitrary than the Gothic and Romantic modes usually viewed as parasitic. Moreover, as Freud suggests, a peculiarly powerful effect is achieved when the writer pretends to move in the world of common reality and then oversteps it, 'betraying us to the superstitiousness which we have ostensibly surmounted'.[8] The grudge which we feel against the attempted deceit is just that retained by readers and critics of *Villette* towards the nun of the Rue Fossette – in whom repression, the uncanny, and the unacknowledged phantom of feminism combine to subvert the novel's façade of realism.

The nun: a realist reading of *Villette* must relegate the nun to the level of Gothic machinery; indicatively, both Kate Millett (for whom the novel is a manifesto of sexual politics) and Terry Eagleton (for whom it is a Marxist myth of power) ignore her ambiguous presence.[9] But just because the device is so cumbrous and unnecessary in realist terms – Ginevra's gallant dressed up for their clandestine assignations – it must have another function. In effect, it symbolises not only Lucy's repression, but the novelist's freedom to evoke or inhibit the *unheimliche*; to lift or impose censorship. The nun thus becomes that phantom or psychic reality which representation represses, evading the censorship of realism as de Hamal himself evades the forbidden ground of the Pensionnat Beck under Mme Beck's censoring eyes. In his medical capacity, Graham Bretton diagnoses 'a case of spectral illusion . . . resulting from long-continued mental conflict' (XXII). But as it turns out, the rationalist explanation is debunked by the fictive reality of the novel itself: 'doctors are so self-opinionated, so immovable in their dry, materialist views' (XXIII), Lucy comments with apparent perversity; yet the text vindicates her. The legend of the nun, buried alive in a

vault under the Methuselah pear-tree 'for some sin against her vow' (XII),
is introduced early on but lies dormant until passion threatens to reassert
itself. The first apparition – summoned up, it seems, by Lucy's love for
Graham Bretton – occurs when she plunges into the vault-like depths
of 'the deep, black, cold garret' (XXII) to enjoy his precious letter:

> Are there wicked things, not human, which envy human bliss?
> Are there evil influences haunting the air, and poisoning it for man?
> What was near me? . . .
> Something in that vast solitary garret sounded strangely. Most
> surely and certainly I heard, as it seemed, a stealthy foot on that
> floor: a sort of gliding out from the direction of the black recess
> haunted by the malefactor cloaks. I turned: my light was dim; the
> room was long – but, as I live! I saw in the middle of that ghostly
> chamber a figure all black or white; the skirts straight, narrow,
> black; the head bandaged, veiled, white.
> Say what you will, reader – tell me I was nervous, or mad;
> affirm that I was unsettled by the excitement of that letter; declare
> that I dreamed: this I vow – I saw there – in that room – on that
> night – an image like – a NUN. (XXII)

The sheerest melodrama? or a bold refutation of 'common reality'?
Lucy's challenge – 'Say what you will, reader' – defies us to find the
narrative incredible or the author unreliable. For the reader, there is
no knowing how to take the nun; is Lucy deceiving us again? A brief
admonitory sighting marks her visit to the theatre (an unexplained light
in the *grenier*); but the next full apparition occurs at a similar moment
of high emotional significance – on the still, dim, electric evening when
she buries her letters from Graham, and her love for him, in a hole
under the Methuselah pear-tree:

> the moon, so dim hitherto, seemed to shine out somewhat brighter:
> a ray gleamed even white before me, and a shadow became distinct
> and marked. I looked more narrowly, to make out the cause of this
> well-defined contrast appearing a little suddenly in the obscure
> alley: whiter and blacker it grew on my eye: it took shape with
> instantaneous transformation. I stood about three yards from a tall,
> sable-robed, snowy-veiled woman.
> Five minutes passed. I neither fled nor shrieked. She was there
> still. I spoke.
> 'Who are you? and why do you come to me?' (XXVI)

Lucy here both hides a treasure and entombs a grief; does the nun confront her to assert their kinship? The third apparition — aroused to vengeful anger — is provoked by M. Paul's declaration of affinity between himself and Lucy (' "we are alike — there is affinity. Do you see it mademoiselle, when you look in the glass?" '). The birth of love and the turbulent re-activation of repression occur simultaneously:

> Yes; there scarce stirred a breeze, and that heavy tree was convulsed, whilst the feathery shrubs stood still. For some minutes amongst the wood and leafage a rending and heaving went on. Dark as it was, it seemed to me that something more solid than either night-shadow, or branch-shadow, blackened out of the boles. At last the struggle ceased. What birth succeeded this travail? What Dryad was born of these throes? We watched fixedly. A sudden bell rang in the house — the prayer-bell. Instantly into our alley there came . . . an apparition, all black and white. With a sort of angry rush — close, close past our faces — swept swiftly the very NUN herself! Never had I seen her so clearly. She looked tall of stature, and fierce of gesture. As she went, the wind rose sobbing; the rain poured wild and cold; the whole night seemed to feel her. (XXXI)

Natural and supernatural are brought ambiguously into play; the nun is at once 'solid', material, and capable of bringing about changes in the weather — 'betraying us to the superstitiousness we have ostensibly surmounted'.

Mirror, mirror . . . : Lucy's question (' "Who are you?" ') remains unanswered, but the nun's ambiguous status — at once real and spectral, both a deceit practised on Lucy and her psychic double — has important implications for the system of representation employed in the novel. The configuration of characters around Lucy is equally expressive of her quest for identity and of her self-estrangement. Mrs Bretton, Mme Beck, Ginevra, the detestable Zélie of St Pierre and the adorable Paulina are the images of women (the good and bad mothers, the rivals and sisters) through whom Lucy both defines and fails to recognise herself, placed as she is at the centre of a distorting hall of mirrors in which each projection is obedient to her feelings of gratitude, rivalry, attraction, hatred or envy. No other woman in the novel has any identity except as Lucy herself bestows it. The absent centre exerts a centripetal force on the other characters, making them all facets of the consciousness whose passions animate them. And yet this is the level which a realist reading of *Villette* would claim as stable, objective, autonomous, in contrast to the phantasmal subjective world represented by the nun and the Gothic hinterland to which she belongs. At this point one must acknowledge the powerful presence of fantasy in Charlotte Brontë's fiction. M. Paul, no less than Lucy's rivals (the images to whom she must submit or over whom she may triumph), is animated by a wish-fulfilment which it is surely justifiable to see as Charlotte Brontë's own. But far from detracting from the fiction, the release of fantasy both energises *Villette* and satisfies that part of the reader which also desires constantly to reject reality for the sake of an obedient, controllable, narcissistically pleasurable image of self and its relation to the world. From the scene in which Ginevra triumphantly contrasts herself and Lucy in the mirror (XIV), to Lucy's unexpected glimpse of herself in public with Graham Bretton and his mother ('a third person in a pink dress and black lace mantle . . . it might have been worse' (XX), to M. Paul's declaration of affinity (' "Do you see it . . . when you look in the glass? Do you observe that your forehead is shaped like mine – that your eyes are cut like mine?" ' (XXXI), we trace, not so much the rehabilitation of the plain heroine, as the persistence of the Lacanian 'Mirror-phase'.[10] Or, to put it in terms of text rather than plot, we too are confronted by an image in which signifier and signified have imaginary correspondence – by a seductive representational illusion which denies the lack or absence central to all signification. The nun stands opposed to this imaginary plenitude of sign or image. Too easily identified as the spectre of repression, or as the double of Lucy's repressed self, she is none the less recalcitrantly other; ' "Who are you?" ', asks Lucy, not recognising her. She is the joker in the pack, the alien, ex-centric self which no image can mirror – only the structure of language. Like the purloined letter in Lacan's reading of the Poe story, where the meaning of the letter (the autonomous signifier) lies in its function in the plot rather than its actual contents, the nun derives her significance from her place in the signifying chain.[11] She has one function in relation to Lucy, another in relation to M. Paul, and another again in relation to Ginevra. The different meanings intersect but do not merge; the threads cross and intertwine without becoming one. Her uncanniness lies in unsettling the 'mirroring' conventions of representation present elsewhere in *Villette*, and in validating Gothic and Romantic modes, not as 'discursive' and parasitic, but – because shifting, unstable, arbitrary and dominated by desire – as the system of signification which can more properly articulate the self.

The TRUTH: so what are we to make of Lucy's extraordinary narrative? which level of the text finally claims priority? Pursuit of the nun to the novel's climax — the phantasmagoric scenes of Lucy's drugged nocturnal expedition to the illuminated park — provides an answer of sorts. The nun has by this time manifested herself in another guise, as the external obstacle to marriage between Lucy and M. Paul; that is, his supposed devotion to the dead, sainted Justine Marie (and, with her, to Roman Catholicism) whose nun-like portrait is pointedly exhibited to Lucy by Père Silas, as well as his guardianship of a bouncing, all-too-alive ward of the same name. Her presence at the climax of the novel perfectly illustrates Charlotte Brontë's deviousness, the strategy by which her heroine's consciousness at once distorts, and, in doing so, creates a truth that is essentially a fiction. In this coda-like sequence, all the characters of the novel are paraded before the apparently invisible Lucy in their happy family parties — the Brettons and Homes; the Becks, Père Silas and Mme Walravens; and lastly, after an elaborate build-up of expectation and delay, M. Paul and his ward. Thus Lucy is ostensibly returned to her original role of excluded spectator. But there is a difference. This time it is she who is *metteur en scène* in a drama of her own making. First comes 'the crisis and the revelation', the long-awaited arrival of the nun or her double, Justine Marie — heightened by Lucy's anticipatory memories of her earlier hauntings:

It is over. The moment and the nun are come. The crisis and the relevation are passed by.

The flambeau glares still within a yard, held up in a park-keeper's hand; its long eager tongue of flame almost licks the figure of the Expected — there — where she stands full in my sight! What is she like? What does she wear? How does she look? Who is she?

There are many masks in the Park to-night, and as the hour wears late, so strange a feeling of revelry and mystery begins to spread abroad that scarce would you discredit me, reader, were I to say that she is like the nun of the attic, that she wears black skirts and white head-clothes, that she looks the resurrection of the flesh, and that she is a risen ghost.

All falsities — all figments! We will not deal in this gear. Let us be honest, and cut, as heretofore, from the homely web of truth.

Homely, though, is an ill-chosen word. What I see is not precisely homely. A girl of Villette stands there . . . (XXXIX)

'*Heimlich* is a word the meaning of which develops in the direction of ambivalence . . .' Once again it is the living not the dead, the familiar not the strange, that becomes uncanny; not least because the bathos fails to proceed as expected. Instead, the transformation of spectral nun into bourgeois belle is followed by yet another audacious reversal — a denial of reality whereby Lucy invents an engagement between M. Paul and his ward, a fiction whose basis ('his nun was indeed buried') is the truth of her own autonomous imagination:

> Thus it must be. The revelation was indeed come. Presentiment had not been mistaken in her impulse; there is a kind of presentiment which never *is* mistaken; it was I who had for a moment miscalculated; not seeing the true bearing of the oracle, I had thought she muttered of vision when, in truth, her prediction touched reality.
> I might have paused longer upon what I saw; I might have deliberated ere I drew inferences. Some perhaps would have held the premises doubtful, the proofs insufficient; some slow sceptics would have incredulously examined, ere they conclusively accepted the project of a marriage between a poor and unselfish man of forty, and his wealthy ward of eighteen; but far from me such shifts and palliatives, far from me such temporary evasion of the actual, such coward fleeing from the dread, the swift-footed, the all-overtaking Fact, such feeble suspense of submission to her the sole sovereign, such paltering and faltering resistance to the Power whose errand is to march conquering and to conquer, such traitor defection from the TRUTH. (XXXIX)

Is this Lucy's final and most outrageous lie? or, as the text insists in the face of its heavily alliterative irony, the novel's central 'truth'? — that the imagination usurps on the real to create its own fictions; that Lucy is essentially and inevitably single. Meanwhile, the self-torturing narrative and masochistic imagery ('I invoked Conviction to nail upon me the certainty, abhorred while embraced') speed her back to her solitary dormitory in the Rue Fossette, to the effigy of the nun on her bed, and the empty garments which signal 'the resurrection of the flesh':

> Tempered by late incidents, my nerves disdained hysteria. Warm from illuminations, and music, and thronging thousands, thoroughly lashed up by a new scourge, I defied spectra. In a moment, without exclamation, I had rushed on the haunted couch; nothing leaped

out, or sprung, or stirred; all the movement was mine, so was all the
life, the reality, the substance, the force; as my instinct felt. I tore
her up — the incubus! I held her on high — the goblin! I shook her
loose — the mystery! And down she fell — down all round me —
down in shreds and fragments — and I trode upon her. (XXXIX)

The phrasing is odd and significant: 'all the movement was mine, so was
all the life, the reality, the substance, the force.' The wardrobe mock-
ingly bequeathed to Lucy by the eloped Ginevra and de Hamal labels
her as the nun of the Rue Fossette — at once accusing her of animating
the spectre from within herself, and forcing her to recognise its true
identity.

The double ending: but of course the narrative doesn't leave things
there, although the ambiguous ending cunningly attempts to do so —
at once uniting Lucy and M. Paul in their educational idyll, and severing
them for ever. The final evasion ('Trouble no quiet, kind heart; leave
sunny imaginations hope' (XLII)) was clearly designed to satisfy the
conventional novel-reader as well as Charlotte Brontë's father. But there
is more to it. Of the two letters she writes to Graham Bretton, Lucy
tells us: 'To speak truth, I compromised matters; I served two masters:
I bowed down in the house of Rimmon, and lifted the heart at another
shrine' (XXIII). The entire novel, not just its ending, bears the marks of
this compromise — between Victorian romance and the Romantic
Imagination, between the realist novel and Gothicism. The relationship
between the two texts is as arbitrary as that between the two letters;
as the signified slides under the signifier, so the buried letter bears an
ex-centric relation to the public version. This is not to say that the real
meaning of *Villette*, 'the TRUTH', lies in its ghostly sub-text. Rather,
the relationship between the two points to what the novel cannot say
about itself — to the real conditions of its literary possibility. Instead of
correcting the novel into a false coherence, we should see in its
ruptured and ambiguous discourse the source of its uncanny power.
The double ending, in reversing the truth/fiction hierarchy, not only
reinstates fantasy as a dominant rather than parasitic version of reality,
but at the same time suggests that there can be no firm ground; only a
perpetual de-centring activity. Fittingly, the sleight of hand is carried
out with the aid of metaphors drawn from the Romantic paradox of
creation-in-destruction. The tempest by which Lucy's earliest loss is
signified becomes an apocalyptic upheaval prophesying rebirth as well
as death when the time comes for her to leave Miss Marchmont ('disturbed volcanic action . . . rivers suddenly rushing above their banks . . .

strange high tides flowing furiously in on low sea-coasts' (IV)). In the same way, Lucy's loss of consciousness before her rebirth into the Bretton household, later in the novel, is heralded by renewed images of Shelleyan storm — 'I only wished that I had wings and could ascend the gale, spread and repose my pinions on its strength, career in its course, sweep where it swept' (XV). There is thus a profound ambiguity in the Romantic cataclysm which shipwrecks Lucy's happiness at the end of the novel:

> The skies hang full and dark — a rack sails from the west; the clouds cast themselves into strange forms — arches and broad radiations; there rise resplendent mornings — glorious, royal, purple as monarch in his state; the heavens are one flame; so wild are they, they rival battle at its thickest — so bloody, they shame Victory in her pride. I know some signs of the sky; I have noted them ever since childhood. God, watch that sail! Oh! guard it!

> .   .   .   .

> That storm roared frenzied for seven days. It did not cease till the Atlantic was strewn with wrecks: it did not lull till the deeps had gorged their full of sustenance. Not till the destroying angel of tempest had achieved his perfect work, would he fold the wings whose waft was thunder — the tremor of whose plumes was storm. (XLII)

John Martin and the Angel of Death transform Lucy's premonition of loss into an apocalyptic victory of the imagination. By admitting to the incompatibility of the world of thought and the world of reality, Lucy at last becomes a truly reliable narrator — single and double at the same time. And by tacitly affirming the centrality of shipwreck, loss and deprivation to the workings of her imagination, Charlotte Brontë also reveals the deepest sources of her own creativity.

The anxiety of influence: Harold Bloom would presumably see the nun as an emblem of repression in a belated text whose sexual anguish, like that of Tennyson's 'Mariana', masks influence-anxiety (note the analogous presence of the Methuselah pear-tree and the famous poplar).[12] A plausible case could be made for misreading *Villette* in the same way. Charlotte Brontë's imagination was nurtured on Romanticism ('that burning clime where we have sojourned too long — its skies flame — the glow of sunset is always upon it'),[13] but the world of Angria had to be repressed in the interests of Victorian realism: 'When I first began to write . . . I restrained imagination, eschewed romance, repressed excitement.'[14] It was no more possible to write a Romantic novel in the mid-nineteenth century than to read one, as the bewildered and imperceptive reviews of *Wuthering Heights* reveal. Unlike her sister, Emily Brontë refused to bow down in the house of Rimmon, and in an important sense, hers is the repressed presence in *Villette*. Lucy's unwilling return to consciousness in the Bretton household ('Where my soul went during that swoon I cannot tell . . . She may have gone upward, and come in sight of her eternal home . . . I know she reentered her prison with pain, with reluctance' (XVI)) resembles nothing so much as Emily Brontë's 'Prisoner' after visionary flight: 'Oh, dreadful is the check — intense the agony/When the ear begins to hear and the eye begins to see . . .'[15] Her invocation 'To Imagination' underlies *Villette*'s paeon to the Imagination in the face of Reason's tyranny (' "But if I feel, may I *never* express?" "*Never!*" declared Reason' (XXI)). Emily Brontë had written, 'So hopeless is the world without,/The world within I doubly prize', and welcomed a 'benignant power,/Sure solacer of human cares' —

> Reason indeed may oft complain
> For Nature's sad reality,
> And tell the suffering heart how vain
> Its cherished dreams must always be;
> And Truth may rudely trample down
> The flowers of Fancy newly blown.
>
> But thou art ever there to bring
> The hovering visions back and breathe
> New glories o'er the blighted spring
> And call a lovelier life from death,
> And whisper with a voice divine
> Of real worlds as bright as thine.[16]

Charlotte Brontë, in turn, creates one of the most remarkable invocations to Imagination in Victorian literature — a passage that criticism of *Villette* has proved consistently unable to assimilate, or even acknowledge:

> Often has Reason turned me out by night, in mid-winter, on cold snow . . . Then, looking up, have I seen in the sky a head amidst circling stars, of which the midmost and the brightest lent a ray sympathetic and attent. A spirit, softer and better than Human Reason, has descended with quiet flight to the waste — bringing all

round her a sphere of air borrowed of eternal summer; bringing perfume of flowers which cannot fade — fragrance of trees whose fruit is life; bringing breezes pure from a world whose day needs no sun to lighten it. My hunger has this good angel appeased with food, sweet and strange, gathered amongst gleaming angels . . . Divine, compassionate, succourable influence! When I bend the knee to other than God, it shall be at thy white and winged feet, beautiful on mountain or on plain. Temples have been reared to the Sun — altars dedicated to the Moon. Oh, greater glory! To thee neither hands build, nor lips consecrate; but hearts, through ages, are faithful to thy worship. A dwelling thou hast, too wide for walls, too high for dome — a temple whose floors are space — rites whose mysteries transpire in presence, to the kindling, the harmony of worlds! (XXI)

The dizzying and visionary prose strains, like Shelley's poetry, away from the actual towards enkindled abstractions that image the human mind. But the deity that the temple of the heart enshrines is female; like the embodiment of rebellion and rage (Vashti), the spirit that succours the mind's hunger has been triumphantly feminised.

Feminism and Romanticism: 'nothing but hunger, rebellion and rage . . . No fine writing can hide this thoroughly, and it will be fatal to her in the long run' — Arnold's prognosis was wrong (Charlotte Brontë died of pregnancy), but revealingly poses a split between rebellion and 'fine writing'. The divorce of the Romantic Imagination from its revolutionary impulse poses special problems for Victorian Romantics. Where vision had once meant a prophetic denunciation of the *status quo* and the imagining of radical alternatives, it comes to threaten madness or mob-violence. Losing its socially transforming role, it can only turn inwards to self-destructive solipsism. Charlotte Brontë's own mistrust erupts in *Villette* with the fire that flames out during Vashti's performance or in the long-vacation nightmare which drives Lucy to the confessional; while the spectral nun (the Alastor of the Rue Fossette?) has to be laid in order to free Lucy from the burden of the autonomous imagination and allow her to become an economically independent headmistress. There are added complications for a woman writer. The drive to female emancipation, while fuelled by revolutionary energy, had an ultimately conservative aim — successful integration into existing social structures (' "I am a rising character: once an old lady's companion, then a nursery-governess, now a school-teacher" ', Lucy tells Ginevra ironically (XXVII)). Moreover, while the novel's pervasive feminisation of the Romantic Imagination is a triumph, it runs the attendant risk of creating a female ghetto. The annexing of special powers of feeling and intuition to women and its consequences (their relegation to incompetent dependency) has an equally strong Romantic tradition; women, idiots and children, like the debased version of the Romantic poet, become at once privileged and (legally) irresponsible. The problem is illuminated by situating Charlotte Brontë's novels within a specifically feminist tradition. *Villette*'s crushing opposition between Reason and Imagination is also present in Mary Wollstonecraft's writing. *The Rights of Woman* (1791) — directed against the infantilising Rousseauist ideal of feminine 'sensibility' — not only advocates the advantages for women of a rational (rather than sentimental) education, but attempts to insert the author herself into the predominantly male discourse of Enlightenment Reason, or 'sense'. Yet, paradoxically, it is within this shaping Rousseauist sensibility that Mary Wollstonecraft operates as both woman and writer — creating in her two highly autobiographical novels, *Mary* (1788) and *The Wrongs of Woman* (1798), fictions which, even as they anatomise the constitution of femininity within the confines of 'sensibility', cannot escape its informing preoccupations and literary influence.[17] Though their concepts of Reason differ, the same split is felt by Charlotte Brontë. In *Villette*, Reason is the wicked and 'envenomed' step-mother as opposed to the succouring, nourishing, consoling 'daughter of heaven', Imagination (XXI). It is within this primal yet divisive relationship that the novelist herself is constituted as woman and writer — nurtured on Romanticism, fostered by uncongenial Reason. The duality haunts her novel, dividing it as Lucy is divided against herself.

Feminist criticism/feminist critic: it is surely no longer the case, as Kate Millett asserts, that literary criticism of the Brontës is 'a long game of masculine prejudice wherein the player either proves they can't write and are hopeless primitives . . . or converts them into case histories from the wilds'.[18] But feminist criticism still has a special task in relation to Charlotte Brontë's novels. That task is not to explain away, but to explain — to theorise — the incoherencies and compromises, inconsistencies and dislocations, which provoked the 'can't write' jibe in the first place; to suggest, in other words, the source of Matthew Arnold's disquiet. It is enough to point to the part played by realism and Reason respectively in Charlotte Brontë's double quest for literary form and for female emancipation. To do so relocates her writing, not in a neurotic northern hinterland ('case histories from the wilds'), but in the mainstream of Victorian literary production — its legacy of

Romanticism complicated in her case by the conflict between a revolutionary impulse towards feminism and its tendency to confine women within irrationality. And what of the feminist critic? Isn't she in the same position as Charlotte Brontë, the writer, and her character, Lucy Snowe? — bound, if she's to gain both a living and a hearing, to install herself within the prevailing conventions of academic literary criticism. To this extent, hers must also be an ex-centric text, a displacement into criticism of the hunger, rebellion and rage which make Lucy an estranged image of self. Constituted within conditions essentially unchanged since those of Mary Wollstonecraft and Charlotte Brontë (i.e. patriarchy) and experiencing similar contradictions within herself and society, the feminist critic faces the same disjunction — removed, however, to the disjunction between literary response and critical discourse. The novel itself becomes the discourse of the Other, making its presence felt in the distortions and mutilations of critical selectivity (*Vashti, The Nun, Feminism and Romanticism*). What strategy remains, beyond unsettling the illusory objectivity of criticism? Surely also to unfold a novel whose very repressions become an eloquent testimony to imaginative freedom, whose ruptures provide access to a double text, and whose doubles animate, as well as haunt, the fiction they trouble. In the last resort, the buried letter of Romanticism and the phantom of feminism both owe their uncanny power to their subterranean and unacknowledged presence — to repression itself, the subject of Charlotte Brontë's most haunting novel, and fiction's special reserve.

Notes

A shortened version of this essay appeared in *Essays in Criticism*, vol. xxix (July 1978), pp. 228-44. I am grateful to the editors for permission to reprint it here, and to the London-based Marxist-Feminist Literary Collective for whom an early version was originally written. Quotations are from the first editions of Charlotte Brontë's novels; references are to chapter divisions.

1. 'The "Uncanny" ' (1919) in James Strachey (trans. and ed.), *The Standard Edition of the Complete Psychological Works of Sigmund Freud* (24 vols., London, 1955), vol. xvii, p. 241. See Hélène Cixous's seminal 'Fiction and its Phantoms: A reading of Freud's *Das Unheimliche* (The "uncanny")', *New Literary History*, vol. vii (1976), pp. 525-48.

2. Matthew Arnold to Mrs Foster, 14 April 1853; see Miriam Allott (ed.), *The Brontës: The Critical Heritage* (London, 1974), p. 201.

3. Kate Millett, *Sexual Politics* (London, 1971), p. 146.

4. To W.S. Williams, 6 November 1852, and George Smith, 3 November 1852; T. Wise and J.A. Symington (eds.), *The Shakespeare Head Brontë: The Life and Letters* (4 vols., London, 1932), vol. iv, pp. 18, 16.

5. Elizabeth Sewell, *Principles of Education* (2 vols., London, 1865), vol. ii, p. 240. See M.J. Peterson, 'The Victorian Governess: Status Incongruence in Family and Society', *Victorian Studies*, vol. xiv (1970), pp. 7-26.

6. To W.S. Williams, 12 May 1848; *Life and Letters*, vol. ii, p. 216.

7. *The Complete Psychological Works of Sigmund Freud*, vol. xvii, pp. 226, 249.

8. Ibid., vol. xvii, p. 250.

9. See Millett, *Sexual Politics*, pp. 140-7, and Terry Eagleton, *Myths of Power: A Marxist Study of the Brontës* (London, 1975), pp. 61-73.

10. See Jacques Lacan, *Ecrits*, trans. Alan Sheridan (London, 1977), pp. 1-7.

11. 'Seminar on "The Purloined Letter" ', trans. Jeffrey Mehlman, *Yale French Studies*, vol. xlviii (1972), pp. 38-72.

12. See Harold Bloom, *Poetry and Repression* (New Haven and London, 1976), pp. 147-54.

13. 'Farewell to Angria', *c.* 1839; see F.E. Ratchford and W.C. De Vane, *Legends of Angria* (New Haven, 1933), p. 316.

14. To G.H. Lewes, 6 November 1847; *Life and Letters*, vol. ii, p. 152.

15. 11. 85-6, no. 190 in C.W. Hatfield (ed.), *The Complete Poems of Emily Jane Brontë* (London, 1941), p. 239.

16. No. 174, ibid., pp. 205-6.

17. See Gary Kelly (ed.), *Mary, A Fiction and The Wrongs of Woman* (London, 1976), pp. vii-xxi, and Margaret Walters, 'The Rights and Wrongs of Women' in Juliet Mitchell and Ann Oakley (eds.), *The Rights and Wrongs of Women* (London, 1976), pp. 304-29.

18. Millett, *Sexual Politics*, p. 147.

3 THE INDEFINITE DISCLOSED: CHRISTINA ROSSETTI AND EMILY DICKINSON

Cora Kaplan

> To fill a Gap
> Insert the Thing that caused it —
> Block it up
> With Other — and 'twill yawn the more —
> You cannot solder an Abyss
> With Air.
>
> (Emily Dickinson, c. 1862)[1]

This curious, compacted lyric is one of a group of poems that form a distinct category in the work of two Victorian women poets, Emily Dickinson and Christina Rossetti. Such lyrics speak directly to and about the psyche, expressing and querying feelings that are deliberately abstracted from any reference to, or analysis of, the social causes of psychological states. They attempt to escape immediate or specific social determination, a project that cannot be finally realised since all representation as such must exist within a cultural discourse. Most of Dickinson's verse, and the larger part of Rossetti's, exclude the social in this way; but in this particular sub-genre their poetry also employs atypical forms of imagery. Instead of straightforward metaphorical constructions, comparisons of like to unlike (as in the metaphysical mode for which Dickinson is famous, or the more traditional late Romantic style preferred by Rossetti), these lyrics are marked by their use of synecdoche, where the part stands for the whole, and metonymy, where the images are narratively or associatively related rather than expressly compared.[2] Images and their meanings are left dangling, as in 'To fill a Gap' where 'Gap', 'Other', 'Abyss' and 'Air' are not meant as metaphors for each other but as substitutes. 'Gaps' are caused by absence and loss and can only be described through an articulation which opens rather than blocks the 'Abyss'.

Such strategies were not vulnerable to the type of textual explication used by Victorian critics, which depended on a text susceptible to paraphrase. Similarly, their richness of reference makes them texts puzzling to modern critics intent on extracting a single or definitive interpretation; dream-form, too, either directly stated or implied,

61

becomes an important means of presenting distorted or unclear images with impunity. While these modes are idiosyncratic to Dickinson and Rossetti, conveying powerful ideas and feelings past internal and external censors, they are by no means the monopoly of women writers. But they deserve the special attention of feminist critics because they seem to 'fill a Gap' in our understanding of women's subjectivity − their sense of themselves − and because their very openness renders the poems at once problematic and vulnerable to particular kinds of misreading. It is too easy to bind them into biographical interpretations of the poets' lives or build them into additional 'literary' evidence to buttress interpretations of women's experience drawn from their prose fiction. Worst of all, because these lyrics are so clearly 'about' the psychological, they can be used to substantiate specific psychoanalytic theories of femininity. The use of psychoanalysis in literary criticism as a way of exploring the conjunction between specific historical ideologies and individual literary works has become popular in recent years, partly in response to the attempt to integrate Marxism and psychoanalytic theory. Feminists have supported and added substantially to such integration, and my reservations about interpretation are intended, not to denounce this enterprise as such, but to serve as a critique of its least useful tendencies.

Why should such common uses of the lyric of feeling, particularly when its meaning is difficult or obscure, be inappropriate? These texts speak to and about psychic phenomena in ways that are unique in women's writing of the period. However formal their presentation, they are, by virtue of their fragmentary and opaque language, torn away from a chain of meaning which would secure them to larger interpretations. Their sybilline quality means that they can be inserted into almost any theory about women as social subjects and about high culture as an expression of women's suppressed and distorted subjectivity. Most of the poems that follow, would, for example support either a phallocentric theory of women's psychological development as espoused by Freud and some of his modern followers, or a concentric theory, lately in vogue in feminist psychoanalysis and already popularised in feminist literary criticism as the concept of 'inner space'.[3] Phallocentric theories see language and gender-socialisation organised around the phallus as a privileged signifier of 'difference'; concentric theory sees the vagina as an equally powerful force in the organisation of women's social, psychic and sexual being, also expressed through their use of language. These theories are still in the early stages of development, and although I am myself tentatively aligned with neo-Freudians such as Lacan, I cannot see the lyrics which I am examining as decisive witness for either side. Their real strength, in relation to the casual reader and the critical theorist alike, is that they are shapes, like ink-blots, from which to decipher related images in our own experience and intellectual orientation. These poems interrogate states for which the poets themselves had no ready explanations; in turn they interrogate our own theory and politics. The symbolic strategies which they employ ensure that this is their main effect, making them stand apart from other lyrics by the same poets which are more precisely metaphorical and more immediately didactic, as well as standing in opposition to narrative, the dominant genre of women's prose writing.

In focusing on the work of two poets who were exact contemporaries (both born in 1830) certain ironic anomalies are apparent. Emily Dickinson's verse, unpublished in her lifetime, has been much more fully worked over by modern critics than Christina Rossetti's, which enjoyed considerable popularity until the turn of the century. Rossetti belongs to the pre-Raphaelite school; her poetry has an obvious niche in English literature, but the twentieth century has virtually ignored her, and for this reason I shall devote more of my attention to her. On the other hand, Dickinson's thousands of short lyrics, as edited by Thomas H. Johnson, have proved a scholar's gift to scholars, a virgin œuvre on which to make their mark. Yet even though Dickinson's poetry has been tackled from almost every critical position, she, like Christina Rossetti, figures much less prominently in the new feminist literary criticism than women novelists of the same period.

One can only suggest some reasons why their work has been slighted by feminists. A large portion of both poets' writing is devotional, it is true; but so is much well-thought-of poetry. More important, perhaps, is the reflexive nature of the verse, its concentration on the inner life, its virtual exclusion of the contemporary or social. Emily Dickinson's approach is analytic, intellectual even; she read more widely than her urban British contemporary. Her lyrics most typically seek to analyse emotions through analogy; that is the way in which she uses the metaphysical. Rossetti's poems offer a sensuous appreciation of emotion. A conscious preoccupation with the constricting demands of femininity does not often surface in the poetry of either. Even in life their protests against the constraints of gender were muted at the social level, where they presented exaggerated examples of retiring women. Unlike contemporary women novelists, many of whom were also perfect Victorian gentlewomen, they hardly ever make combative social relations with lovers or family the subject of their poetry. Instead, their verse is preoccupied with a melancholy inner struggle for peace of mind. This introspective, almost morbid preoccupation marked not only their verse but also that of many lesser women poets of the century — so much so that in the mid-1890s the young Alice Thompson, who would become the poet and feminist Alice Meynell, wrote bitterly of her 'rhyming faculty' that 'whatever I write will be melancholy and self-conscious, as are all women's poems.'[4]

Dickinson's and Rossetti's lyrics are so meagre in description of their cultural surroundings that they do not date, except in certain turns of speech, and therefore withhold the crucial historical distance that places the nineteenth-century novel in a convenient conceptual past; the modern reader cannot see them through the wrong end of the binoculars, from a progressive present in which a better world for women is implicit. Such poetry accentuates the way in which the female psyche has a recalcitrant tendency to remain recognisable in its supposedly 'weaker' aspects, despite a variety of ostensible improvements in women's social and political status. This emphasis may suggest the difficulty which they present for a new feminist criticism. The women's movement today — Marxist, bourgeois or radical feminist — tends to endorse women's struggle through social and political action and to resist as weakening those psychoanalytic interpretations of femininity which seem to confirm or eternalise women's passive and masochistic behaviour. Both Rossetti and Dickinson represented very fully the internal struggles of women of their day as well as ours, without the comforting assurance that their spiritual malaise would be cured by egalitarian marriage, revision of the laws of inheritance, education, employment, a more equitable division of labour, the loosening of sexual prohibitions, or the curtailment of parental authority.

Since the most intractable problem facing feminists today is the relationship between the psychological components of femininity, female socialisation, and the social and political elements of women's subordination, it is not surprising that the writing of Dickinson and Rossetti should provide much thought but small comfort. Their poetry — particularly at its most arcane and difficult points — does, however, help us to understand the relationship between the imaginative act and the dominant ideology. Despite considerable prejudice against women writers in the nineteenth century, imaginative writing was, of all forms of public discourse, the one in which women were most able to participate and, in England, become prominent. Perhaps it was thought to be the least dangerous to bourgeois hegemony and hence to patriarchal power. This being so (and it is, of course, open to debate), we might come at their poetry in a new way, understanding that even when its overt intention is revolutionary it is only rarely a force which ruptures or alters existing social and political forms. In their most radical sallies it may be said that Rossetti and Dickinson conformed to the judgement of an approving contemporary critic who compared Christina Rossetti favourably with Elizabeth Barrett Browning because Rossetti accepted 'the burden of womanhood'. Where their strategies of subversion are subtle, even subliminal, the effect may still be to confirm traditional arrangements by substituting fantasy for anger. Both a clearer definition of the place of literary discourse in women's oppression and the place of literature in resistance to it is needed. Such an approach would begin by accepting the contradiction posed by women's writing as simultaneously a historical record of their oppression and a definitive mark of their defiance, hence making the conservative implications of the work of these two major poets less embarrassing for feminist criticism.

Christina Rossetti

Two recent feminist readings of Christina Rossetti's *Goblin Market* (1862) may help to distinguish between useful and misleading analyses of such poetry. *Goblin Market* has for some years had an underground reputation as a forgotten feminist classic. Christina Rossetti adamantly resisted attempts to press an interpretation on the poem, insisting that it was what its surface suggests – a fairy story. It unquestionably belongs to the genre of 'faery' which had a long tradition in English and underwent a late-nineteenth-century revival. A narrative (like many of Rossetti's longer poems), it is the story of two sisters, Laura and Lizzie, who live alone together. Wilful Laura looks at and listens to the fairy men, then buys and sucks the goblins' magical fruit which produces a violent addiction. The goblins sell only once to each buyer and Lizzie, older and more careful, watches her sister waste away in 'baulked desire'. Finally she takes a silver penny and seeks out the goblins who literally assault her with their wares, but cannot make her open her lips to eat the fruit herself. The sexual analogy is quite explicit:

> Like a royal virgin town
> Topped with gilded dome and spire
> Close beleagured by a fleet
> Mad to tug her standard down.[5]

Finally they toss back her penny and, covered in juice, 'In a smart, ache, tingle', Lizzie rushes back to Laura crying 'Hug me, kiss me, suck my juices'.[6] Laura obeys and recovers; Lizzie does not suffer, and the two sisters live to marry and tell their tale to their own children, both as cautionary and as heroic, with the moral that 'there is no friend like a sister'.[7]

My first example, Maureen Duffy's interpretation in *The Erotic World of Faery*, is full of suggestive insights culled from psychoanalytic theory; but it is never clear how the text is being defined in relation to her analysis. It is not just that the text is left unspecified as a product of Christina Rossetti's conscious intention or as unconscious displacement – the problem of conscious or unconscious production of images is never even taken up. Sometimes it seems as if Duffy views the poem as a loose but evocative series of representations in which each reader can find a metaphor to suit his or her fantasy; at other points the poem is seen to be grounded in Victorian sexual taboos; at still others the text is used as a 'timeless' example of the way in which the unconscious displaces and condenses sexual meanings. We might start by asking what conscious sexual under- and overtones Rossetti meant the poem to carry. To the extent that it is allegorical, the goblins' fruit and the serpent's apple are constant, implied metaphors. The lines already quoted about the 'virgin town' make clear Rossetti's basic analogy between goblins-with-fruit and sexual temptation. But the last thing *Goblin Market* intends is a recapitulation of Eve's fall. The analogy is there to set up a different, contradictory set of relations to the story of Adam and Eve. While the snake's apple produces sensations of shame in the Edenic couple, the goblins' fruit gives Laura knowledge of desire but not shame. This, and the fact that Laura and Lizzie are sisters instead of mates, constitutes the deliberate contrast which Rossetti establishes between her fairy tale and the Edenic myth.

Duffy's basic assumption is that the poem concerns fantasy sex, desire and masturbation. But read as an allegory (bad thoughts equal bad fairies, forbidden fruit is the female body itself), the narrative breaks down; the point about the goblins is that they represent – whether consciously, unconsciously, or as a result of ambiguity – both real tempters of the other sex (i.e. males) and paranoid projections of temptation. Duffy sees Laura devouring the fruit as 'a powerful masturbatory fantasy of feeding at the breast', quoting Rossetti in support: 'She sucked until her lips were sore.'[8] But even this simple image is too condensed to be reduced to a single connotation; childish greed and undifferentiated sensual pleasure may be indicated, but a contradiction remains: children can get sore lips from eating too much tart fruit, but babies don't get sore lips from breast-feeding. *Mothers* do, however, get sore nipples from being sucked, and if we are to pursue the masturbatory implications of Duffy's reading then presumably sore lips must be transposed from mouth to vagina. But what is important about the passage is not the physical site or source of sensual excitement, but the moral overtone: you can hurt from too much pleasure, oral or genital. As with Duffy's suggestion that the goblins' invitation to Lizzie to 'Bob at our cherries/Bite at our peaches' is a temptation closer to fellatio (surely the sexual practice least likely to have been known to the author), we are confronted by the poem's ability to induce fantasy, its power to stir further erotic association in the reader.

Duffy's attempt to historicise the poem produces further difficulties. Quoting William Acton's *The Functions and Disorders of the Reproductive Organs* (1857), she suggests that the symptoms of Laura's decline are those which Acton ascribes to the habitual masturbator. Although Acton's text conveniently precedes the poem's writing by a few years, it is highly unlikely that Christian Rossetti, who refused to dip into a racy novel, would have read it. True, Acton simply repeats and gives spurious scientific valorisation to current beliefs about masturbation, but his symptoms are punitive projection rather than medical reality. If one wanted to look for a 'real' medical anaology for Laura's decline, and one moreover that Christina Rossetti might have witnessed, one could point to drug addiction, of course, but possibly to anorexia, now commonly thought to be associated with pubescent crises at the onset of adult female sexuality. This explanation is equally hypothetical; its only advantage is that it is less specific and coincides both with the mysterious ailments of adolescence and with the traditional malaise following fairy curses on either sex. But pursuit of Laura's disease distracts from what is really important: its place in the moral narrative. Laura is ill with 'baulked desire', not guilt; Lizzie goes out determined to cure, not absolve, her, by getting her sister more of what she wants. Most important for the structure of the poem, Laura's illness is an excuse for the next 'erotic' episode in the poem, Lizzie's assault by the goblins.

Finally, Duffy sees in Laura and Lizzie 'the sisters who appear repeatedly in paintings and drawings from Millais to Sargent. This double female image is an interesting component of the period's eroticism akin to the heterosexual desire to see blue films about lesbians.'[9] The sisterly relationship in the poem has definite and unsuppressed sensuous elements, but are we really to believe that Christina

Rossetti produced a representation of female eroticism pandering to male taste? Blue films about lesbians are made for and by men, as distinct from representations by lesbians about lesbian relationships made by and for women. Both may satisfy the erotic fantasies of either sex in different ways, but it is hardly useful to talk about a 'period's eroticism' as if it were a unified phenomenon. In addition, the 'erotic' encounter between Laura and Lizzie is far more daring than any scene, however suggestive, portrayed in the high art of the period. It is protected from censure through its enclosure in fairy tale and through the pain and anguish of the cure (Lizzie's embrace) which now tastes of bitterest wormwood. The poem operates its own internal censorship by making joint motifs of pleasure and punishment strongest at the most significant erotic moments. What such historicising in relation to Victorian sexual attitude and high art may locate is the site of contradiction within a poem which struggles to represent female sexual fantasy while being constrained nevertheless by the guilt inherent in even the most displaced expression of such fantasy.

Ellen Moers, in *Literary Women*, provides a much tauter commentary on the poem. More careful in her use of psychoanalytic interpretations, she contributes to our understanding of the punitive elements in *Goblin Market* by examining the mixed elements of sensuality, sadism and violence in the sisters' confrontation with the goblins. Moers places the poem within her discussion of female Gothic, a genre in which violence to women in supernatural settings is a leading trope. However, Moers' argument for the prominence of hand-to-hand sadism, pinching and plaguing is based on her assessment of the limited heterosexual experience open to single women writers in the nineteenth century. Their sexual experience and subsequent sexual fantasy are linked to the night side of the Victorian nursery, where siblings, cousins and friends were allowed a pre-pubescent freedom denied to young men and women:

> Women authors of Gothic fantasies appear to testify that the physical teasing they received from their brothers — the pinching, mauling, and scratching we dismiss as the most unimportant of children's games — took on outsize proportions and powerful erotic overtones in their adult imaginations . . . (it was not only sexual play but *any* kind of physical play for middle-class women that fell under the Victorian ban).[10]

Moers extends her argument by pointing to the prominence of the nursery-tussle motif in the writing of many other Victorian women. Her clear and cautious use of the relation between socialisation, fantasy and literature is a model for feminist criticism. She does not attempt to prove anything about Christina Rossetti's individual experience; rather, she generalises illuminatingly about the social components of women's sexual imagination. She is, if anything, a little too eager to clean up the poem by locating its more disturbing elements in a harmless practice which demonstrates the poverty rather than the richness of women's sexual fantasy.

While *Goblin Market* cannot be decoded as an elaborate adult sexual scenario, it undoubtedly remains an exploration of women's sexual fantasy which includes suggestions of masochism, homoeroticism, rape or incest. The images are incomplete and blurred for several possible reasons. Most obviously the blurring can be seen as a form of both conscious and unconscious censorship; it is also (perhaps primarily) the result of sexual ignorance. Christina Rossetti was sexually un-initiated, and while we may not have to fix her imagination at the level of a ten-year-old, we may legitimately see transformed fantasies as in-distinct, referring characteristically to sensations rather than particular practices. Blurring occurs typically in fantasy anyway, where images condense and overlay each other, while condensed images often con-tract pleasure and punishment into a single act. The most interesting element of the poem remains this obscure level of internal reference combined with its very precise form. The narrative shape of the poem signals the primacy of erotic fantasy. The two sisters are given to the reader without social context. The absence of all social detail except their apparently orphaned state fits in well with the conventional frame of the fairy or folk tale as well as that of sexual fantasy, where too much specificity can impede the erotic message. The encounters with the goblins, and Laura's and Lizzie's embrace at the end of the poem, are presented within a surprisingly threadbare narrative scheme; the poet's words and attention are lavished instead on the 'erotic' incidents.

This rich concentration on the sensuous moment is typical of erotic fantasy; but the fairy story or folk tale similarly often contains irrele-vant narrative elements which have little direct bearing on the dramatic crises. Thus the closing of the poem, like its opening, is compatible with both. Rather than leaving the girls locked in the annealing embrace, Rossetti projects them forwards into marriage and motherhood. This social ending — traditional in many narrative forms — is odd here only because the poem does not begin with a typical fairy story introduc-tion. Instead it dives right into the heart of the matter: 'Morning and evening/Maids heard the goblins' cry . . .' My analysis of the poem does not attempt to refute Duffy and Moers by going one better. Rather, it attempts to locate the poem within Christina Rossetti's work, and to identify particular strategies, conscious or unconscious, for conveying the pleasurable but forbidden past the Victorian censor. More important, I have tried to suggest the difficulty of disentangling the text as a historical structure of meaning and the text as read by the critic at any point after its production. Most simply, I suppose, *Goblin Market* can be seen as a comical-tragical view of the erotic from the women's position with conscious and unconscious elements inextricably mingled. A brief funny-sad lyric of *c.* 1861 by Emily Dickinson reads like a marginal gloss on Rossetti's poem:

Over the fence—
Strawberries—grow—
Over the fence—
I could climb—if I tried, I know—
Berries are nice!

But—if I stained my Apron—
God would certainly scold!
Oh, dear—I guess if He were a Boy—
He'd—climb—if He could![11]

Like a number of Victorian poets, Christina Rossetti used dream-form as a favourite device when she wanted to exempt her poems from the demands of clarity. Poetry did not have to be very difficult to be thought obscure — witness contemporary verdicts on Robert Browning. Fancy, faery, dream-form and the absurd, as in Edward Lear's verse, were acceptable ways round the expectation that each metaphor be complete in itself, not too far-fetched, and related to the one that followed. For Tennyson, too, dream-form was a means of introducing irrational, private states of being into a canon built round a literature concerned with socially conventional ideas and feelings. Such alien psychic levels find their representation elsewhere in Victorian writing not only through the convention of the dream (both Alice's adventures are dreams), but through methods of displacement such as setting poem or novel in the past or in another country where things can be ordered differently. English writers themselves (the Brownings are perhaps the most celebrated example) went abroad in order to be released from the claustrophobic mores of their class and culture. The other scenes —

Wonderland, the world of Tennyson's *The Princess*, *Goblin Market*, Arthur's Court — are all in part used to suspend social rules; the dream-state, as one of these other worlds, permits the expression of feelings and the enactment of dramas taboo in genteel households.

Christina Rossetti's work represents part of this movement away from the Victorian ideal of the socialised and accessible poet, but the evolution of an alternate aesthetic was very gradual as well as being practised well in advance of any theory to defend it. Midway between the fantasy world of *Goblin Market* and the stated dream-form of 'My Dream' and 'On the Wing' is *An Old-World Thicket*, another long poem by Rossetti which uses reverie, the state between sleep and waking. *An Old-World Thicket* has Dante's 'una selva oscura' as its epigraph, and its scene and structure are meant to remind the reader of the opening of *The Divine Comedy*:

> Midway this way of life we're bound upon,
> I woke to find myself in a dark wood,
> Where the right road was wholly lost and gone.[12]

For Christina Rossetti, Dante was a deeper poet even than Tennyson, one of the few contemporaries to whom she gave whole-hearted admiration.[13] *An Old-World Thicket* is about her own mid-life crisis, but for English readers not familiar with Dante, Rossetti's opening lines — 'Awake or sleeping (for I know not which)/I was or was not mazed within a wood' — might also recall Tennyson's 'A Dream of Fair Women', where reverie gives way to dream so that the poet 'At last methought that I had wandered far/In an old wood' (11.53-4). Dante's dark wood and Tennyson's 'old wood', peopled with tragic heroines from the past, are brought together in Rossetti's poem, where the tragedy's queen is the poet-speaker herself. Tennyson's wood, like Dante's, is dark and menacing —

> There was no motion in the dumb dead air,
>   Not any song of bird or sound of rill;
> Gross darkness of the inner sepulchre
>   Is not so deadly still . . . ('A Dream of Fair Women', 11. 65-8)

There are forests and forests; Rossetti's wood is full of mother-birds and their broods in a shade that 'danced and twinkled to the unseen sun', a world where

Branches and leaves cast shadows one by one,
    And all their shadows swayed
In breaths of air that rustled and that played.

Her birds 'challenged each desire . . . Like anything they seemed, and everything'.[14] Tennyson's fair women are legendary figures, doomed and sexually active phantoms from the past brought, at their moment of grief and trauma, to the dead forest. Rossetti presents a single active female consciousness, the poet's own, in an alive, feminine and sensualised forest.

The future of this modern female psyche is unresolved, sometimes in harmony with, occasionally in counterpoint to, the mood of the surrounding nature. Often it is rebellious — 'Such revolt . . . That kicks and breaks itself against the bolt . . . And vainly shakes, and cannot shake the gate.'[15] *An Old-World Thicket* concerns anger, depression, resignation, loss of faith, represented in a deliberately abstracted form relieved by natural symbol — the birds, the aspens and the 'widening waters'. It is bracketed by two significant and comprehensible images, the 'mother-bird' and her brood of the opening lines, and 'A patriarchal ram' and 'all his kin' whose moonlit figures represent the final peace and resignation of the poet-speaker. Tennyson's poem (in which the poet-dreamer is a passive observer) looks at women as archetypal representations; Dante's journey is into the self. Rossetti's self-conscious use of the two frames is a daring sleight of hand by which the reader is tricked into accepting a female Dante as an appropriate epic searcher for inner truth and peace. Tennyson's poem is almost a self-parody of male dreams about female sexual power: Rossetti's is a moody evocation of female impotence. Yet, as in *Goblin Market*, the images of *An Old-World Thicket* can no more be made to fit a coherent psychic schema than translated into social or autobiographical narrative. The poem seems to move from the fantasy world of magical birds who 'speak more wisdom than we speak' to the social symbol of the ram's tinkling bell which controls the flock, from forest to farm. But within the poem the imagery is wilder; the fluctuating mood of the poet-speaker, 'Adrift upon life's sea without an ark', is all contradiction and conflict, in revolt against a life in which 'habit trains us not to break but bend'. The 'mazed' world of the forest orchestrates the speaker's mood; the dream state indicates that the poet sees the ram's control as illusory. The Gothic shifts from outer scene to inner feeling are not metaphorical but metonymic, contiguous statements about the positioning of the self in relation to the scene. Though these shifts are contained within an overarching metaphor (the belief that man's submission to God brings salvation and relief) we need not follow Christina Rossetti's ram all the way home, responding instead to the multiple meanings projected through the dreamer and her forest.

The dream-state poem allows a suspension of the real and a representation of mood rather than narrative. Dream-form gives the writer still more permission, for it disclaims all conscious responsibility for the statement in the poem, and repels an interpretation of its content. There is a witty example of the ability to deflect analysis in Christina Rossetti's 'My Dream', written *c.* 1855. The poem is a delicious fantasy about a 'crew' of royal crocodiles who emerge from the Euphrates and are eaten by their king, represented as a sort of natural monarch —

> His punier brethren quaked before his tail,
> Broad as a rafter, potent as a flail.
> . . . .
> He knew no law, he feared no binding law,
> But ground them with inexorable jaw.

The cannibal crocodile sleeps, and in sleep dwindles 'to the common size'. Reduced, he watches a 'wingèd vessel' tame the wild waters and sheds 'appropriate tears':

> What can it mean? you ask. I answer not
> For meaning, but myself must echo, What?
> And tell it as I saw it on the spot.[16]

Christina Rossetti is wickedly proprietary about this 'dream'; its first line ('Hear now a curious dream I dreamed last night') mimics the sort of breakfast-table clarion that submits the rest of the family to the dreamer's monologue. The 'dream' itself is overloaded with symbols — heathen, phallic and patriarchal — but they are as elusive as a gnomic folk tale. The poem irritated William Rossetti, for he could make little of it. As long as he was convinced his sister was writing up a real dream he was content to leave it as an example of

> the exceptional turn of mind of Christina Rossetti — the odd freakishness which flecked the extreme and almost excessive seriousness of her thought . . . It looks like the narration of a true dream; and nothing seems as if it could account for so eccentric a train of notions, except that she in fact dreamed them. And yet she did not;

for, in a copy of her collected edition of 1875, I find that she has marked the piece 'not a real dream.' As it was not a real dream, and she chose nevertheless to give it verbal form, one seeks for a meaning in it, and I for one cannot find any that bears development. She certainly liked the poem, and in this I and others quite agreed with her; I possess a little bit of paper, containing three illustrations of her own to *The Dream*, and bearing the date 16 March '55. There is (1) the dreamer slumbering under a tree, from which the monarch crocodile dangles; (2) the crocodile sleeping with 'unstrung claw,' as the 'wingèd vessel' approaches; and (3) the crocodile as he reared up in front of the vessel and 'wrung his hands.'[17]

Christina Rossetti's choice of passages for illustration is almost as tantalising as the poem itself. 'My Dream' is a joky lesson to critical headhunters tracking either phalluses, patriarchs or oppressors, or all three; Christina Rossetti's illustrations suggest that she 'did it to annoy' because she knew it teased.

'My Dream' teases, but it also gives pleasure, as William Rossetti ruefully admits. So too does a much more intense lyric in dream-form, 'On the Wing' (1862), which reiterates the themes of love and loss so familiar in Rossetti's poetry:

Once in a dream (for once I dreamed of you)
    We stood together in an open field;
    Above our heads two swift-winged pigeons wheeled,
Sporting at ease and courting full in view: —
When loftier still a broadening darkness flew,
    Down-swooping, and a ravenous hawk revealed;
    Too weak to fight, too fond to fly, they yield;
So farewell life and love and pleasures new.
Then as their plumes fell fluttering to the ground,
    Their snow-white plumage flecked with crimson drops,
        I wept, and thought I turned towards you to weep:
    But you were gone; while rustling hedgerow tops
Bent in a wind which bore to me a sound
        Of far-off piteous bleat of lambs and sheep.[18]

As in *Goblin Market*, the speaker is careful not to confuse punishment (the loss of 'life and love and pleasures new') with guilt, which remains deliberately unassigned. The poem contains a series of highly condensed visual images in which the supposed lovers are both participants and witnesses of a roughly sketched primal scene, but one which contains pre-lapsarian innocence too. The hawk is the agent of vengeance for the 'open', 'full in view' courting in which birds and bird-watchers are engaged. Caught in the act by father, fate, authority, the birds are too 'weak' and too 'fond' to fly. Death and lost virginity mingle in the crimson drops on white plumage. Memory and prophecy are bound up in the vision; how or why the dream-lover is excised from the scene we do not know. Without his presence, the piteous bleat of 'lambs and sheep' (the mother-child dyad), calls the dreamer back to the lonely world of women and children to which all unwedded females are consigned.

Both the dream-form and the allegorical scene release the poem from a conventionally moral conclusion. The dreamer and her lover are spectators of, not actors in, a drama which enacts a 'natural' tragedy. The pigeons' fate is connected to the dreamer's largely through narrative contiguity: they watch the fate of others. The interpolated conclusion, 'So farewell life and love and pleasures new', is ambiguously related to both human and animal couples. But the 'ravenous hawk' is the poem's villain – emphasised, even over-emphasised, as a natural, not divine, avenger. No sexual or social transgression is implied by the words of the poem, so that we have no means of connecting the traumatic scene in the air with the history of loss attributed to the dreamer. Dreamer and lover remain in a metonymic relation to the pigeons and hawk; unspecified, incomplete. Although 'On the Wing' is more coherent in its internal narrative, potentially easier to reduce to a psychological analogue, it too is essentially a fragment snipped out of a fuller social or psychological history. Since the dreamer is not 'responsible' for developed meaning the reader is free to fill up the space between the field and the air with her own connotative meaning. One might ask why such a poem requires a feminist reading. Although the images may evoke memories and fears in either sex, the closing link between dreamer, lambs and sheep makes it clear that it is spoken from the female position. Women readers may thus find it a particularly poignant focus around which to organise their own emotions. I came across a comment of William Rossetti's in his memoir of Christina which is in no way a gloss on any particular poem, but suggests one determining factor among others on all of them. Rossetti wrote that Christina had 'a rather unusual feeling of deference for "the head of the family," whoever he might be – my father, Dante Gabriel, and finally myself.'[19]

Emily Dickinson

Christina Rossetti's verse offers up the dream-scene as fantasy in bursts of rich sensuous confusion. Emily Dickinson only rarely uses indirect or 'permissive' forms when she wishes to project sensuous or lascivious images. She is more likely to go for overt statement, as in 'Wild Nights'. Dream-state, rarely signalled by the expressed convention of dreaming, is used to emphasise the dislocation between the poem's images — shifts from inner to outer representation, from realism to fantasy. Perhaps because she did not anticipate a wide reading public for her verse she had little hesitation about using metonymic or synecdochic tropes such as 'If end I gained/It ends beyond/Indefinite disclosed—.'[20] Queries about the 'Indefinite disclosed' are common in her work, applying equally to the human and to the divine condition. The use of the word 'blank' to signify an unrepresentable emotion or position is typical — 'From Blank to Blank—/A Threadless Way/I pushed Mechanic feet—' or 'Pain has an element of blank.'[21] The dream scene is, however, implicitly invoked in certain poems, not all of them within the sub-genre of 'difficult' verse discussed here. The famous lyric 'Because I could not stop for Death'[22] is an instance where the dream is a secondary frame for a poem in which the primary convention is a classical or medieval reference to death as driver, boatman or charioteer — here, in genteel bourgeois disguise as the carriage-man. Within the poem the landscapes of school, fields and cemetery seem arbitrary choices, laconic milestones viewed as in a dream. The final thrust of the poem turns in part on the distortion of time as it might be experienced in a dream-state: the moment of recognition of death is longer than the centuries of eternity themselves. Here a traditional metaphor brackets a more eccentric and obscure series of events.

Two other poems in unstated dream-form are more ambitious and less easily understood. Both are well known. 'I started Early — Took my Dog —' moves from a realistic opening to a deliberately fantastic centre. 'The Mermaids in the Basement . . . And Frigates — in the Upper Floor' invite the speaker as grounded mouse into a Gothic sea mansion. In the last section, Gothic, fantasy and reality are elided and the 'Tide' as man engulfs 'Shoe', 'Apron', 'Belt' and 'Bodice' until the speaker starts and heads back towards the 'Solid Town' where 'with a Mighty look —/At me — The Sea withdrew —.'[23] The overt formalised allegory in this poem notifies us that it is a daytime fantasy, on the surface a comic one. The inversion of the looker and the looked-at is funny; the mermaids stare at the conventionally dressed speaker, the frigate invites the land mouse on board. The 'Tide' — nature, lover, rapist, gentleman

— strands the retreating speaker in her safe social world. Because both sex and death are incorporated in the sea as symbol, as an unstable reference, and because the dreamer's desire in relation to this lover-destroyer is also unstable, the mermaids and the frigate act as displacing images to decoy the reader away from the more erotic and unnerving implications of the poem, joking up its tragic overtones. The strategies of disguise here bear a strong resemblance to those used by Christina Rossetti in both 'My Dream' and 'On the Wing'.

Much more powerful and unpleasant is 'My Life had stood — a Loaded Gun.'[24] Surely we are at least safe in the land of metaphor: the speaker is the gun; God/lover/man is represented in the 'master' as the omnipotent figure who will shoot the gun. Indeed he is all of these. But wait a moment, guns? Guns and bullets, the 'Yellow Eye', 'emphatic Thumb', are phallic objects. The Victorian model marriage, where masters are men and slaves are obedient women, is broken up in this poem. Master and gun, hunter and weapon are hardly God and his servant Emily, lover and mistress. Instead they are two parts of the phallic actor, the speaking gun and the silent but ambulatory gun-toter. It is unclear throughout the poem who is in command, and the bullet-gun-master are welded into an androgynous fantasy — violent, fetishistic and atavistic. The poem toys with omnipotence, banishes femininity. The 'Life' that had 'stood' 'in Corners' is decoded into something quite other than the familiar poet-speaker whose bodice and apron mark both her subjectivity and subjection.

Anne Sexton, talking about her own poetry in an interview some years ago, supports the concept that the poet herself may not want to know too much of what's going on in a poem. 'An image might come to me, a line — you don't know where it's going to go. It goes its own way.' She asks that a poem 'be what it means to its *readers*' as well as to the army of critics. 'I feel that the poems I love by other people belong to *me*. I don't need to hear what these poems mean, because they may have a meaning so deep I don't *want* to know.'[25] To accept Sexton's point as poet and reader is not to beg the question of meaning, to return literature to a purely subjective relationship between text and audience, or to valorise all individual interpretations. But it may be that these complex lyrics of Rossetti and Dickinson were designed to circumvent the resistance of writer and reader as well as to defy contemporary critical reduction. Female lyric poets of the last century, I would argue, chose to cut out the social in order to foreground the psychic subject, though they were often without a traditional language with which to describe its antics. It is tempting to see their poetry as historical verification of the theories about femininity and the unconscious available to us — even, to credit them with a barely suppressed, subversive anticipation of Freud. But while these poems do throw psychological states into sharp relief and avoid realistic reconstructions of social relations, they cannot transcend the ideological orientation of their authors; the very absence of the ideologies of social realism in the texts signals the binding strength of their presence in the material world of the poems' creation. Further, it signals women's difficulty in speaking their psychological conflicts through its rational discourse. Writing criticism, like writing poetry, is — among other things — a political act; and the writing of Marxist-feminist literary criticism is not a neutral activity, but speaks from within a specifically defined political dialectic. This group of lyrics pierces to the root of a particularly painful, unresolved contradiction in feminist theory — the contradiction between progressive social struggle and the recalcitrant female psyche — and so moves us further towards an interrogation of our own positions.

Notes

1. Thomas H. Johnson (ed.), *The Complete Poems of Emily Dickinson* (London, 1975), p. 266. All references are to this edition.
2. My use of these distinctions is largely drawn from Roman Jakobson, *Studies on Child Language and Aphasia* (The Hague, 1971), pp. 44-5 and *passim*.
3. The leading modern theoretician of phallocentric theory is the French psychoanalyst, Jacques Lacan. See *Ecrits*, trans. Alan Sheridan (London, 1977). For concentric theory see Karen Horney, *Feminine Psychology* (London, 1967). More recent discussion of 'phallocentric' versus 'concentric' include Luce Irigaray, 'Women's Exile', *Ideology and Consciousness*, vol. i (1977), pp. 62-76; Parveen Adams, 'Representation and Sexuality', *m/f*, vol. i (1978), pp. 66-82; and Michèle Montrelay, 'Inquiry into Femininity', *m/f*, vol. i (1978), pp. 83-101.
4. See *Salt and Bitter and Good: Three Centuries of English and American Women Poets* (New York and London, 1975), p. 181.
5. William Michael Rossetti (ed.), *The Poetical Works of Christina Rossetti with Memoir and Notes etc.* (London, 1904), p. 6. All references are to this edition.
6. Ibid., p. 7.
7. Ibid., p. 8.
8. Maureen Duffy, *The Erotic World of Faery* (London, 1972), p. 290.
9. Ibid., pp. 288-9.
10. Ellen Moers, *Literary Women* (New York, 1976), p. 105.
11. Johnson, *Complete Poems of Emily Dickinson*, p. 115.
12. *The Divine comedy, I: Hell*, trans. Dorothy L. Sayers (London, 1977), Canto I, 11. 1-3.
13. She was not, however, above parodying him; I suspect that Rossetti's much undervalued poem, *The Prince's Progress* in which a wayward prince lets his betrothed die of grief and age while he is kept Ulysses-like on a series of adventures, is partly an impish send-up of Tennyson's *The Princess*, where an over-

eager prince wins his reluctant feminist fiancée by breaking into her all-women's university. Tennyson conjures up an Amazonian enclave of radical feminists: Rossetti counters with the reality – docile princess waiting in vain for an errant knight who arrives 'Too late for love, too late for joy' (*Poetical Works*, p. 34).

14. *Poetical Works*, p. 64.

15. Ibid., p. 65.

16. Ibid., pp. 315-16.

17. Ibid., p. 479.

18. Ibid., pp. 352-3.

19. Ibid., p. lxvi.

20. Johnson, *Complete Poems of Emily Dickinson*, p. 345.

21. Ibid., pp. 373, 323.

22. Ibid., p. 350.

23. Ibid., pp. 254-5.

24. Ibid., p. 369.

25. Gregory Fitz Gerald, 'The Choir from the Soul: A Conversation with Anne Sexton', *The Massachusetts Review*, vol. xix (1978), pp. 69-88.

4 BEYOND DETERMINISM: GEORGE ELIOT AND VIRGINIA WOOLF

Gillian Beer

In this essay I want to look at the particular patterns of intelligibility implied by determinism and to think about ways in which the dominance of deterministic organisations of experience in the later nineteenth and earlier twentieth centuries bore upon women, and in particular upon two writers: George Eliot and Virginia Woolf. In the course of the argument I hope to demonstrate some of the ulterior or alternative patterns created by the two novelists. These fictive patterns question, dilate or surpass the deterministic ones which were so vigorous a part of their intellectual and emotional upbringing. To put it at its simplest: can the female self be expressed through plot or must it be conceived in resistance to plot? Must it lodge 'between the acts'? Virginia Woolf said that she could not make up plots and George Eliot that conclusions are at best negations. At the end of *Middlemarch* George Eliot writes of Dorothea's two marriages:

> Certainly those determining acts of her life were not ideally beautiful. They were the mixed result of young and noble impulse struggling amidst the conditions of an imperfect social state, in which great feelings will often take the aspect of error, and great faith the aspect of illusion. For there is no creature whose inward being is so strong that it is not greatly determined by what lies outside it.[1]

Here the conditions of an imperfect social state bear in upon young and noble impulse, changing its aspect and cramping its powers without obliterating its nature. The ironic transformation of 'great' into 'greatly' registers this diminishing and enclosing: 'great feelings', 'great faith', 'greatly determined'. The passage also brings out an issue which I should clarify at the outset. The determinants of gender, upbringing, heredity, class, historical period, are all constituent elements in our experience. The idea of determinism is newer, and is in itself perhaps the most powerful single determinant of the past hundred years. It is with the system-making powers of this idea and their bearing on women's experience that I am chiefly concerned.

Determinism is a comparatively recent word. The first instance noted by the *Oxford English Dictionary* is 1846. In 1844 it was still possible for Marx to see free, conscious activity as man's species-characteristic, a view he was not to hold for long. So George Eliot wrote at a time when determinism was still a fresh idea which seemed to promise the possibility of a knowable world without godhead. For Virginia Woolf it is a pattern associated with her father's generation, and with the authority of a male-organised world. Before determinism, necessity required, or Fate struck. In the idea of Fate the apparent autonomy of the human being is interrupted by Fate's interventions and the individual proves to be part of a plot not of his own making. But Fate's interventions are selective, determinism is all-inclusive. In determinism autonomy is extinguished and 'the consciousness of freedom rests chiefly upon an oblivion of the antecedents to our choice'. That quotation from William Thomson's *Oxford Essays* (1855) illustrates how already the idea of preconsciousness or even of the unconscious was becoming a needed element in the definition of determinism. Freud's analysis of the role of the unconscious in conscious motive extended the area of the determined and made it impossible for consciousness ever fully to encompass or control it.

The *Oxford English Dictionary*'s earliest instance emphasises the rationalism of the deterministic idea; Hamilton Reid contrasts the two schemes of necessity, one that of 'brute or blind Fate', the other 'rational Determinism'. In all the early instances there is a suggestion that although the individual may be inattentive to the sources of his own state, determinism represents a knowable order which is to be preferred to the aberrant and unscrupulous interventions of 'brute Fate'. Fate reverses or propels, is an external force. Determinism implies an inherent and irreversible order capable of including all phenomena. The Freudian concept of over-determination emphasises the multiple pathways by which one arrives at the same place. The individual is directed into a restricted time, space and activity. Although she cannot know all the conditions that have brought her there, they are, according to this arrangement of experience, ineluctably present, intertwined and matted so thick that there is no space, no interruption, no moment, which can escape from sequence. Determinism emphasises relations, but relations fixed in a succession which more and more acutely delimits and characterises. It is a process we recognise in *Middlemarch*'s melancholy.

The all-inclusiveness which is essential to deterministic organisation of experience means that any method of seeking escape from its omniverous powers will be cast as wish-fulfilment, impossibility, something freakish and fitful, something delusory. Feelings take the aspect of error and faith the aspect of illusion. So all such assertion of apparently other perceptions – the indeterminate, the reversible, the reality of that which might have been, the multiplicity of the future, the moment broken away from sequence, broken away from relations, fear without object, lack without object – is seen as second-order experience, doomed and negative. It is perceived as either failing to recognise the laws which underlie apparent heterogeneity or as merely fancifully ignoring them. Virginia Woolf in her essay on George Eliot explores the nature of desire in George Eliot's women:

> In learning they seek their goal; in the ordinary tasks of womanhood; in the wider service of their kind. They do not find what they seek, and we cannot wonder. The ancient consciousness of woman, charged with suffering and sensibility, and for so many ages dumb, seems in them to have brimmed and overflowed and uttered a demand for something – they scarcely know what – for something that is perhaps incompatible with the facts of human existence.[2]

Virginia Woolf does not specify what those facts may be, though she says that George Eliot had too strong an intelligence to tamper with them. As so often in her critical writing, she draws back, leaving only that 'perhaps' to suggest an alternative view of possibilities. In the ordering of her fiction she is bolder. Indeed, both these writers are more exploratory in the ordering of their fiction than in polemics. They work askance from the expected rather than confront it.

I have written up to now of determinism as a concept in a way which might be held to bear both on men's and women's idea of the self. Of all the figures who gave energy to the concept of scientific determinism Darwin is the most influential. In *The Origin of Species* (1859) he wrote that chance is the name we give to 'as yet unknown laws' – a passage which trawls the future back into the deterministic net. In *The Origin of Species* the radical insistence that transformation *has* occurred and species *do* change disguised for a time the equal insistence upon order, upon things being inevitably as they are because of their antecedents, upon a gradualistic process so extended as to be always beyond the horizon of the individual human life. In *The Descent of Man* (1871) the emphasis upon the determined and the irremediable is much more marked. If women have a quarrel with Darwin, this study, with its use of anthropological even in preference to biological evidence, must be its source. Eliza Gamble, indeed, challenged Darwin's reading of the evidence in her book *The Evolution of Woman: An Inquiry into the Dogma of her Inferiority to Man*, published in 1894. In *The Descent of Man* Darwin concentrates on sexual selection as one of the controls in evolutionary process. He wished to emphasise that random mutation was not the sole, or indeed the dominant mechanism, in man's development. Darwin bases his argument on a fixed notion of sexual distinction. 'Man is more courageous, pugnacious and energetic than woman, and has a more inventive genius. His brain is absolutely larger, but whether or not proportionately to his larger body, has not, I believe, been fully ascertained.'[3] Writing at exactly the same time George Eliot comments ironically in the 'Prelude' to *Middlemarch* on society's reaction to women's yearnings:

> Some have felt that these blundering lives are due to the inconven-
> ient indefiniteness with which the Supreme Power has fashioned the
> natures of women: if there were one level of feminine incompe-
> tence as strict as the ability to count three and no more, the social
> lot of women might be treated with scientific certitude.[4]

One of the still crucial issues of debate among theorists in the women's movement, such as Montrelay and Kristeva, drawing for example on Karen Horney, is whether biological determinism is a dangerous under-lying element in our insistence on the distinctiveness of women's psycho-sexual understanding of the world. Darwin identified women with a position intermediate between child and man and used the analogy with 'the childhood of the race'. Extending the then current metaphor of the varying races as being at different points in the growth towards adulthood, he places women in the position of a less deve-loped race, one closer to the childhood of humanity:

> It is generally admitted that with women the powers of intuition,
> of rapid perception, and perhaps of imitation, are more strongly
> marked than in man; but some, at least, of these faculties are charac-
> teristic of the lower races, and therefore of a past and lower state of
> civilization.

Moreover, he suggests that 'during manhood' men 'generally undergo a severe struggle in order to maintain themselves and their families; and this will tend to keep up or even increase their mental powers, and, as a consequence, the present inequality between the sexes.'[5] A passage like this clearly gives particular pungency to Virginia Woolf's ironic glance at the collapse of manhood at the discovery that the women servants (a neat condensation of terms) are getting along very nicely without his providing for them:

He has been out all day in the city earning his living, and he comes home at night expecting repose and comfort to find that his servants — the women servants — have taken possession of the house. He goes into the library — an august apartment which he is accustomed to have all to himself — and finds the kitchen maid curled up in the arm chair reading Plato. He goes into the kitchen and there is the cook engaged in writing a Mass in B flat. He goes into the billiard room and finds the parlourmaid knocking up a fine break at the table. He goes into the bed room and there is the housemaid working out a mathematical problem. What is he to do? He has been accustomed for centuries to have that sumptuous mansion all to himself, to be master in his own house. Well of course his first instinct is to dismiss the whole crew. But he reflects that then he would have to do the work of the house himself, and he has not been trained to do it. — Nature has denied him certain (quite essential) gifts. He therefore says that these women servants may practise their silly little amusements in their spare time, but if he finds them neglecting the sacred duties which nature has imposed upon them he will do something very dreadful indeed.

I am the bread winner; how am I going to support a wife and family if my wife and family can support themselves? No, I will make it as hard as possible for my wife and family to support themselves because [I then hope they will give up doing it, and they will let me support them and it] for reasons which I need not go into but they have to do with the most profound instincts of my nature it is much pleasanter to support a wife and family, than to allow a wife and family to support themselves.[6]

Darwin does acknowledge that educating women when they are close to adulthood might produce some changes:

In order that woman should reach the same standard as man, she ought, when nearly adult, to be trained to energy and perseverance and to have her reason and imagination exercised to the highest point; and then she would probably transmit these qualities chiefly to her adult daughters.

But for these effects to spread he notes that such women must, statistically, bear more children than their less educated sisters. Darwin is not without irony in his attitude to the relations between the sexes; of music in courtship he observes, for example, that:

> Women are generally thought to possess sweeter voices than men, and as far as this serves as any guide, we may infer that they first acquired musical powers in order to attract the other sex. But if so, this must have occurred long ago, before our ancestors had become sufficiently human to treat and value their women merely as useful slaves.

However, he goes on to state that in contra-distinction to the idea of slavery, 'In civilised life man is largely, but by no means exclusively, influenced in the choice of his wife by external appearance.'[7] Therefore sexual selection will always emphasise the predominance of beauty over other characteristics. Significantly, Darwin assumes that among humans, as opposed to other species, it is always the men who do the selecting. The implication of his argument is that women's characteristics will be determined by their acceptability to men. It's a way of squeezing and defining the identity of women which George Eliot glances at ironically in one of the epigraphs for *Daniel Deronda* — a novel preoccupied with the conditions of the marriage market and inheritance:

> What woman should be? Sir, consult the taste
> Of marriageable men. This planet's store
> In iron, cotton, wool, or chemicals —
> All matter rendered to our plastic skill,
> Is wrought in shapes responsive to demand:
> The market's pulse makes index high or low,
> By rule sublime. Our daughters must be wives,
> And to be wives must be what men will choose:
> Men's taste is woman's test. You mark the phrase?
> 'Tis good, I think? — the sense well winged and poised
> With t's and s's.[8]

Women are shaped, like other natural matter, into forms 'responsive to demand'. The rancorous ironies generated by this situation spread throughout society and throughout this novel whose space and whose ellipses condense the pretensions of the present-day English upper-class assumptions into pilulous smallness.

It is in the context of such arguments: from zoology (women's brains are smaller), from social evolutionary theory (women are fixed in a state analogous to that of less developed races), from sexual conditions (women must be wives and can become so only by representing what men value in them), that the major determining argument about sexual distinction grows. Darwin's book appeared in 1871, just before *Middlemarch* was published. In the succeeding years George Eliot was at work on *Daniel Deronda*. Virginia Woolf selects the 1880s as the period on which she offers analytical intervening commentaries revealing the oppression and denial internalised by a young middle-class woman in the 1880s. *The Pargiters* attempts to distinguish with tonic clarity between the socially determined elements in women's *understanding* of their experience, the constraints of that experience, and what is endemic to experience. Clearly there are some processes which are inescapable and irreversible: physical growth is one of them. Virginia Woolf comments in 'A Sketch of the Past':

> But somehow into that picture must be brought, too, the sense of movement and change. Nothing remained stable long. One must get the feeling of everything approaching and then disappearing, getting large, getting small, passing at different rates of speed past the little creature; one must get the feeling that made her press on, the little creature driven on as she was by growth of her legs and arms, driven without her being able to stop it, or to change it, driven as a plant is driven up out of the earth, up until the stalk grows, the leaf grows, buds swell. That is what is indescribable, that is what makes all the images too static, for no sooner has one said this was so, than it was past and altered.[9]

Here Virginia Woolf seizes upon the rapidity, the silently expanding kaleidoscope of childhood growth. The driving power of growth is an ungainsayable and successive element in experience — an experience which she ceases to recount here as she reaches puberty and the day of her mother's death. The particular organisation implied by evolutionary theory and determinism borrows the idea of irreversible onward sequence from the experience of growth. It can't run backwards, though it may include equally convergence and branching. Nor can it stay still. George Eliot wrote just after the appearance of Darwin's *Origin of*

Species, 'But to me the Development theory and all other explanations of processes by which things came to be, produces a feeble impression compared with the mystery that lies under the processes.'[10] Though she tended in her early work to identify this mystery with origins, George Eliot never entirely does away with a sense of some slumberous and unchanging mystery outside – or as she puts it – 'under' process. I think it is possible to see the recrudescence of this sense as part of an attempt to move beyond determinism which is most subtly organised in *Daniel Deronda*.

But I would like first to look at the book in which she seems to be working most acceptingly within the confines of that which is determined: *The Mill on the Floss*. The onward movement in determinism has a particular implication for narrative. Our *understanding* of events must run in reverse order. We can understand the present only in terms of its past, which is seen as stable and irremediable. If Virginia Woolf emphasises the unfurling and lapsing of time in her images of physical growth, George Eliot emphasises the passionate slowness of childhood in *The Mill on the Floss*. Though the narrative is arranged like memory with crystal-clear episodes of recall, the book dwells upon the shaping elements of Maggie's emotional growth – within a particular small community for which George Eliot provides not only a full account of the present trading activities, but a history of its past and an eponymous saint's story. Narrow as the society and environment are, George Eliot remarked in conversation that the conditions for a young girl in such a community in her youth were in fact far worse than she had shown them to be in *The Mill*. A series of episodes dramatise the development and the starvation of Maggie's possibilities: there is a superabundance of intelligence and emotion which can find no answering form in its environment; Maggie's father ruminates: 'a woman's no business wi' being so clever; it'll turn to trouble, I doubt.'[11]

The organicist form of the *Bildungsroman* is invoked, with its emphasis upon the gradual assimilation of the young man (say, *Wilhelm Meister*) to his environment. In that organicist form we are left with a sense both of completion and disillusionment – the autocratic self acquiesces at last in the humdrum terms of its own survival within society. But *The Mill on the Floss* demonstrates that for the heroine, as opposed to the hero of *Bildungsroman*, there can be no such accommodation. (Kingsley makes a similar point about the proletarian hero of *Alton Locke* who must die at the book's end on the way to a new life abroad because there is no place for him in current society.) Death may become the only means of escape from the determining bonds of a particular society — especially is this so if the author subscribes intellectually to the idea of determinism. So at the end of *The Mill on the Floss* George Eliot reverses the novel's flow, allowing Maggie to escape the parsimonious anguish of a misunderstood life amidst a narrow community. Instead she sweeps back upon the flood waters over the scenes of her youth, over the Red Deeps to childhood, back to the Mill and her brother, to 'the strong resurgent love . . . that swept away all the later impressions of hard, cruel offence and misunderstanding, and left only the deep, underlying, unshakable memories of early union'.[12] The transformations of growth and development are reversed; the past is recoverable; Maggie appears as the active rescuer of her alienated brother Tom. When she had floated down the stream with Stephen Guest (set off from the community by his name) her will was in abeyance. At the end she is endowed with a kind of natural freedom. The chapter is entitled 'The Final Rescue' and the uneasiness which many readers feel with the conclusion is, I think, hinted at defensively in that address from author to reader: it is George Eliot who rescues Maggie from the grim, cramped future that the social determinism of the plot has seemed to make inescapable.

George Eliot chose always to imprison her most favoured women — Dinah, Maggie, Dorothea. She does not allow them to share her own extraordinary flight, her escape from St Oggs and from Middlemarch. She needs them to endure their own typicality. But at the end of *The Mill* her obduracy fails. She allows to Maggie the fulfilment of an infantile, passionate, incestuous recovery of love: 'In their death they were not divided.' The solution exceeds the book's terms because George Eliot permits to herself in addition that fulfilment of immersion and self-denial, the obliteration of self in familial love, which she steadfastly resisted in her own adult life. What we have in *The Mill* is an apparently deterministic order which in its conclusion whirls backwards into desire, instead of into understanding and rationalisation. George Eliot is fascinated by the unassuageable longings of her heroine. She allows them fulfilment in a form of plot which simply glides out of the channelled sequence of social growth and makes literal the expansion of desire. The river loses its form in the flood. This total dowsing of the self is an uncontrolled challenge to the idea of necessary sequence. It lacks bleakness, is even lubricious, and yet that sense of the inordinate and of full satisfaction which George Eliot creates in the conclusion does realise confused and passionate needs. For women under oppression such needs can find no real form within an ordering of plot which relies upon sequence, development, the understanding and renunciation of the past, the acceptance of the determined present. The end of *The Mill* is symbolic outcry. It goes outside the forms of social realism to which determinism is at that period so closely linked. Social realism later becomes for Virginia Woolf the enemy of the real.

So even in as early a novel as *The Mill*, we can see George Eliot straining the idea of 'necessary sequence' which she at the same time found so reassuring. It seemed to imply secure pathways, channels for the 'persistent self' of which she wrote in *Middlemarch*: 'Strange, that some of us, with quick alternate vision, see beyond our infatuations, and even while we rave on the heights, behold the wide plain where our persistent self pauses and awaits us.'[13] The persistence of the self is important to her, but the idea of persistence admits also that of transformation in her work: 'Character is not writ in marble.' This sense of 'self' as the enduring core of being, capable of being the object of its own attention, is a surprisingly recent sense for the word. For George Eliot the topic is complicated by the high value she places upon self-abnegation. Maggie's self can be fully asserted only in death; in life she is striving for compliancy. George Eliot is preoccupied with the interplay of organism and medium, but in her work tragedy is generated out of the impassibility of the medium — the very slow rate at which society accepts change, particularly change of assumptions whatever the diversity of practice, so that a quick being like Maggie or Dorothea will be trapped in time, in a medium whose rate of change lags, and so forecloses their futures. Virginia Woolf, too, recognises the 'immense forces society brings to play upon each of us' — but the image she uses to express this emphasises the rapidity with which sensibility shifts:

> Consider what immense forces society brings to play upon each of us, how that society changes from decade to decade; and also from class to class; well, if we cannot analyse these invisible presences, we know very little of the subject of the memoir; and again how futile life-writing becomes. I see myself as a fish in a stream; deflected; held in place, but cannot describe the stream.[14]

'The present moment' is indescribable, or flat, she suggests at the end of *Orlando*. Language, even at its most feverish, is writing its own elegy and that of the experience which prompted it. It cannot, therefore, escape the past. But it can select and compress the past, surveying it instead of being embedded in it — and that is the function of pastiche in both *Orlando* and *Between the Acts*. It's a form of celebration and revenge simultaneously which allows her to rupture the continuities of language by fixing our attention on them. *Orlando* creates an order which shows the self as fantastically autonomous, jubilantly intact through changes of gender, of nation, of historical period. *Orlando* is play, coming immediately after *To the Lighthouse* and its grave exploration of sexual polarities and of the self at the mercy of its historical place in time. *Orlando*'s jesting reminds us of the *power* of what it frees us momentarily from believing in: the determinants of gender, individual ageing, history. Yet the suppression of such belief has its own authority: it unravels accustomed patterns and suggests other orders of possibility. The disjunction between the self and history, the speeding up of time, create an unreflective victory over evolutionary determinism. The self in this book is clad in gender and history and survives them.

Elaine Showalter in *A Literature of their Own* dismisses *Orlando* as 'tedious high camp', but this, I think, is because she is preoccupied with her attack on androgyny. Indeed she is impatient with all Virginia Woolf's later books which she holds 'show signs of a progressive technical inability to accommodate the facts and crises of day-to-day experience'.[15] I do not believe that Virginia Woolf had lost a technical ability she earlier commanded, but rather that she had come to distrust the day-to-day as a sufficient register of reality. By concentrating her attention on the polemical writing it seems to me that Elaine Showalter has missed considering the narrative politics of Virginia Woolf's re-organisation of experience in a work like *The Waves*. If Virginia Woolf moves away from facts and crises it is because she denies the claim of such ordering to be all-inclusive. Escape is not necessarily a form of retreat or failure. Escape can mean freedom and the trying out of new possibilities after imprisonment. Similarly in her discussion of George Eliot, Showalter pays most attention to *The Mill on the Floss* where she tracks the fate of the 'feminine heroine' and barely mentions *Middlemarch* or *Daniel Deronda* which far more radically question assumptions about the limits of women's experience.

Julia Kristeva in *Polylogue* entitles one discussion 'La femme, ce n'est jamais ça'. She distrusts the new romanticism which places its belief in feminine identity — a practice which she sees as the inverse of 'phallocratisme'. She recommends 'cet aspect du travail de l'avant-garde qui dissout les identités, y compris les identités sexuelles'.[16] I will return to this in the discussion of *The Waves*. Here she is in argument with, for example, Michèle Montrelay whose 'Inquiry into Femininity' in *L'Ombre et le Nom* (1977) suggests that femininity is 'the blind spot' of the symbolic processes analysed by Freud. 'Two incompatible, heterogeneous territories co-exist inside the feminine unconscious: that of representation and that which remains the "dark continent".'[17] The themes of lack and absence become in Montrelay, as in Lacan, specific to women's primary psychosexual experiences, and hence to their art. Clearly such arguments draw upon Lacan's emphasis upon language as a pre-existing system which orders and constitutes the subject as the other, the object of desire, that which can never be fully known or realised through articulation.[18]

Without arguing a fully theorised case it is possible to see ways in which these suggestions do throw light upon the practice of the writers with whom I am concerned. But each of them is also held within a specific ideological situation related to determinism and I think that it is important to understand the means by which, as writers who are women, they bring that dominant order into question. Neither of them is content to remain within the sanctuary of women's issues. Nor did they acquiesce in that form of imperialism which claims all reasoned modes of discourse as male and accords to the female, lyrical interventions only. George Eliot, as Virginia Woolf remarked, reached beyond the sanctuary of womanhood into men's preserves and 'plucked for herself the strange bright fruits of art and knowledge' while not renouncing 'her own inheritance – the difference of view, the difference of standard'.[19] It is probably no coincidence that *The Mill on the Floss* and *To The Lighthouse*, the most autobiographic novels of their authors' careers, are also those which most emphasise the polarisation of sex roles. *Daniel Deronda* and *The Waves* are the works in which they each explore to the furthest reach possible the relationship between plot and the self, and study ways of loosening the ties between them. One way of doing this is to destabilise the idea of origins. This topic includes the relationship of writer and text and I would like briefly to discuss that first.

George Eliot, with her massive, eloquent and finely discriminate concern with intellectual issues, saw the question of origins in relation to evolutionary theory. She probably, like Lewes, perceived the theistic and patriarchal indications of Darwin's idea of 'the one form' and preferred the idea of the earth at the dawn of life as 'like a vast germinal membrane, every slightly diversified point producing its own vital form'.[20] After *Romola*, in which a succession of fathers and father-figures are killed and rejected, fathers are notably absent from her work (Caleb Garth has the appearance of a survivor from some other era).

One kind of origin has lost its power for her. But there remains in *Middlemarch* the problem of the narrator who is also the originator, the maker. The narrator is a source of succession and of determining interpretation, accorded an objectivity which has been shown to be impossible through the study of the partial knowledge of the characters. Does she simply exempt her own creativity and presence from her distrust of origins and teleology? She attempts ways out of the dilemma — the use of 'we' as a form of address, multiplicity and variability of event. But 'she' remains a hidden alternative, one that is not offered, allowed or mentioned, within what appears to be the absoluteness of the books ordering. Dorothea is permitted no transformation. She escapes from Middlemarch, not to create any substantive event, but to work through others. George Eliot, that figure of androgynous power for the 1870s, is inscribed within the work because of the presence of the author's name. Her surviving presence is part of the text, and she seems to stand, perhaps delusively, for ways out of the determinations of the book. In her case the organism did change medium. It's a dilemma which reminds us that the apparent all-inclusiveness of Middlemarch the town is a matter simply of its own pretensions. But it also suggests that the apparent all-inclusiveness of *Middlemarch* the book is dubious too and permits a doubtful optimism which runs counter to its own mordant study of entrapment.

In *Daniel Deronda* George Eliot renounces the advantages of her position as originator, determining sequence:

> Men can do nothing without the make-believe of a beginning. Even Science, the strict measurer, is obliged to start with a make-believe unit, and must fix on a point in the stars' unceasing journey when his sidereal clock shall pretend that time is at Nought. His less accurate grandmother Poetry has always been understood to start in the middle . . .[21]

Time sequence is disrupted and the author's location is blurred. There is no longer a gap between characters' discourse and writer's discourse. Instead of the attribution of linear or arboreal sequence, time is shuffled, overlapped, suspended. Origins become a theme, and are thus brought into the area of that which may be questioned and debated. But much of the imagery is proleptic, and second sight is a reality in the consciousness equally of Gwendolen and of Mordecai. Cycle, recurrence, the reversal of time and its suspension are all admitted. The book's surface is clandestine. The characters dwell in a formidable state of passivity amidst the buzz of unspoken obsession. The two men in Gwendolen's life are notably passive: Deronda with the passivity of the therapist and Grandcourt of the domineering. The figure of the mother becomes the predominant source of emotion — fathers simply do not count as origins in this text (even the Meyrick family is dominated by the mother). Gwendolen's mother is her only emotional concern beyond herself. Deronda's mother has liberated herself from the demands of race, love, motherhood, in order to follow her stupendous career as an opera singer; she appals and compels Deronda. She is punished but indomitable:

'Oh — the reasons of our actions!' said the Princess, with a ring of something like sarcastic scorn. 'When you are as old as I am, it will not seem so simple a question — "Why did you do this?" People talk of their motives in a cut and dried way. Every woman is supposed to have the same set of motives, or else to be a monster. I am not a monster, but I have not felt exactly what other women feel — or say they feel, for fear of being thought unlike others. When you reproach me in your heart for sending you away from me, you mean that I ought to say I felt about you as other women say they feel about their children. I did *not* feel that.[22]

Mothers are no longer Madonnas — Gwendolen avoids being either. Her triumph is that of barrenness; she does not conceive an heir to Grandcourt. Moreover George Eliot herself has renounced the role of mother towards her creations which had so powerfully drawn her earlier in her career. George Eliot lurks now in the periphrases of the text, no longer retaining for herself some space unblemished by the confusion of her characters' consciousness. This is signalled particularly by the way the ending abuts the present of herself and her first readers, permitting no retrospect from a vantage point of intervening years. That structure would settle and confirm a deterministic reading. Instead we are left — perhaps unsatisfactorily — with Mira and Deronda sailing off to the East to make a then seemingly impossible Zionist state (heredity triumphs over environment); while Gwendolen is left indeterminate, no longer emotionally and sexually dependent on Deronda, sustained by the outflaring of her own fear and need. Her future is not mapped for us: it is hard to imagine any activist outcome for Gwendolen, but this time the woman has not drowned. She is still there, not George Eliot's favourite kind of woman but permitted to survive that too — insistent, fertile, positive, undetermined. The eliding of the distance between writer and text and at the same time the opening up of gaps within the text perturb any sense of necessary sequence. At the same time the emphasis upon heredity as Daniel discovers his Jewishness suggests a contrary issue. It is too easy since Macherey to praise fissures simply for being there, for wrecking any pretence at wholeness, and in *Daniel Deronda* George Eliot certainly mourns the loss of cultural integrity rather than accepting it; the book strives structurally for a unity its perceptions will not fully permit. But in the image of Gwendolen, not quite wrecked, surviving into a future no one has charted for her, we glimpse a woman who has survived the business of sexual selection. Her image of herself is no longer simplified into a hierarchy of what is acceptable. Gwendolen has come to care for her own heterogeneity.

Now is life very solid or very shifting? I am haunted by the two contradictions. This has gone on for ever; will last for ever; goes down to the bottom of the world — this moment I stand on. Also it is transitory, flying, diaphanous. I shall pass like a cloud on the waves. Perhaps it may be that though we change, one flying after another, so quick, so quick, yet we are somehow successive and continuous we human beings, and show the light through. But what is the light?[23]

Virginia Woolf's books reject plot. Plot insists on origins, sequence, consequences, discovery, exclusion and closure. She reads the formulation of experience as being essentially social, and conforming to the particular rigid structure of English society. Plot gives primacy to our acted parts. 'She was convinced that society is man-made, that the chief occupations of men are the shedding of blood, the making of money, the giving of orders, and the wearing of uniforms, and that none of these occupations is admirable.'[24] This insistence on occupation and action she saw as part of a patriarchal ordering and it is an element in her quarrel with Arnold Bennett in 'Mr. Bennett and Mrs. Brown'. For her Bennett was an example of a masculine world of fixity and determination. His naturalistic novels emphasise the details of daily life and delineate that which is internal through a record of the external. She wanted, in contrast, to 'stand further back from life'. 'The psychological novelist has been prone to limit psychology to the psychology of personal intercourse . . . We long for some more impersonal relationship. We long for ideas, for dreams, for imaginations, for poetry.'[25] She wants a novel that will 'give the relation of the mind to general

ideas and its soliloquy in solitude . . . the outline rather than the detail'.
She distrusted what was called 'reality'; she sought to 'insubstantise'.[26]

At the time that she began writing *The Waves* Virginia Woolf experienced a particularly intense dislike of what she called 'this appalling
narrative business of the realist'.[27] All the usual elements of plot are
discarded or made peripheral: Bernard's marriage and four children,
Louis and Rhoda's affair, Louis's career in the city, the imperial theme
of the raj in India. We do in a veiled and unclimactic way know of all
these things but the book sloughs off most of the complexities of social
thriving and personal possession. The characters exist alongside each
other, partaking of each other's imagery, meeting at intervals in situations which reveal a hieratic dignity in their long acquaintance. The
book substitutes rhythm for plot. It makes no pretence at the busy
inclusiveness of social or scientific determinism. Instead it surveys
tides, waves, phases of human life, which have their own inescapable
forms but which require – and this, I think, is crucial – no prognosis,
no concealment, no fixing and polarisation by the writer. In other of
her works Virginia Woolf allowed genealogy the role of plot: *Night and
Day*, *The Years*. She liked to select rhythms for our attention which are
not purely human rhythms (the turn of tides, of night and day, a day).
But common to all her novels is the quietistic recognition of the single
life span.

The eschewing of plot is an aspect of her feminism. The avoidance
of narrative climax is a way of getting outside the fixing properties of
event. The effect of recurrences in *The Waves* is a kind of stasis. Im-
mobility becomes as important as evanescence, and as much a challenge
to deterministic plot. Moments are incandescent, but do not transform.
Doing without transformation means that perceptions abide and are
not cast into irreversible succession. The characteristics of style replace
plot. Virginia Woolf described the effect of Proust's style on her own
desire to write:

> Oh if I could write like that! I cry. And at the moment such is the
> astonishing vibration and saturation and intensification that he pro-
> cures – theres something sexual in it – that I feel I *can* write like
> that, and seize my pen and then I *can't* write like that.[28]

'Saturation' is the word that Virginia Woolf used to describe what she
desired to produce in *The Waves*, 'a saturated unchopped completeness'.[29] The author is all-penetrative because expressed through style,
not plot. In this way the question of origins is suspended. The style

with its heightened sense-perceptions creates arousal without climax.

Arnold Bennett had earlier seen an 'utter absence of feeling for form' as typically feminine. Writing of George Eliot in his *Journals* he comments:

> Her style, though not without shrewdness, is too rank to have any enduring vitality. People call it 'masculine.' Quite wrong! It is down-right, aggressive, sometimes rude, but genuinely masculine, never. On the contrary it is transparently feminine — feminine in its lack of restraint, its wordiness, and the utter absence of feeling for form that characterises it.[30]

This confident attribution of male and female characteristics to style is still to be found at quite a simple level in criticism of Virginia Woolf and should make one wary of easy polarisations which reproduce embedded assumptions about male and female character. James Naremore, for example, in *The World Without a Self* (1973) complains that in *The Waves*,

> There are times when Virginia Woolf seems untrue to her characters, making them all speak with a peculiarly feminine sadness and wonder, as when Bernard the child says 'The air no longer rolls its long, unhappy, purple waves over us', or when he excitedly declares 'Let us take possession of our secret territory, which is lit by pendant currants like a candelabra.' In neither case does he sound much like a child, but more especially he does not sound like a boy.[31]

But *The Waves* shifts attention away from polarised forms of sexuality (it was originally conceived as a multiple autobiography of a woman) — *not*, I would suggest, into the kind of vigorous androgyny that Herbert Marder argues for in *Feminism and Art*, where the old oppositions are preserved in a new form of marriage. He comments in this style on a quotation from *A Room of One's Own*:

> For if Chloe likes Olivia and Mary Carmichael knows how to express it she will light a torch in that vast chamber where no-body has yet been. It is all half lights and profound shadows like those serpentine caves where one goes with a candle peering up and down. (pp. 145-6)

Here Virginia Woolf sketches the movement toward liberation, as far as it has gone: the personal freedom that makes it possible for Mary Carmichael to be an artist; the economic independence that enables her to make use of her freedom; the ability to see women in relation to each other; the struggle to find a new style appropriate to new subject matter; the opening of hitherto obscure regions of women's minds. Undoubtedly the illumination of the cavern, the increase in self-knowledge, would bring women one step closer to androgyny.[32]

Virginia Woolf works rather through a dislimning of the edges of identity, an acknowledgement of how much of our life is to do with primary perceptual experience: not humanistic, but tactile, auditory — she called *The Waves* an 'abstract . . . eyeless book'[33] — in which the self is in undetermined relations with objects, surfaces, heat and cold. These depend, only fitfully, on memory; they do not depend upon a current social system, or upon modes of order created by society, nor, she suggests, are they exclusively based upon gender (Naremore imagines a peculiarly deprived kind of boy child who is incapable of sniffing the candelabra of currants).

In *The Waves* we can observe some of the qualities shared by feminist and *avant-garde* writing, such as Kristeva commented on in her remark about the dissolution of identities, even sexual identities. But this community of practice should not lead us to assume that their motives are identical. *The Pargiters* reveals how much Virginia Woolf felt herself fixed in historical time, in the conditions of her own generation, because of her need to work through language, which imposes current social forms. She tells her imagination:

> I cannot make use of what you tell me — about women's bodies for instance — their passions — and so on, because the conventions are still very strong. If I were to overcome the conventions I should need the courage of a hero, and I am not a hero.
>
> I doubt that a writer can be a hero. I doubt that a hero can be a writer.[34]

To that extent Virginia Woolf lives in a determined situation. She does not tell about women's bodies but in *The Waves*, having driven out authoritarian narrative, she uses women's special experience of time as one of the two underlying orders of the book. The book accepts the common human condition of growth and ageing, while relying for its particular order on recurrence and cycle. The menstrual relationship to time is implicit in the tides, the recurring waves, the stilled episodes of reunion and dissolution.

Gender, in so far as it determines, always reminds us of our 'unacted parts'.[35] In many of Virginia Woolf's books, lack and absence are crucial to the form of the experience – and this theme may well have psychosexual bearings on her self as woman. Such explanation is, I think, valid but not all-sufficient. For the theme clearly has also to do with her individual experiences of early bereavement and her generation's experience of the Great War. In her earlier novels closure is assembled about an absence: Jacob, Septimus, Mrs Ramsay. What *does* seem to me to be specific to her situation as a woman is her insistence that relations other than enacted ones – other even than binary ones, such as that between man and woman – are essential to full life.

George Eliot saw the range of immanent worlds about us, and their ever-extending relationships, as ways out of the thickening and fixing properties of determinism. She drives her characters through plot, and in *Daniel Deronda*, out beyond it. Virginia Woolf avoids the condensations of plot, which to her imply the inevitability of an established order. She moves beyond the male-female polarisation, not into androgyny, but into a sense of movement, lapsing, of identity flowing out into the moment. Neither George Eliot nor Virgina Woolf escaped entirely the assumptions of determinism, but each of them drew upon 'her own inheritance – the difference of view, the difference of standard', to test the patriarchal implications of the idea and to explore territories beyond it, seeking 'more knowledge and more freedom'.[36]

Notes

1. *The Works of George Eliot*, Cabinet Edition (Edinburgh and London, 1878-80), *Middlemarch*, vol. iii, p. 464. All references to her novels are to this edition.
2. 'George Eliot' in *The Common Reader* (London, 1925), p. 217. Collected in *Collected Essays*, vol. i (London, 1966), pp. 196-204.
3. *The Descent of Man, and Selection in Relation to Sex* (2 vols., London, 1871), vol. ii, pp. 316-17.
4. *Middlemarch*, vol. i, pp. 2-3.
5. *The Descent of Man*, vol. ii, pp. 326, 329-30.
6. M.A. Leaska (ed.), *The Pargiters* (London, 1978), pp. xlii, xliii; speech of 21 January 1931. The second passage is a deleted section.
7. *The Descent of Man*, vol. ii, pp. 329, 337, 338.
8. *Daniel Deronda*, vol. i, p. 144.
9. Jeanne Schulkind (ed.), *Moments of Being* (London, 1976), p. 79.
10. Gordon Haight (ed.), *The George Eliot Letters* (7 vols., New Haven, 1954-6), vol. iii, p. 227.

11. *The Mill on the Floss*, vol. i, p. 20. George Eliot's remark is recorded in an unpublished letter in Girton College Library.

12. Ibid., vol. ii, p. 395.

13. *Middlemarch*, vol. i, p. 231.

14. 'A Sketch of the Past', *Moments of Being*, p. 80.

15. Elaine Showalter, *A Literature of their Own: British Women Novelists from Brontë to Lessing* (Princeton, New Jersey, 1977), p. 291.

16. Julia Kristeva, *Polylogue* (Paris, 1977), pp. 517, 519, 520.

17. Michèle Montrelay, 'Inquiry into Femininity', trans. Parveen Adams, *m/f*, vol. i (1978), p. 92.

18. See Jacques Lacan, 'The Subject and the Other: Alienation' in *The Four Fundamental Concepts of Psychoanalysis*, trans. Alan Sheridan (London, 1977).

19. 'George Eliot' in *The Common Reader*, pp. 217-18.

20. 'Mr. Darwin's Hypotheses', *Fortnightly Review*, n.s., vol. iv (November 1868), p. 494.

21. *Daniel Deronda*, vol. i, p. 3.

22. Ibid., vol. iii, p. 127.

23. Virginia Woolf, *A Writer's Diary* (London, 1953), p. 141 (4 January 1929).

24. E.M. Forster, Rede Lecture (Cambridge, 1942). Quoted in Nigel Nicolson (ed.), *The Question of Things Happening, The Letters of Virginia Woolf*, vol. ii (London, 1976), p. xviii.

25. 'The Narrow Bridge of Art' (1927) in *Collected Essays*, vol. ii (London, 1966), pp. 225, 226.

26. *A Writer's Diary*, p. 57 (19 June 1923).

27. Ibid., p. 139 (28 November 1928).

28. *The Question of Things Happening*, p. 525.

29. *A Writer's Diary*, p. 164 (30 December 1930).

30. *The Journals of Arnold Bennett*, compiled by Newman Flower (New York, 1932), pp. 5-6.

31. James Naremore, *The World Without a Self* (New Haven, 1973), p. 159.

32. Herbert Marder, *Feminism and Art* (Chicago and London, 1968), p. 124.

33. *A Writer's Diary*, p. 137 (7 November 1928).

34. *The Pargiters*, p. xxxix.

35. Virginia Woolf, *Between the Acts* (London, 1941), p. 179.

36. 'George Eliot' in *The Common Reader*, p. 218.

5 SUE BRIDEHEAD AND THE NEW WOMAN

John Goode

I

Criticism of *Jude the Obscure* usually takes it to be a *representation*; hence, however hard such analysis tries to come to terms with the novel's radicalism, it is inevitably ideological. Criticism of this kind necessarily dissolves the specific literary effect of the text, the author's 'production', into its component sources which are situated in 'reality' — that is to say, the ideological structure of experience by which we (including Hardy) insert ourselves into the hegemony. But *Jude* is such a truly radical novel precisely because it takes reality apart; that is, it doesn't merely reproduce reality, even as a 'series of seemings', but exposes its flaws and its mystifications. You cannot come to terms with the novel either as a moral fable or as an exhibition of social reality because it is the very terms of those structures, their ideological base, that it interrogates. After the death of her children, before she has, as they say, *broken down*, Sue tells Jude: 'There is something external to us which says, "You shan't!" First it said, "You shan't learn!" Then it said, "You shan't labour!" Now it says, "You shan't love!" ' (VI. ii) This very precisely defines the overdetermined form of the novel. Learning, labour and love — the three human activities on which bourgeois ideology bases its libertarian pride — are shown to be denied by 'something external'. In most novels, including Hardy's own earlier work, these three are accommodated within 'the interstices of a mass of hard prosaic reality' (*Far from the Madding Crowd*, LVI); even Tess is left free finally to love. Here it really doesn't matter what the external is, whether nature's inexorable law or social oppression. What matters is that it is external; it might as well be God. But although Jude comments that this is bitter, he does not answer when Sue replies that it is true. Because he cannot answer, he has no way to stop her from seeking to propitiate this external with the mortification of the flesh, the terrible flesh. A further precision is needed in our reading of this passage. Sue can say this because she is more articulate than Jude, who has *already broken down* by returning absurdly to the centre of his dream (Christminster). That is why he is horrified by her denial of love. Jude on his own account, even with Sue's aid, can confront and articulate what forbids learning and labour (and confront it as ideological). But it is only Sue who can demystify love and identify its determinants. And that is what most critics cannot take, and why criticism of the novel tends to sprawl from fiction to reality when it comes to Sue.

Most accounts of *Jude the Obscure* cannot cope with Sue except by reference to some ideologically structured reality. This usually enables the critic to say one of two things, both of which are demonstrably false representations of the text: either that Hardy's presentation of Sue is inconsistent, or that she is a neurotic type of the frigid woman. The most extreme version of the second reading is, of course, Lawrence's, which sees Sue as 'no woman' but a witch, whose attraction to Jude in the first place is in reaction to the incomprehensible womanliness of Arabella:

> And this tragedy is the result of over-development of one principle of human life at the expense of the other; an over-balancing; a laying of all the stress on the Male, the Love, the Spirit, the Mind, the Consciousness; a denying, a blaspheming against the Female, the Law, the Soul, the Senses, the Feelings.[1]

I don't need to stress the sexism of Lawrence's account; it is remark· ably like that of the reactionary reviewers such as Mrs Oliphant and R.Y. Tyrell whom Havelock Ellis implicitly rebuked when he said that to describe Sue as neurotic was to reveal an attitude which considers 'human sexual relationships to be as simple as those of the farmyard'.[2] But I think that Lawrence is important because what he identifies as Sue's 'maleness' is her articulateness:

> That which was female in her she wanted to consume within the male force, to consume it in the fire of understanding, of giving utterance. Whereas an ordinary woman knows that she contains all understanding, that she is the unutterable which man must forever continue to try to utter.

What is unforgivable about Sue is her utterance, her subjecting of experience to the trials of language. Lawrence, underneath the hysterical ideology, seems very acute to me, for he recognises that Sue is destructive because she utters herself — whereas in the ideology of sexism, the woman is an image to be uttered. That is to say, woman achieves her womanliness at the point at which she is silent and therefore can be inserted as 'love' into the world of learning and labour; or rather, in Lawrence's own terms, as the 'Law' which silences all questions.

The most available feminist inversion of Lawrence's ideology makes the inconsistencies of Sue's character part of the limitations of the novelist himself. Kate Millett on the one hand affirms Sue's rationality ('Sue is only too logical. She has understood the world, absorbed its propositions, and finally implemented that guilt which precipitated her own self-hatred. Nothing remains to her but to destroy herself')[3]; but on the other hand she clearly feels that Hardy loads the dice against Sue because of his own uncertainty, so that a woman who can be articulated by the feminist as 'an intelligent rebel against sexual politics' is presented to us as 'by turns an enigma, a pathetic creature, a nut, and an iceberg'. She complains that we are never allowed to see Sue's motivation and processes of change, but decides that the clue to Sue, as to Arabella, is that they both despise womanhood, and that in Sue's case, this makes her hold sexuality in terror. It is not that Millett doesn't recognise the validity of Hardy's representation; it is rather that Hardy himself doesn't understand what defeats her.

I want to try to show that both approaches to Sue are wrong, but more than this, that a significant silence in both critics indicates the way in which they are wrong — and that this, in turn, indicates where the fictive effect of the novel displaces its own ideology in a mirror. For it is quite remarkable how many critics either despise Sue or blame Hardy for the confusion without ever asking whether the difficulty resides in the ways in which we articulate the world. Perhaps the most revealing recent account is John Lucas's.[4] Lucas finds *Jude* a less achieved novel than *Tess*, because by making Sue so unrepresentative, and failing to place her against some concept of womanhood ('we need more in the way of women than the novel actually gives us') Hardy fails to enable us to decide how much of the tragedy resides in the artificial system of things, and how much in the 'inexorable laws of nature' which make women what they are. Hardy, it is true, had already created a 'pure woman', but maybe we should ask whether the woman in *Jude* isn't precisely the question that is posed against that strange creation. Tess is the subject of the novel: that makes her inevitably an object of the reader's consumption (no novel has ever produced so much of what Sontag required in place of hermeneutics, namely, an erotics of art). But Sue is not the centre of the novel, she exists as a function of Jude's experience, hence as an object for him. It is surely possible that the questions come from her inability to take shape as that object. Lucas says that while we can understand why Sue shies away from Phillotson, the fact that she shies away from Jude makes her pathological, for although sex can be oppressive, it '*is, or ought to be* mutual' (my italics). Millett, we have noticed, says that Sue hates her sexuality; Lawrence, that she is sexless. First of all, as I shall show, this is not really true. What is true, however, is that Sue exposes the ideology of Lucas's statement. You can't, I think (as Millett says), be solid about the class system and muddled about sexual politics. These critics are muddled about both, and they are muddled because neither Hardy nor Sue will let go of the questions.

II -

When Sue has retreated back into her marriage with Phillotson, Jude poses what I take to be the fundamental ideological question posed by the novel and found unforgivable by the critics who cannot take Sue:

'What I can't understand in you is your extraordinary blindness now to your old logic. Is it peculiar to you, or is it common to woman? Is a woman a thinking unit at all, or a fraction always wanting its integer?' (VI. iii)

If this question is asked in the novel it is surely naïve to ask it of the novel. What is more important is that this question should be asked; it poses for Sue only one of two possibilities – that the nature of her blindness to her own logic must be explained either by her 'peculiarity', or by her belonging to womanhood. Either way, she is committed to being an image, and it is this that pervades the novel. Nobody ever confronts Jude with the choice between being a man or being peculiar. The essential thing is that Sue must be available to understanding. We might want to deduce that Hardy feels the same way as Jude at this point, but I think to do so would go both against the consistency of the novel and against Hardy's whole career as a writer. Twenty years before he wrote *Jude*, Hardy had made Bathsheba Everdene say: ' "It is difficult for a woman to define her feelings in language which is chiefly made by men to express theirs" ' (*Far from the Madding Crowd*, LI). He built a career as a writer out of the very mediations that woman as subject has to create to define her own subjectivity. The plots that turn on caprice, the scenes which reach outside the interaction of manners, the images which embody contradiction, are all constructs made by the novelist to articulate those unspeakable (though not unutterable) feelings. In *Jude*, for the first time in his major fiction, the woman is no longer the vessel of those mediations, but the object of male understanding. Sue not only speaks for herself because she is an intelligent rebel; she is called on to speak for herself – to place herself in relation to other women and to their ways of feeling. She several times has to relate her particularity to what all women are like 'really'. In other words, she has to affirm that she is *a woman*, or admit her ethereal nature – her 'peculiarity'. If we think about the novel naturalistically, without any ideological idyllicising of love (it *'is or ought to be* mutual'), we might ask ourselves about the absurdity of Jude's lack of understanding. Sue has been driven around the country by prejudice and poverty, she is stuck in Christminster by Jude's obsession, and now all her children have been killed by Jude's son whom she has made her own. Our perfect union, she tells Jude, is stained with blood. But of course we don't consider it naturalistically, because we don't ever ask what is happening to Sue; because it is rather a question of Sue happening to Jude. So what matters is where this reaction puts her, rather than why it comes about.

Sue is more than anything an image; that is literally how she comes into Jude's life, as a photograph, and how she is continually represented to us throughout the novel – dressed in Jude's clothes, walking in the distance with Phillotson, looking like a heap of clothes on the floor of St Silas's church. But if she is an image, it is a vital part of this image that it has a voice, and hence a logic. Although logic and image play contrasting and reinforcing roles in relation to one another at different points in the novel, it is the relationship between them which calls in question the ideological alternative between peculiarity, on one hand, and the nature of woman, on the other. Sue thus has an instrumentality which makes it irrelevant to ask what kind of ordeal she is undergoing, at least until the novel moves towards the shared experience of Jude and Sue in the Aldbrickham section. For example, at the very beginning Jude sees her haloed in the Christminster ecclesiastical art shop, while we see her buying pagan statues: a relatively simple juxtaposition of false image and conscious decision. But although Hardy presents her logic as having a potential subjectivity (that is, Sue's purchase of the statue is private, tentative, naïve and confused – it could be the frail start of an emancipation), by the time this logic has come to Jude's notice it is formed and decisive, something for him to understand and adjust his own attitude by. I don't think that this confusion entails confusion on Hardy's part, for it is as a confusing image that Sue is effective in breaking down Jude's illusions. Nor do I think that it is because she is in some way pathological. Sue has a potential coherence which is kept at bay by her function. If she is in any sense to be seen as abnormal, it is only in the sense that neurosis becomes normative in Freud because it exposes what a 'healthy' state of mind represses.

The question of her sexuality is crucial in this. It isn't an easy question. Jude himself calls her sexless before the consummation, then explicitly withdraws it when she gives in, only to repeat it in the last section when he is confronted with her return to Phillotson. And that seems to me what we are supposed to feel — an extreme confusion. But this confusion is not seen to reside in her personality; rather, it resides in the insertion of her dual role of image and logic into the world experienced by Jude. From the start this opens up a gap between what she actually says and the way that it is taken. When she tells Jude about the undergraduate who is supposed to have died of unrequited love, she cites it as an example of ' "what people call a peculiarity in me" ' but immediately goes on to affirm that her peculiarity lies merely in having no fear of men because she knows they are not always out to molest you. The differentiation here is cultural: ' "I have not felt about them what most women are taught to feel." ' Jude makes it biologistic. Equally there is no mystery about why she never became the under-graduate's mistress: ' "He wanted me to be his mistress, in fact, but I wasn't in love with him" ' (III. iv). It seems very straightforward, and the undergraduate's claim that he died of a broken heart is surely in-tended to be preposterous. That is, until Jude's reception of the story is defined: 'Jude felt much depressed; she seemed to get further and further away from him with her strange ways and curious unconscious-ness of gender' (III. iv). The only sexual terror in this seems to me to be Jude's — the sense that there must be something unnatural in a woman who won't give way to a man she doesn't love. And yet at the same time, what Sue affirms seems to offer very different possibilities: ' "I suppose, Jude, it is odd that you should see me like this and all my things hanging there? Yet what nonsense! They are only a woman's clothes — sexless cloth and linen" ' (III. iii). It seems to suggest, if only fragmentarily (though it goes with Aunt Drusilla's story of Sue as a child, her resistance to invidious comparison with Arabella, the adop-tion of Jude's son, and 'that complete mutual understanding' between her and Jude at the fair), a repressed version of a sexuality not possible in the novel itself.

That is all very well, but it is still true that Sue clearly doesn't want to consummate her relationship with Jude, and that she retreats into the most conventional guilt about their sexual relationship when the children are dead. But I think that if we take Sue's function into account, we cannot make the mistake of thinking that there is some inherent inconsistency in her characterisation. Again it is a question of the relationship of the image to the logic. For what seems to me to be most truly radical about this novel is that sexuality is not left as a kind of idyllic enclave within the oppressive social system. Loving is subject to that external denial too. We have to bear in mind what the meaning of the marriage to Phillotson is. It comes out of that dislocation between logic and image which Sue enacts and which Jude never emancipates her from. Marriage has to do, as Phillotson makes clear, with the regularisation of the sentiments, the ordering of sexuality in terms which will be socially effective. The evocation of Mill in this context is not, as Eagleton says, bourgeois liberalism;[5] it is rather the taking of that affirmation into the area at which the ideology works most opaquely, the point at which the artificial system of things leagues itself with the laws of nature. Lucas quotes as an example of Hardy's muddle the passage about the young women in the dormitory:

> their tender feminine faces upturned to the flaring gas-jets which at intervals stretched down the long dormitories, every face bearing the legend 'The Weaker' upon it, as the penalty of the sex wherein they were moulded, which by no possible exertion of their willing hearts and abilities could be made strong while the inexorable laws of nature remain what they are. (III. iii)

Strictly theoretically, this might constitute an evasion (is it social oppression or the laws of nature that make women the weaker sex?), but the same point has to be made about this that is made about Sue's representativeness: it is the area of confusion between the two which constitutes the basis of the novel's question. Does Hardy mean to suggest the possibility that the laws of nature might change? Surely to do so calls into question the whole phenomenology of the narrative. This is a 'pretty, suggestive, pathetic sight', like the sleeping young women, an arena of understanding that slips out of our grasp as soon as it is glimpsed. Such contiguity of nature and society is exactly what constitutes the ideology of marriage. Sue's challenge to marriage is a challenge to the social structure itself, as Gillingham realises: ' "if people did as you want to do, there'd be a general domestic disintegration. The family would no longer be the social unit" ' (IV. iv). The Shelleyan counter to this is not marked by its sexlessness. *Epipsychidion*, which Sue invokes shortly after this, is about a love which evolves itself in transcendence of a prison, as some of the lines she omits make clear.

High, spirit-wingèd Heart! who dost forever
Beat thine unfeeling bars with vain endeavour,
Till those bright plumes of thought, in which arrayed
It over-soared this low and worldly shade,
Lie shattered; and thy panting, wounded breast
Stains with dear blood its unmaternal nest! (11. 13-18)

The last line surely reminds us of the blood-stained perfect union. Physical sexuality is continually implicated with marriage, and those early chapters in Aldbrickham are about the subject of marriage and 'the other thing' (sexuality) together, because sexuality is blood-stained. Once they have children, Jude and Sue have to live the economic life of the couple. In a sense Sue is right to see the children's death as retribution. It is the payment for a return to 'Greek joyousness'. Throughout the novel, what Jude and Sue aspire to is comradeship. This has to define itself against marriage, and thus against 'sexuality'. And yet, there can be no doubt that the real making of this comradeship comes in those few pages between the consummation and the return to Christminster. It is just, however, that it cannot descend into the world of actuality without being destroyed. And that is what Sue recognises in her mortification at the end. She and Jude were wrong to make their relationship physical because you cannot be comrades in a world of domestic gins.

As I have argued, Sue has to perform the function of articulating all this. The pattern of openness and retreat recognises the war between logic and image. But that is to put it too metaphysically; Sue is only bodiless in so far as the body of the woman is a basis of capitalist reproduction, and therefore not her own. At this point I should stress that I am not trying to find an apologetic for Sue. It is not a question of discovering a psychology or making her representative. What makes Sue effective is her function in the novel, which is the function of an exposing image — that is to say, of an image carrying its own logic which is not the logic of the understandable, comprising both what she utters and what she seems, the gap between them and the collusion they make. As this image she destroys the lives of the order-loving individuals who aspire out of their loneliness through her. It is this destruction, however, that uncovers the determinants of both their aspiration and their loneliness. The sexual fascination of Sue and its demand for comradeship exposes the very impossibility of sexuality. Outside the field of possibility which she calls attention to, there is always the external that limits the field. Where I think we can go so wrong in this novel is to treat it in terms of a representation which we then find incomprehensible. It is the incomprehensibility that constitutes the novel's effect; the incomprehensibility of Sue (who as an image is offered for comprehension) is one way at least in which the incomprehensibility of the world (i.e. bourgeois ideology) is offered. To seek to tie her down to representativeness, or to the explicable, would be to postulate that ideology is 'false consciousness'. But we are talking about a literary effect and it is the literary function of Sue as part of what Hardy produces in this novel that constitutes the basis of our understanding. And the case of Sue is relatively specific.

III

Hardy in the 'Postscript' of 1912 cites, perhaps disingenuously, a German critic who said that Sue was the first delineation in fiction of the woman of the feminist movement. In fact, as Elaine Showalter establishes, feminism is dominant in fiction already by the time Hardy writes *Jude*.[6] And more than this, Sue clearly belongs to a literary variant of the feminist heroine which became fashionable in English fiction after the first performance in England of *Hedda Gabler* in 1891, and which came to be known as the New Woman. A.R. Cunningham gives an informative account of this variant in 'The "New Woman Fiction" of the 1890s',[7] showing how other texts before *Jude* have heroines who cite Mill and Spencer and aspire to the emancipation which is doomed 'either through personal weakness or social law', and who even in some cases retreat like Sue into Christianity. While the better-known writers such as Grant Allen and Sarah Grand celebrate the New Woman largely as a figure of purity, other writers (most notably George Egerton) use the type as a means of confronting the displaced sexuality of woman. What I think characterises Hardy is that he uses this literary device not as a subject offered to the reader's amazement, but as an active force within the novel which answers to the buried ideology of the questing hero. In other words, whereas Arabella limits Jude's dream, Sue translates his dream into questions, taking him beyond the bewilderment of 'the artificial system of things' into the bewilderment of nature's inexorable law. Nevertheless she does this as an image, and what makes for her coherence is neither her consistency nor Hardy's, but the persistent way in which she exposes the limits of meaning. Although this is clearly a subject requiring elaboration, I want (rather than placing Sue in her immediate context as the New Woman) to see the novel in terms of the larger context of feminist literature at the end of the nineteenth century by relating it briefly to the best feminist text of that period, *The Story of An African Farm*.

Olive Schreiner's novel appeared in 1883 and there was a first edition in Hardy's library, though I have no idea whether he read it, and I am not trying to claim that it influenced him. More importantly, it seems to me, the relationship of Schreiner's novel to ideology shares a great deal with that of Hardy's. It is not accidental that Schreiner's text gets treated in very similar ways to Hardy's. Even Elaine Showalter says that matters of plot and construction were beyond Schreiner, and that what marks her writing is its ardour rather than its art. Schreiner as a writer, in fact, gets treated rather like Sue as a character – the talented neurotic who was unable to keep up any significant level of productivity. Of course there isn't much after *The Story of An African Farm*, but to have achieved that much seems fairly remarkable, and it is clear to me at least that it is a carefully structured text, positing many voices against one another, not – obviously – in a way that makes for an identifiable coherence or for a comfortably distanced fiction. But the relationship of Waldo to Lyndall is a liaison of speech, each of them stimulated into thought and given voice by a 'stranger' (the traveller who interprets Waldo's carving, the lover through whom Lyndall experiences the conditions of female sexuality); they are only able to communicate because they do not get entrammelled in sexuality: ' "I like you so much, I love you." She rested her cheek softly against his shoulder. "When I am with you I never know that I am a woman and you are a man; I only know that we are both things that think." '[8] As well as this possibility of a comradeship making language the bridge which 'reality' denies to both of them, what is also important in relation to *Jude* is that Lyndall should define the difference between man and woman as the difference between expecting to work and being expected to seem:

'It is not what is done to us, but what is made of us,' she said at last, 'that wrongs us. No man can be really injured but by what modifies himself. We all enter the world little plastic beings, with so much natural force perhaps, but for the rest – blank; and the world tells us what we are to be, and shapes us by the ends it sets before us. To you it says – *Work*; and to us it says – *Seem*! To you it says – As you approximate to man's highest ideal of God, as your arm is strong and your knowledge great, and the power to labour is with you, so you shall gain all that human heart desires. To us it says – Strength shall not help you, nor knowledge, nor labour. You shall gain what men gain, but by other means. And so the world makes men and women.

'Look at this little chin of mine, Waldo, with the dimple in it. It is but a small part of my person; but though I had a knowledge of all things under the sun, and the wisdom to use it, and the deep loving heart of an angel, it would not stead me through life like this little chin. I can win money with it, I can win love; I can win power with it, I can win fame. What would knowledge help me? The less a woman has in her head the lighter she is for climbing. I once heard an old man say, that he never saw intellect help a woman so much as a pretty ankle; and it was the truth. They begin to shape us to our cursed end,' she said, with her lips drawn in to look as though they smiled, 'when we are tiny things in shoes and socks. We sit with our little feet drawn up under us in the window, and look out at the boys in their happy play. We want to go. Then a loving hand is laid on us: "Little one, you cannot go," they say; "your little face will burn, and your nice white dress be spoiled." We feel it must be for our good, it is so lovingly said; but we cannot understand; and we kneel still with one little cheek wistfully pressed against the pane. Afterwards we go and thread blue beads, and make a string for our neck; and we go and stand before the glass. We see the complexion we were not to spoil, and the white frock, and we look into our own great eyes. Then the curse begins to act on us. It finishes its work when we are grown women, who no more look out wistfully at a more healthy life; we are contented. We fit our sphere as a Chinese woman's foot fits her shoe, exactly, as though God had made both — and yet He knows nothing of either. In some of us the shaping to our end has been quite completed. The parts we are not to use have been quite atrophied, and have even dropped off; but in others, and we are not less to be pitied, they have been weakened and left. We wear the bandages, but our limbs have not grown to them; we know that we are compressed, and chafe against them.'[9]

That is what constitutes the unattainability of the woman; being expected to seem, she cannot talk unless she is able not to be a woman. In that gap between talking and seeming exists not only the character of Lyndall, but also the very form of the novel. The reality of the novel is more highly fragmented than many other texts of the period, and yet the writing itself acts out its ideological commitment to the Emersonian unity which is so often noticed in *The Story of An African Farm* — noticed, without its being seen as the instrument which makes possible the novel's own particular version of comradeship. Formally, this Emersonian unity comes to a head when Waldo's life is suddenly presented as phases of our life. In terms of the novel's meaning it is there in the final consolation of the hunter (a feather from the white bird of Truth) and the commitment Waldo makes to dreams. The form of the novel, that is to say, is instrumental.

But the instrumentality which the text achieves through its form must be defined in terms of its ideological recognition. When the stranger is telling Waldo of the hunter's search for truth, he makes it a precondition of that search that the hunter releases the birds of certain concepts from their cage: 'He went to his cage, and with his hands broke down the bars, and the jagged iron tore his flesh. It is sometimes easier to build than to break.'[10] The Emersonian commitment has to be seen in the context of this total demystification. Patiently the novel erodes all the ideological supports of the characters, so that it is the very fracturing of form that gives the novel its instrumentality. Now a fiction is a representation — it is itself an image, so that to provide a text which is a coherent representation would be the same as being understandable. And I have tried to show what constitutes Sue's effectivity is that she isn't — that she constitutes an image which breaks down the certainties through her own logic. This is, self-consciously, the aesthetic of *The Story of An African Farm*: the preface to the second edition clearly foreshadows the 'series of seemings' which follow ('the method of the life we all lead [where] nothing can be prophesied', as opposed to 'the stage method'). Significantly, both Schreiner and George Egerton move towards fragmented form. An Egerton story is not only short, it is chopped. And it is also strictly speaking incomprehensible. The heroine of 'A Cross Line', for example, is able to speak to the stranger, but what she says is enigmatic and she only goes to him because he accepts the enigma. The account of woman here picks up all the themes — image, enigma, liar:

Then she fancies she is on the stage of an ancient theatre out in the open air, with hundreds of faces upturned towards her. She is gauze-clad in a cobweb garment of wondrous tissue. Her arms are clasped by jewelled snakes, and one with quivering diamond fangs coils round her hips. Her hair floats loosely, and her feet are sandal-clad, and the delicate breath of vines and the salt freshness of an incoming sea seems to fill her nostrils. She bounds forward and dances, bends her lissom waist, and curves her slender arms, and gives to the soul of each man what he craves, be it good or evil. And she can feel now, lying here in the shade of Irish hills with her head resting on her scarlet shawl and her eyes closed, the grand intoxicating power of swaying all these human souls to wonder and applause. She can see herself with parted lips and panting, rounded breasts, and a dancing devil in each glowing eye, sway voluptuously to the wild music that rises, now slow, now fast, now deliriously wild, seductive, intoxicating, with a human note of passion in its strain. She can feel the answering shiver of feeling that quivers up to her from the dense audience, spellbound by the motion of her glancing feet, and she flies swifter and swifter, and lighter and lighter, till the very serpents seem alive with jewelled scintillations. One quivering, gleaming, daring bound, and she stands with outstretched arms and passion-filled eyes, poised on one slender foot, asking a supreme note to finish her dream of motion. And the men rise to a man and answer her, and cheer, cheer till the echoes shout from the surrounding hills and tumble wildly down the crags. The clouds have sailed away, leaving long feathery streaks in their wake. Her eyes have an inseeing look, and she is tremulous with excitement. She can hear yet that last grand shout, and the strain of that old-time music that she has never heard in this life of hers, save as an inner accompaniment to the memory of hidden things, born with her, not of this time.

And her thoughts go to other women she has known, women good and bad, school friends, casual acquaintances, women workers — joyless machines for grinding daily corn, unwilling maids grown old in the endeavour to get settled, patient wives who bear little ones to indifferent husbands until they wear out — a long array. She busies herself with questioning. Have they, too, this thirst for excitement, for change, this restless craving for sun and love and motion? Stray words, half confidences, glimpses through soul-chinks of suppressed fires, actual outbreaks, domestic catastrophes, how the ghosts dance in the cells of her memory! And she laughs, laughs softly to herself because the denseness of man, his chivalrous conservative devotion to the female idea he has created blinds him, perhaps happily, to the problems of her complex nature. Ay, she mutters musingly, the wisest of them can only say we are enigmas.[11]

The point about this passage is that it is a self-communing — it offers what the understanding of the good husband leaves out, what is inexplicable to the new lover. I'm here trying to talk about form and content at once: both the structure and the portrayal move towards that inconsistency which constitutes Sue's effectiveness. The New

Woman is most effective in that sense, not because she reads John Stuart Mill, has reservations about the exploitation of her sexuality, or submits to the external (death, the lover, God), but because that dance opens up the ideological structure of reality. The end of *Hedda Gabler* sums up the challenge to intelligibility: ' "People just don't do things like that." '

Notes

References in the text are to the chapter divisions of Hardy's novels.

1. 'Study of Thomas Hardy' in E.D. McDonald|(ed.), *Phoenix: The Post-humous Papers of D.H. Lawrence* (London, 1967), p. 509.

2. R.G. Cox (ed.), *Thomas Hardy: The Critical Heritage* (London, 1970), p. 311.

3. Kate Millett, *Sexual Politics* (London, 1972), pp. 130-4.

4. *The Literature of Change: Studies in the Nineteenth-Century Provincial Novel* (Hassocks, Sussex, 1977), pp. 188-91.

5. Introduction to *Jude the Obscure*, New Wessex edn. (London, 1975), p. 15.

6. Elaine Showalter, *A Literature of Their Own: British Women Novelists from Brontë to Lessing* (London, 1977), pp. 182-215.

7. *Victorian Studies*, vol. xvii (1974), pp. 177-86.

8. Olive Schreiner, *The Story of An African Farm*, 2 vols. (London, 1883), vol. ii, p. 94.

9. Ibid., vol. ii, pp. 39-42.

10. Ibid., vol. i, p. 301.

11. George Egerton, *Keynotes* (London, 1893), pp. 19-21.

IBSEN AND THE LANGUAGE OF WOMEN

Inga-Stina Ewbank

'How do we know,' my son asked me recently, 'that God is a man and not a woman?' As he is of an age (eight) much given to metaphysical speculations and investigations of First Causes, I found myself hastily casting around for an argument which would be adequate to this disturbing question. At the time, it was a relief to discover that the answer was written on a lolly-stick and went: 'Because we sing hymns, not hers.' But afterwards both the question and the answer went on niggling — perhaps because, in a manner which I hope is not altogether frivolous, they are tied up with the subject of this essay. Anyone proposing to discuss 'the language of women' — and thus positing the possibility of differentiating meaningfully between a male and a female language — runs the risk of making statements as absurd as that of the author of the lolly-stick joke. We all know about 'History' being changed to 'Herstory'.[1] And yet the absurdities are not merely amusing (any more than it is merely amusing to wonder why we should assume that God is male). They seem to be the ultimate manifestations of a kind of despair, a female version of modern man's[2] sense of absurd alienation, reflecting the fear that language itself is a con-trick; part of a male conspiracy. *Genesis* does not help, for after the haunting image of equality in the first chapter — 'So God created man in his own image, in the image of God created he him; male and female created he them' (1:27) — the second chapter tells us that Adam invented language *before* Eve was there to share in the process:

> And out of the ground the Lord formed every beast of the field and every fowl of the air; and brought them unto Adam to see what he would call them: and whatsoever Adam called every living creature, that was the name thereof. (2:19)

Only then did the Lord make Eve from one of Adam's ribs, whereupon Adam decided that 'she shall be called Woman, because she was taken out of Man' — thus beginning the linguistic tradition whereby women, as Elaine Showalter says, have been trained to think of themselves 'in prepositions'.[3]

We need not be fundamentalists to feel that the relative positions

114

(and I use the noun advisedly) of men and women in the world are connected vitally with their relative attitudes to, and uses of, language. Nor do we need to be embattled to feel that the history of language 'really is *his* story, not hers'. A just-published discussion of a major Swedish project for research into linguistic sex differentiation opens unequivocally: 'Our sciences have been biassed by patriarchal attitudes. They make women invisible.'[4] Just over a hundred years ago Henrik Ibsen made Lona Hessel, in the closing lines of *Pillars of the Community* (1877), throw much the same accusation at the society embodied in that play: 'You never see the women.' The moral of this sad echo is not merely a *'plus ça change'*; it is also — and more to my point — one to do with the interrelatedness of society, language and literature. *Pillars of the Community* marks Ibsen's deliberate turn to prose drama on contemporary themes; it is (among other things) about a man who is initially deaf to women's language but who has eventually to learn to listen to it. Ibsen was not a sociolinguist — he would have scorned the term, had it existed in his day — but the terms and findings of sociolinguists *may* help us to understand his art. And, conversely, his art may do more than scientific research can, to reveal to us whether there is such a thing as woman's language and, if so, when and why and how it is spoken.

Let me show what I mean, by a specific example. In Act IV of *Pillars of the Community*, as the tension is building up for the climax of the play (the public procession to honour Karsten Bernick, the Pillar who has built his life and reputation on a lie), there is a confrontation between Bernick and Lona Hessel — the 'new' woman whose love he sacrificed long ago for the sake of money and respectability. In so far as a man so soaked in hypocrisy and self-deceit can come to any genuine recognition of who he is and what he has done, this is Bernick's moment of *anagnorisis*; he sees the 'hollowness' of all he has achieved. He also thinks he sees where he went wrong:

> *Bernick.* . . . Oh, Lona, why didn't I really know you . . . in the old days?
> *Lona.* What if you had?
> *Bernick.* I would never have let you go; and if I had kept you, I wouldn't be where I am now.[5]

Lona, recognising the loophole of self-pity which Bernick is preparing for himself, attempts to close it with a realistic challenge —

Lona. And the woman you chose instead of me . . . don't you ever think what *she* might have been to you?

— only to find that the self-pity is stronger:

Bernick. All I know is that she hasn't been to me any of the things I needed.

At this point, the printed version of the play goes on to one of those radical attacks from Lona which establish her as the play's truth-teller:

Lona. Because you've never shared your purpose in life with her; because you've never let her be free and true in her relationship with you . . .

But in the fifth (and last preserved) draft of the play, Ibsen here instead gives Bernick a long speech, to explain what it was he 'needed'; and in doing so, he also gives in a nutshell a definition of how woman thinks, feels and functions which would seem to sum up in an ironic fashion central nineteenth-century attitudes — and some would say twentieth-century, too:

Bernick. All I know is that she hasn't been to me any of the things I needed. You would say the fault is mine . . . but that's no help. She might have tried to meet me half-way; might have shared my interests; might now and then have given me a glimpse of those inconsequential and intuitive thought processes which a man can't, of course, use directly, but which have a rousing and purifying effect on his whole being, all the same. It's this power that our women are not allowed to exercise . . . most of them don't even have it. Lona . . . not one in a thousand has the courage to be as you are . . .
Lona. That is . . . to be themselves.[6]

The reason why Ibsen cut this out must have been not only to shorten the speeches in the dialogue (as was often his way between draft and finished manuscript), but also because — as Bernick goes on — the tone becomes very difficult for an audience to catch. The male chauvinist, the *user* of women and condescending admirer of their 'inconsequential and intuitive thought processes', becomes himself just as inconsequential, realising as he speaks that most women don't have the 'power' he is attributing to them; or — even more damaging to his own position — that, if they do, his society does not allow them to 'exercise' it. Who is speaking woman's language now? To cancel any momentary sympathy called for by the end of Bernick's speech, the draft then returns him to an orthodox chauvinist position of blatant and self-condemning callousness:

> *Bernick.* You don't understand. You don't know the urge a man has
> to achieve something in this world. It's different for you women.
> You need something to love: a cat or a dog or a canary, if nothing
> else . . .

This is not a very subtle scene. Dramatically and thematically it has a kind of Morality structure: Lona, the truth-teller, opposing Bernick, the obfuscator of truth, the self-deceiver. But in the two long speeches which Ibsen eventually cut, the scene provides a very full statement of those attitudes to the generic intellectual and psychological differences between man and woman which prevailed in Ibsen's day, and which still prevail, albeit in a more underground fashion. The planners of the Swedish project for the study of sex differentiations in language, to which I have already referred, point out that they wish to avoid the common circular argument which begins with a conventional definition of sex roles and goes on to find these roles proved and authenticated in the language men and women speak, respectively. The conventional definition they describe as 'man: rational, active, instrumental, assured; woman: emotional, passive, expressive, uncertain.'[7] Every bit of this definition underlies both the text and the sub-text of the scene from *Pillars*; it is there both in what Bernick says and in his attitude — presented with open but effective irony — to Lona in the dialogue, epitomised by his 'You don't understand. You don't know . . .' These are phrases which are going to recur in Ibsen's plays, right through to his 'Dramatic Epilogue', *When We Dead Awaken*, as men and women face each other across a gulf which, though not as spectacular, is just as deep as that in the plays of his contemporary Scandinavian dramatist, August Strindberg. But, for my purposes at the moment, what interests me is that implicitly the nineteenth-century dramatist presents exactly the dilemma which the twentieth-century sociolinguists make explicit. The scene is based on, but also questions, traditional assumptions. What is more, the dramatic purpose of the scene and the play as a whole could be paraphrased in the same linguists' declaration of their purpose. The aim of their research, they say, 'is not to legitimize oppression (as in the circular argument described), but to reveal it and thereby to help to liberate human potentials'.[8]

The liberation of human potential, and the various forms of oppression which meet us, openly or insidiously, wherever we look, would seem to be — if one dare generalise about an art so full of contraries — the central theme of all Ibsen's plays, from *Catiline* in 1849 to *When We Dead Awaken* in 1899. More often than any other playwright Ibsen finds such potential in women characters. And, lest we should too easily identify him with an optimistic view of the 'New Woman', we might remind ourselves that his plays resolve themselves either in the tragic impossibility of his women characters being liberated into anything other than death, or else in a liberation so tenuous and self-defeating that, as with Nora, it has been felt to be a fate worse than death. Mrs Alving is left, at the end of *Ghosts*, 'in speechless horror' at her discovery of where the combined forces of oppression and liberation have brought her; Hedda Gabler chooses the equally speechless, if noisier, act of suicide by pistol to assert herself against apparently overwhelming oppression; Rebecca West is silenced by the mill-race and Irene (in *When We Dead Awaken*) by an avalanche — both sharing their deaths with their male partners. Ella Rentheim and Gunhild Borkman are in a manner liberated at last by the death on the snowy mountainside of John Gabriel Borkman, but all their language can do, by then, is to state the utter devastation of their own lives:

> *Mrs Borkman.* We two . . . twin sisters . . . over the man we both loved.
> *Ella.* We two shadows . . . over the dead man.[9]

Only a few of Ibsen's women are given the full opportunity to find out who they are ('to be themselves', as Lona puts it) and to live and act upon it: Nora, perhaps, though we leave her as soon as she slams the door of the matrimonial home; Ellida Wangel, in *The Lady From the Sea*, certainly, though there is loss as well as gain in her achievement of 'freedom with responsibility'. Lona Hessel seems in a sense to have got there before the play started, and her language to be the normative language of *Pillars of the Community*. But Bernick's conversion to truth is so partial and the whole ending of the play so ambivalent that there is more than a shade of irony around her final, apparently triumphant line: 'the spirit of truth and the spirit of freedom: *those* are the pillars of the community.'

Most of Ibsen's women are either dead or in a state beyond the limits of language by the time they understand the real nature of their predicament. For that reason alone, it would be absurd to pretend that Ibsen's understanding of women can be measured solely, or even mainly, by the language he gives them to speak. Another reason is the simple fact that he was a dramatist, and that therefore much of his language was non-verbal, residing in the visual imagery and the acts or movements on stage. The pregnant Hedda Gabler burning Eilert Løvborg's manuscript is a stage image which speaks more eloquently than any words could do (and certainly more explicitly than any late-nineteenth-century dramatic dialogue could have done) of the peculiar sexual frustrations of the heroine and of the paradox of creative and destructive urges inherent in womanhood. Even in a play as dependent as *Rosmersholm* on characters merely talking, until the final off-stage joint suicide, the realisation of the heroine's predicament as a woman – the tension between her urge towards power and intellectual dominance, on the one hand, and her sexual need to love and be loved, on the other – lies as much in what is not said as in what is said. And, of course, this is not squeamishness but part of Ibsen's essential dramatic technique of teasing us out of any comfortable preconceived assumptions about the motives and impulses behind human behaviour (male and female). What his most discriminating admirers took away from his plays, when they first broke upon the English stage, was that the life of their texts lay in their ability 'to make people think and see for themselves'.[10]

Yet, however perversely, it is to the study of the language of women within Ibsen's verbal texts that I am committed. There is, I think, room for such a study; but all I can do within the scope of a single essay is to suggest its directions and, above all, the limits it should observe. Perhaps the first point to remember is that none but the most documentary playwright (if such exist) uses his dialogue as if he were playing a tape: Ibsen's women may, up to a point, speak their own language; but over and above all they speak Ibsen's language. What they say and how they say it are part of his peculiar use of language, of what we would call his 'style'. It is particularly important to recognise this in the case of Ibsen who, in this country, is nearly always read in translation, and whose language has far too readily and easily been assumed by English critics to be a not very important element of his dramatic art: a plastic wrapping round 'themes' and 'symbols' and 'characters', rather than a formative element in its own right.

We might do well to think for a moment, in order to get things into perspective, if and how playwrights who are less professedly naturalistic arrive at a woman's language. Webster's Duchess of Malfi is part of the play's total vision of innocence and goodness engulfed in a world of disorder and evil; and in that sense her speeches make their contributions to a developing dramatic poem — to the image-chains of trapped birds, or of beautiful, fragile beings preyed upon by beasts, which carry the vision of that poem. But the poem *is* also a play, and in that play she is supremely a woman, defying the conventional limitations of womanhood (as women in plays are wont to do) by marrying the man she loves, and speaking a language whose vocabulary reflects what Webster presumably saw as the normal preoccupations of woman as wife and mother. The notorious cough syrup as well as the vision of herself as Fate's whipping-top belong here. In the end, the play and the poem are *one* as she meets death — a lonely woman against a crowd of madmen and, later, a group of executioners — with a mixture of courage and humility which is communicated to us by her language:

> Pull, and pull strongly, for your able strength
> Must pull down heaven upon me:
> Yet stay, heaven gates are not so highly arch'd
> As princes' palaces; they that enter there
> Must go upon their knees.
> (*Duchess of Malfi*, IV. ii. 226-30)[11]

Karsten Bernick might say that this is female speech, in its inconsequentiality ('Yet stay . . .') and its intuitive grasp of the situation, and I think he would have hold of a corner of the truth. Webster depends both on the typicality and the extraordinariness of this speech, on the interaction of the two qualities; just as he depends on the interaction of the calm centre within the speech with the disordered violence of the situation without. The Duchess is a woman, and an aristocratic woman ('Duchess of Malfi still') facing death — unlike her waiting-woman who bites and scratches — with a courage which might conventionally be termed manly fortitude. But needless to say, I hope, our experience in the theatre is not directed towards characteristics of sex or class as such; our emotions are wrung by a complex of emotions of pity and pride, horror and admiration as, through the specific situation of the Duchess, we sense something about the condition of man (which includes woman).

In a similar, though not identical fashion, Shakespeare's tragic heroines (leaving aside his often epicene comic heroines, who would take us too far astray) both have and have not a language of their own *as* women. Lady Macbeth in her early speeches — the call on the spirits to 'unsex' her, and her appeal to Macbeth by way of the suckling babe whose brains she would have dashed out — speaks both as part of the dark imaginative world of the play and as a woman ready to defy her own womanhood. When Duncan's murder has been discovered she relies in her swoon on stereotyped notions of such womanhood; and in her sleep-walking scene she both shows us her womanhood stealing up on her and projects, as an integral part of the play, a larger sense of the mysteriousness and ultimate self-destructiveness of evil. In her purposefulness, coupled with a traditionally female practicality, she is just such a wife as Bernick might have 'needed' (or John Gabriel Borkman) — although 'When all's done/You look but on a stool' turns out to be an inadequate defence against the metaphysical horrors unleashed by Macbeth's crime and hers. With Ophelia, Cordelia and Desdemona, we might well seem to have versions of a female stereotype: often silent or inarticulate, submissive to their men and ultimately unable to control their own destinies.[12] Each of them is distinguished from the society she inhabits by characteristics of style — brevity, simplicity and directness. Where the men around them continually get language and reality confused (Lear believing in Goneril's and Regan's protestations of love is an extreme example; Othello's acceptance of Iago's *words*, rather than Desdemona's *being*, is another), they hold on to a closeness between word and deed, language and felt reality. Whereas Othello really seems to believe that Desdemona's falling in love with him was a matter of verbal persuasion, of enthralment by the romantic tale of his love and adventures, to Desdemona it is a matter of essences: 'I saw Othello's visage in his mind.' They seem to apprehend the words they use like tangible realities, whether it is Cordelia asserting her love for her father 'According to my bond; no more nor less', or Ophelia trying to insist, before Polonius, on the reality of the 'vows' which Hamlet has sworn to her (*Hamlet*, I. iii. 114), or Desdemona being unable to get the word 'whore' across her lips (*Othello*, IV. ii. 119-20). It makes them desperately vulnerable and tragically defenceless when confronted with those who do not speak the same language. Ophelia and Desdemona each find that the man they love has become absorbed in a version of reality which he himself has created — again largely by his language. In that world, Ophelia's name is 'frailty', Desdemona's 'whore'; and neither makes sense. 'I understand a fury in your words,/ But not the words', Desdemona tells Othello (IV. ii. 33-4). The inability to translate, in George Steiner's sense, has such vast tragic dimensions that it clearly transcends any simple issue of male *versus* female language.[13] Yet the issue is there. It is there, too, in the quality of sympathy which seems to characterise the language-uses of these Shakespearian women, and especially that of Cordelia. She seems vicariously to re-live her father's sufferings in the storm, hovelling 'with swine and rogues forlorn,/In short and musty straw' (*King Lear*, IV. vii. 39-40). No doubt this is a female quality; a somewhat similar moment occurs in *Brand*, near the opening of Act IV, where Agnes, mourning her dead baby, *feels* how cold he must be out there in the churchyard, 'on the pillow of cold wood-shavings'. In pointed contrast with Brand's insist-ence on keeping his terms separate —

> *Brand.* The *corpse* lies under the snow;
> The *child* has been borne to Heaven.

— Agnes insists on the emotional oneness of the two:

> *Agnes.* . . .
> That which you harshly call the *corpse*,
> Is still to me the *child*.
> . . .
> Alf, who sleeps under the snow,
> Is my Alf up there in Heaven.[14]

Agnes's womanly feelings and language serve in the dramatic structure to throw an ironic light on Brand's sacrificial zeal. Cordelia's serve as a kind of norm in the play of *King Lear*: both her sympathy and her tendency to subordinate language to experience are what the play as a whole moves towards, and what Edgar clinches in the final lines: 'Speak what we feel, not what we ought to say./The oldest hath borne most . . .' In both cases the dramatist has given his heroine a language which characteristises her as a woman but also, and more importantly, is a vital part of the play's total structure of language and meanings.

I have laboured the Shakespearian comparison because I trust it will illuminate what I now wish to go on to say about Ibsen and the lang-uage of women. After he had turned from verse drama to what he termed 'the far more difficult art of prose',[15] Ibsen's few theoretical statements about his own language tend to refer to life-like characterisa-tion and to the task of creating an illusion of reality.[16] But he also persisted in referring to his creative activity by that untranslatable word 'digte' (it means writing poetry, but it also means making up any kind of fiction); and as he uses the word, it is qualitative rather than merely descriptive, referring to imaginative ways of seeing things as well as (and more than) ways of saying them. His plays are not meant to be slavish imitations of life, couched in a language such as men, and women, do use, but imaginative projections of his vision of life — making contact, of course, with their audience and readers by their likeness to life such as we know it, but not stopping there. Similarly, his language, while like enough to what we hear around us to make us feel that we are listening to 'real' men and women, is primarily in the service of his vision — part of works written in prose, but with the imaginative coherence of poems.

Relatedly, the social issues which his prose plays often raise — and in particular those written in the late seventies and early eighties — are not there for their own propagandist value but as part of a larger vision of life. It is well known that, when the Norwegian Society for Women's Rights in 1898 gave a banquet for Ibsen, the aged playwright disconcerted his hostesses by making a speech in which he disclaimed any connection with women's rights. 'Of course,' he said, 'it is incidentally desirable to solve the problem of women; but that has not been my whole object. My task has been the portrayal of human beings.'[17] Obviously his statement contains a false dichotomy: the problem of women *versus* the portrayal of human beings. And of course he knew it. He was not betraying the insights of *A Doll's House* and the other twenty-three plays he had written but was teaching his listeners the lesson that the portrayal of women is not a separate issue from the portrayal of human beings generally; and that, if you portray human beings with the sensitivity of a poet, then you are, if not solving, at least exploring the problem of women. The lesson could apply as well to Shakespeare as to Ibsen.

This said, it would be wrong to suggest that Ibsen is just like Shakespeare, and that a study of his language of women raises exactly the same questions as would a similar study of Shakespeare. Very early Ibsen indeed has certain Shakespearian — or rather pseudo-Shakespearian — qualities. His first play, *Catiline*, is a verse drama in the mode of Romantic German Shakespeare translations and of their offspring in early-nineteenth-century Scandinavian poetic drama. Its language depends very much on metaphor — the image, as in early Shakespeare, sometimes becoming almost an end in itself. The whole play is held together by an obvious image pattern of dark—light, day—night. For the first time in Ibsen there appears a structure of character relationships which is going to persist throughout his works: a man torn (or at least suspended) between two women, one (to whom he is often married) soft and sweet and ordinary; the other more intense, aggressive, even violent, but also far more imaginatively exciting. (One thinks of the two women in *The Vikings at Helgeland*, of Betty and Lona Hessel in *Pillars of the Community*, of Beate and Rebecca in *Rosmersholm*, of Mrs Elvsted and Hedda in *Hedda Gabler*, Gunhild and Ella in *John Gabriel Borkman*, and Maia and Irene in *When We Dead Awaken*.) The position of Catiline between the two women in his life, Aurelia (his wife) and Furia (his inspiration), is explored by verbal metaphor. Furia becomes consistently associated with 'flame' or 'fire', or such light as 'the blue sulphurous torch' of Hades. Aurelia, on the other hand, is the light of natural day, and when he has stabbed her to death, Catiline turns to Furia in a set of images which clearly — many generations removed — has its ancestry in *Othello* and *Antony and Cleopatra*, as well as being the first germ of the closing scene in *John Gabriel Borkman*:

> . . . the light is out.
> Now is the whole wide circle of the earth
> Transformed into a cold and boundless grave,
> And covered with a vault of lead,
> And under this vault stand you and I,
> Abandoned by both light and darkness,
> By death and life — two restless shadows.[18]

Not only is the emphasis throughout the play on what the women mean to the man, as part of a thematic dialectic (much as in *Brand*, or *Peer Gynt*), but clearly this kind of idiom is also incapable of developing into anything which could meaningfully be called the language of women.

It is in his early prose plays that we see such a development, as the needs of his subject matter produce their own idiom. In the earliest extant notes (written in 1870) towards what was to become *Pillars of the Community*, Ibsen begins with a paragraph describing the basic motif of the piece as the position of women in a men's world of self-important business.[19] But even by the end of the notes, as characters and action are taking shape, the play is beginning to appear to him more as a web of small-town life than just as a structure of male-female relationships:

> There is a significance underneath; something symbolical, the libera-
> tion from all narrow conventions; a new free and beautiful life. This
> is what the piece turns on. This matter to be illuminated from all
> sides.[20]

In the event, *Pillars* turned into the most *Middlemarch*-like of all Ibsen's plays, and in this picture of a stultifying community the rights of industrial workers and of sailors are more dramatically prominent than those of women. But the liberation of women remains thematically dominant. Not, of course, that they all *want* to be liberated; one of the (for Ibsen) unusual features of this play is the background chorus of conventional lower-middle-class ladies whose adoration of their husbands (whom they call by their surnames) is matched only by their worship of social proprieties. They speak with the callousness of those proprieties, and as echoes of their husbands. Here, for example, is the arch gossip, Mrs Rummel, summing up the fate of Dina Dorf's mother with a terrifying literalness —

She didn't last long, either. She was a fine lady, you know, and not used to working. So it went to her chest, and then she died.

— and then immediately turning to the rhetoric of the Pillars to describe how this 'ugly business' affected the Bernick family:

It's the dark spot in the sunlight of their happiness, as Rummel put it once.

The society of the Pillars is very much created for us by its language; they revel in 'poetic' metaphors which are obviously empty clichés. Their rhetoric cries out to be seen as false. Against this, the three women who in various ways seek (or find) liberation — Dina, Lona and Martha — are set off as the plain-speakers, those whose language comes from the centre of their being, not just from the social surface. Lona, on her truth-mission, is deliberately provoking in her vocabulary — as 'unfeminine' in her use of swear-words and adjectives which are 'not nice' as in her dress and in the activities she is reputed to have been engaged in in America. In this way she deflates the rhetoric of the 'moral' people and asserts the rights of the free woman. But she also has an emotional rhetoric of her own when she wants to make a point — to ask for 'fresh air' or to tell Bernick that his whole life is built on 'quicksands'. In the end, as I have already suggested, I think we are meant to see her womanly emotions overcome her clear-sightedness. 'Old love does not rust,'[21] she tells Bernick when he asks for her motives in coming back to save him from himself; and as an audience we are uneasily aware that her final triumphant belief in Bernick's full conversion to 'the spirit of freedom and the spirit of truth' is less than justified.

Dina is, throughout, simple and direct, both in vocabulary and in syntax. As befits a girl who declares that she does not want to be 'a thing which is taken', she very obviously does not speak the received standard language of the community. She asks awkward, literal-minded questions in the moral sewing-party with which the play opens; and at other times, such as the revelatory group scenes which conclude Acts II and III, she is almost inarticulate. For an actress, to portray Dina is a difficult task because she has so little verbal underpinning of her emotions, reactions and decisions — momentous as they are (Dina and Johan are, after all, the only people who get away from the 'narrow conventions'). Ibsen seems to be making the point that for Dina there is really no meaningful language in this community.

While both Lona and Dina are in opposite ways perhaps as close as Ibsen gets to a kind of programmatic language for women, Martha Bernick both softens and widens the picture by showing Ibsen's insight into the thoughts and feelings of the one who did not get away, and never will. Martha, the spinster, a convenience in the Bernick household (as Bernick volubly tells us), might well have remained a two-dimensional shadow. Instead Ibsen gives her a scene, in Act IV, after Johan and Dina have run away — a dialogue with Lona, with no plot motivation as such, in which we learn of her hopeless love, longing and waiting for Johan. The lyrical quality of the scene, as Martha opens her heart and bares her feelings, makes it different from anything else in this argumentative-rhetorical play, almost threatening the convention of naturalism (in the recent Royal Shakespeare Company production, the actress had the help of speaking after a drink from the celebratory punch-bowl). The emotional effect is produced entirely by verbal means — by words in comment on what we have seen and are now seeing. The means are almost entirely literal statements, in a series of simple main clauses. Starkly she pinpoints the female tragedy of ageing: when Johan went away, they were contemporaries; now she is far older than he. Some of the words are in themselves emotive, like the repeated 'alone'; some are made peculiarly emotive by their repetition:

> I have loved him and waited for him. Every summer I waited for him to come. And then he came . . . but he didn't see me.

Martha's experience of not being seen by Johan, as he returns, transforms the play's thematic statement, 'You never see the women', into personal tragedy. The one exception to the literalness of the language in the scene is Martha's image of herself waiting and waiting for Johan:

   Martha. . . . and meanwhile I had been sitting here, spinning and
      spinning . . .
   Lona. The thread of his happiness, Martha.
   Martha. Yes, it was gold I spun. No bitterness.[22]

Like the girl in *Rumpelstiltskin*, Martha — by caring for Dina and bringing her up, and thus spinning the thread of Johan's happiness — has
spun straw into gold. There is a threat of mawkishness in the fairy-tale
reference; but it is, I think, held in check by the idea, also present, of
Martha as one of the Fates, or Norns, spinning the destiny of Johan.
And then there is the ineluctable sadness which comes from quite a
different echo — the song sung in every Scandinavian nursery:

   'Spin, spin, spin daughter mine:
   Soon your suitor will come.'

   And the daughter spun,
   And her tears did run.
   But never did that suitor come.[23]

Martha's is indeed the tragedy of the spinster, and in writing this scene
Ibsen extended his register of women's language. The interesting thing
— and the reason why I have dwelt at such length on the scene — is that
in doing so he also shows stylistic qualities which are going to become
characteristic of his later plays. These qualities, regardless of the sex of
the speaker, are: plain and literal statements which act as the tip of
icebergs of repressed emotions; a simple, repetitive vocabulary, where
the repetitions signify the obsessiveness with which ideas are held and
feelings examined; sudden leaps, under emotional pressure, from the
colloquial into metaphors which evoke quite other, non-realistic,
realms; a syntax of staccato sentences which enacts the movement of
the mind as it painfully unburdens itself of its oppressive load.

   But these, as I said, are features of Ibsen's later style: from *Rosmersholm* (1886) onwards (if I am to put a date to it). In the play which
followed *Pillars of the Community*, *The Doll's House*, the language of
both men and women is still largely tied to the exploration of a social
theme. Not that the play stands or falls on Women's Rights; in the role-
playing relationship of Nora and Thorvald Helmer there are insights
into the gap between woman and man, the failure of communication
between husband and wife, which are quite timeless — or, as some
would prefer to put it, surprisingly modern. But the language which is

given to Nora is clearly meant to outline for us the curve of her development, from being Thorvald's plaything to discovering that she must leave her doll's house and go out to find herself. Until her moment of recognition, it is made very clear that man enforces on woman a type of behaviour *and* a language to go with it. Nora speaks with the 'female helplessness' which Thorvald expects of her, when she speaks to *him*: she has a different idiom when she speaks to Mrs Linde, though this is still governed by her notion of what a clever little wife should sound like, just as her flirtation with the dismal Dr Rank seems very much made up to an expected pattern; only in the odd moments of lonely agony, when the suicide decision looms, does she seem to have anything of a voice of her own. But she can switch from this to the language Thorvald expects, at the drop of a hat, or the appearance of a husband; as at the end of Act II:

> *Nora (stands for a moment as though to collect herself, then looks at her watch).* Five. Seven hours to midnight. Then twenty-four hours to the next midnight. Then the tarantella will be over. Twenty-four and seven? Thirty-one hours to live.
> *Helmer (in the doorway, right).* What's happened to our little skylark?
> *Nora (running towards him with open arms).* Here she is![24]

Nora is a living — or, as Ibsen would have said, a '*digtet*' — proof of the point maintained by many modern sociolinguists: that women have to be bilingual in a male society. Indeed she has several languages. In the last scene, when she is facing her husband after her recognition and resolution, she yet again speaks a different one: restrained, simple, but logically connected statements. I think Ibsen may be trying to do what Wesker did with Beattie Bryant at the end of *Roots* — to show a woman finding her own, new language. Dramatically, I doubt if he is even as successful as Wesker; in recent productions, at least, I have found this scene affecting me more with the inadequacy of Helmer's language to deal with the situation than with any really *felt* sense of discovery in Nora. But then this might have been exactly Ibsen's intention — not to underline a thesis but, in his own words, 'to portray human beings' (of either sex).

It is perhaps a pity that it was Nora who first created 'Ibsenism' in this country and who came to connect the name of Ibsen with the idea of the new, liberated woman. The first performance of an unexpurgated Ibsen play was that of *A Doll's House* (with Janet Achurch as Nora) at the Novelty Theatre on 7 June 1889 and it brought him overnight fame and notoriety. As the editor of *Ibsen: The Critical Heritage* points out, 'for years — in some quarters even today — it was impossible to discuss Ibsen without referring to the position of women in society.' One wonders what might have happened if a different play had introduced him in England. For by 1889 he was about to write *Hedda Gabler* and had already written plays like *Ghosts, The Wild Duck, Rosmersholm* and *The Lady from the Sea*; and even the wildest simplification of what he was writing about could hardly have justified the following, Bernick-like, rebuke:

> The women who are so infuriated at the notion of being treated as mere toys, are, of course, perfectly in the right; but they should beware of confounding the feelings of men who look to them for nothing better than pleasant sensations and mental distraction, with the feelings of men who look to them to raise their ideal of mental and moral grace and beauty. (An unsigned notice in *The Spectator*, 21 June 1888)[25]

Mrs Alving in *Ghosts* is, in a sense, created out of the joint experiences of the women in *Pillars of the Community* and *A Doll's House*. She has, in her early conversations with Manders, the deflatory style and argumentative assurance of Lona Hessel and, in her increasingly troubled dialogues with her son, she has some of the tentativeness and wistfulness of Martha. Like Nora, she has a language which changes, so as to describe the curve of her (and the play's) development, from the assured statements in the opening Act, to the painful series of antitheses with which she makes clear her discovery, in the third and last Act, of what life must have been like for her husband. And there are worse discoveries to come: Osvald's breakdown under his inherited syphilis. Fine stylistic details signal this final horror. She who has always spoken so articulately and relied so largely on active verbs in the indicative ('I had to do so-and-so'; 'We shall do so-and-so') is reduced to repeating a dreadful, depersonalising, passive outcry — 'This cannot be endured' — then to a series of inarticulate Yes's and No's, and ultimately to 'speechless horror'. With Mrs Alving, I do not think Ibsen is in fact so much trying to write a woman's language as to chart, in action and language, the frustrated attempt of a soul to free itself from the 'ghosts' of past oppression.

With the speechless horror of Mrs Alving, like the arrested scream on one of Francis Bacon's faces, the woman question passes — for good in

Ibsen — into the condition of modern man. When, in later plays, his women seem to speak a different language from the men, they do so in the service of the whole play's exploration of 'human beings'. Gina, in *The Wild Duck*, provides linguistic comedy with her malapropisms, but she also has a quality akin to Cordelia's of undercutting, by her literal-ness and her attention to concrete details of experience, the elaborate metaphors which the men, Gregers Werle and Hjalmar Ekdal (one genuine, one fake), jointly mistake for truth. Her knowledge is not merely the practical one that hysterical 'idealism' can be cured by coffee with bread *and* butter, but also the intuitive insight that know-ing comes through seeing, not speaking: 'Look at the child, Ekdal!'

It becomes increasingly true, as we move into the later stages of Ibsen's career, that his language is in the service of each play as a whole. *John Gabriel Borkman* is, in some ways, a latter-day *Pillars of the Community*, but its world has lost the social stratification and particu-larity; it is made up of two bleak rooms where three people — John Gabriel and the two women whom he has both betrayed — tear away at each other and all struggle for dominance over Erhart, the son who gets away. In a sense, the women's experience gives them a different language from Borkman's: Ella, in the final scene, pits the 'cold, dark kingdom' of Borkman's visions against her own reality, 'a warm, living human heart'. But we are back here with patternings of the male-female predicament that are symbolical and image-based, rather than verbal and linguistic. In another sense, all the characters of the Bork-man household speak the same language: stark, obsessively repetitive, simple words carrying an almost unbearable emotional load which is as likely to issue into wordless agony — like Mrs Borkman's at the end of Act I — as into the rare, haunting metaphor.

Statistical surveys conducted by contemporary researchers into linguistic sex differences seem ironically, for all the desire not to fall back on stereotyped notions of sex roles, to have found a set of pre-dictable characteristics applying to female as against male language: it is simpler, using shorter sentences and fewer subclauses; and this also involves it being, in construction and syntax, more illogical and inco-herent. It is also more emotional; and, finally, it is more adapted to the situation in which the speech occurs than its male counterpart.[26] It is a curious fact that these characteristics could also be said to describe the style of Ibsen, as against the standard literary Norwegian of his day. I hasten to say that I have not written this essay to prove that Ibsen was really a woman, nor even to suggest, as James Joyce does, a womanli-ness in his nature:

Ibsen's knowledge of humanity is nowhere more obvious than in his portrayal of women. He amazes one by his painful introspection; he seems to know them better than they know themselves. Indeed, if one may say so, of an eminently virile man, there is a curious admixture of the woman in his nature.[27]

If I have to draw a conclusion at all, it is that Ibsen came to see the predicament of modern man (in the sense of 'human being') as most acutely realised in the predicament of modern woman; and that, to write his plays about human beings, he needed the emotional quality, the inconsequentiality, the staccato of simple sentences, the sense that experience is constantly outstripping both the vocabulary and the structure of language, which he found in the language of women. But conclusions are precarious when we deal with Ibsen whose favourite retort was 'On the contrary!' – and who would have been the first to point to one ineluctable but logically devasting flaw in this paper; that it is composed in woman's language.

Notes

1. As a leading article recently confessed in the research bulletin published by the Linguistics Department of Stanford University, 'researchers involved in women's language often admit to being far from disinterested observers of women's position in society': *Women and Language* (September-November 1976), quoted by Claes-Christian Elert, 'Rapporter inom planeringsarbetet för forskningsprojektet "Könsroller och Språk" ', in *Könsroller i Språk*, vol. ii, Report no. 61 from the Research Committee in Uppsala for Modern Swedish (FUMS) (Uppsala, 1978), p. 13. Robin Lakoff's book, *Language and Woman's Place* (New York, 1975), seems to me an unhappy example of the trivialising effect which such an approach can have upon a serious subject.

2. 'Man' here meaning, of course, 'men and women'. Writing as a Scandinavian, brought up – like Ibsen – in a language with a neutral word (Norwegian 'menneske'; Swedish människa') for men and women together, I am constantly frustrated by the lack of such a word in English. Ibsen often uses this word, and it generally has to be clumsily rendered by 'human being' (as later in this paper). The problem is clearly more than semantic.

3. Elaine Showalter, 'Review Essay: Literary Criticism', *Signs: Journal of Women in Culture and Society*, vol. i, no. 2 (Winter 1975), p. 452. Admittedly, she is thinking not of the Bible but of Donne's poem 'To his Mistris Going to Bed': 'Licence my roving hands, and let them goe/Behind, before, above, between, below' (11. 25-6).

4. Tove Skutnabb-Kangas and Olaug Rekdal, in *Könsroller i Språk*, vol. ii, p. 77.

5. For quotations from *Pillars of the Community* I use the translation which I prepared for the Royal Shakespeare production of the play at the Aldwych Theatre, London, which opened in August 1977.

6. This is my literal translation from the fifth draft of the play, as printed in vol. viii of Francis Bull, Halvdan Koht and Didrik Arup Seip (eds.), *The Centenary Edition of Ibsen's Collected Works* (*Hundreårsutgave: Henrik Ibsen's Samlede Verker*) (21 vols., Oslo, 1928-57), p. 230.

7. *Könsroller i Språk*, vol. ii, p. 81.

8. Ibid., vol. ii, p. 81.

9. *John Gabriel Borkman*, English version by Inga-Stina Ewbank and Peter Hall (London, 1975), p. 94.

10. William Archer, 'Ibsen and English Criticism', *Fortnightly Review*, vol. xlvi (July 1889), pp. 30-7; reprinted in Michael Egan (ed.), *Ibsen: The Critical Heritage* (London, 1972), pp. 115-23 (the quoted passage is on p. 119).

11. Quoted from Elizabeth M. Brennan (ed.), *The Duchess of Malfi* (New Mermaids, London, 1964).

12. I have attempted to discuss the language of these heroines in a paper delivered at the International Shakespeare Congress, Washington, DC, 1976, and published in D. Bevington and J.L. Halio (eds.), *Shakespeare: Pattern of Excelling Nature* (Newark, Delaware, 1978), pp. 222-9.

13. George Steiner, *After Babel: Aspects of Language and Translation* (London, 1975), Chapter I, 'Understanding as Translation'; see especially p. 47.

14. I quote my own literal translation of *Brand*, in order to bring out the balanced antithesis of the passage in the original.

15. Letter to Lucie Wolf, 25 May 1883 (*The Centenary Edition*, vol. xvii, p. 511). Some of the points made in this essay unavoidably overlap with my essay on 'Ibsen and "The Far More Difficult Art of Prose" ' in D. Haakonsen (ed.), *Contemporary Approaches to Ibsen*, vol. ii (Oslo, 1971), pp. 60-83.

16. See his comments on the language in *The Wild Duck*, 6 March 1891 and 21 November 1884 (*Centenary Edition*, vol. xviii, pp. 288, 50), and in *Ghosts*, 2 August 1883 (*Centenary Edition*, vol. xvii, p. 520).

17. Ibid., vol. xv, p. 417.

18. Again, to bring out what is going on in the original, I supply my own literal (not literary) translation.

19. *Centenary Edition*, vol. viii, p. 154.

20. Ibid., vol. viii, p. 156 (my translation).

21. This is Lona's phrase in the fifth draft (ibid., vol. viii, p. 240); in the printed version she says 'Old friendship does not rust.' The former version is the natural, proverbial expression, and we kept this in the Royal Shakespeare production of the play.

22. The bitter-sweetness of Martha's position is further emphasised in the fifth draft, but not in the printed version of the play, by Martha's continuation: 'The object is not so much to be happy as to deserve to be' (ibid., vol. viii, p. 228).

23. I have discussed this song, which has folk-song antecedents, in a paper, 'Ibsen's Language: Literary Text and Theatrical Context', forthcoming in *The Yearbook of English Studies*, vol. ix (1979), pp. 102-15.

24. Again, I have supplied a literal translation.

25. Reprinted in *Ibsen: The Critical Heritage*, p. 113.

26. Kerstin Nordin and Gun Nordmark, 'Forskning kring könsroller i språk', *Könsroller i Språk*, vol. ii, pp. 63-76.

27. 'Ibsen's New Drama', James Joyce's review of *When We Dead Awaken*, appeared in *Fortnightly Review*, n.s., vol. lxvii (1 April 1900), pp. 575-90. It is reprinted in *Ibsen: The Critical Heritage*, pp. 385-91; the quoted passage is on p. 388.

7 POETRY AND CONSCIENCE: RUSSIAN WOMEN POETS OF THE TWENTIETH CENTURY

Elaine Feinstein

Two women, Anna Akhmatova and Marina Tsvetayeva, stand among the greatest Russian poets — indeed, the greatest European poets — of the twentieth century. They are regarded with veneration both among émigrés and inside Russia now. And yet during their lifetime an almost superhuman courage was to be required from them, and their poetry was either ignored or suppressed. Love for the poetry of Akhmatova and Tsvetayeva has been, of course, expressed by men as well as women, and by poets as different as Brodsky and Yevtushenko; but I shall be dealing in this essay with women poets, who seem to have drawn an assurance from their great predecessors which sets them apart from women poets in the West.

In a poem Bella Akhmadulina read to me in Paris she described a sense of almost personal responsibility towards them:

This generation demands performance. The guilt of that
I take on without either gift or desire for it,
for your sake I take on the shame of pretence
so that in me may be seen some hint of the past,
of how it might be with Marina and Anna alive
when poetry and conscience could live together.

The two women's lives were as different as their personalities. In 1910 Akhmatova married Gumilyov, who was one of the most colourful figures in Russian poetry before the Revolution, at a time when she was not yet sure she would become a poet (Gumilyov thought of her as more suited to ballet), while Tsvetayeva was very much the dominant partner in *her* marriage to a gentle Sergei Efron and was certain of her role as poet from adolescence. Yet both women's lives were in some way framed by their first attachments, even though Akhmatova's marriage to Gumilyov was not happy, and Tsvetayeva was to be more intensely in love with other men. Gumilyov was shot in 1921 and the echoes of that death sentence were to reverberate through the rest of Akhmatova's life, bringing danger not only to Anna herself, and everyone who came close to her, but most terribly to the son of her marriage

133

to Gumilyov, whose long imprisonment under threat of death was to be the greatest torment of her life.

In the case of Tsvetayeva, it was her need to rejoin Efron which led her to leave Russia in 1922 when she heard that he had found refuge in Prague. As a White Officer, however disillusioned with that cause, he could not hope to return to Russia. And so began her long isolation as a poet, dependent on émigrés in Prague and Paris who welcomed her initially but soon rejected her. Akhmatova, on the other hand, though she loved Paris, always proudly refused to go into exile; as she declares in one of her best-known poems:

> I am not one of those who left the land
> to the mercy of its enemies.

Tsvetayeva's life in exile was one of poverty and neglect; by a curious irony, it was in exile that her husband Efron joined the Communist Party, and became a Soviet agent. He returned to Russia in 1937, soon followed by his daughter Alya, leaving Marina isolated and distrusted by her émigré friends in Paris, and with a young son who was desperate to return to his own homeland. And so in 1939, Marina once again followed Efron; and once again things went badly. Efron was imprisoned and shot; Marina's daughter Alya was taken to a labour camp; and when Hitler's war began Marina was evacuated with her son to Yelabuga, which lay on the other side of the river Kama from Chistopol where more acceptable writers had been billeted. There, in August 1941, she hanged herself.

Akhmatova began as a poet with a perfect command of lyrical forms; by the time *Requiem*, her longest, and perhaps greatest, poem comes to be written, the pain she has to record is so different in scale and intensity that it calls from her new rhythms, almost a new voice, a voice that can flow with the misery not only of her own waiting and fear, but the misery of all the other women waiting at prison walls to hear some news of those who have been taken from them. The poem is preceded by a note describing the woman with blue lips who recognises Akhmatova in the queue and asks her if she can put all their suffering into words. It is this duty which means there is no arrogance in Akhmatova's appropriating the position of Mary at the foot of the cross. She is looking at the crucifixion through Mary's eyes; but her voice is the voice of all the other women who know what is happening to their sons:

Requiem

Remembrance hour returns with the turning year.
I see, I hear, I touch you drawing near:

the one we tried to help to the sentry's booth,
and who no longer walks this precious earth,

and that one who would toss her pretty mane
and say, 'It's just like coming home again.'

I want to name the names of all that host,
but they snatched up the list, and now it's lost.

I've woven them a garment that's prepared
out of poor words, those that I overheard,

and will hold fast to every word and glance
all of my days, even in new mischance,

and if a gag should blind my tortured mouth,
through which a hundred million people shout,

then let them pray for me, as I do pray
for them, this eve of my remembrance day.

And if my country ever should assent
to casting in my name a monument,

I should be proud to have my memory graced,
but only if the monument be placed

not near the sea on which my eyes first opened —
my last link with the sea has long been broken —

nor in the Tsar's garden near the sacred stump,
where a grieved shadow hunts my body's warmth,

but here, where I endured three hundred hours
in line before the implacable iron bars.

Because even in blissful death I fear
to lose the clangour of the Black Marias,

to lose the banging of that odious gate
and the old crone howling like a wounded beast.

And from my motionless bronze-lidded sockets
may the melting snow, like teardrops, slowly trickle,

and a prison dove coo somewhere, over and over,
as the ships sail softly down the flowing Neva.

Akhmatova's poems of this period have a direct passion very different from her early writing. Tsvetayeva's greatness, though she also matured and grew, never lay in static perfection. It was always a matter of a passionate onward flow of feeling, that rhythm of which Pasternak spoke when he described her earliest poems as 'soaring . . . over the difficulties of creation'. She was one of those rare spirits to whom poetry has an almost supernatural importance of its own. Her daughter writes of her: 'She was able to subordinate any concerns to the interests of her work. I insist *any*.' But her daughter also testifies that if this led her to make severe demands on those around her, she treated herself with even greater severity. The conditions of Marina's Paris life, for example, would have been hard for anyone. At first, the four members of the Efron family lived cramped into one room. Their poverty was unremitting. They had so little spare cash that Marina has to beg 'a simple washable dress' to replace the woollen one she had been living in all winter. To Anna Teskova she wrote: 'We are devoured by coal, gas, the milkman, the baker . . . the only meat we eat is horsemeat.' Impractical and disorganised as she thought herself (and there are many descriptions of her Moscow flat which bear out her domestic eccentricity), she nevertheless coped with the daily necessity of shopping, with an eye always to the cheapest goods.

She did all the cooking. And yet she continued to write. The poet Rimma Kazakova makes it clear that she resents any grouping of poets together simply because they happened to be female, although she well understands the particular problems that a poet who is a woman has to face:

I think a man or woman who is a great personality is not afraid of stepping beyond the norms of ordinary behaviour. And if you speak about Tsvetayeva, I must say that I never think of her first as a woman, but always as just such an outstanding human spirit. And yet she worked like a horse for her family as a woman.

She did, and it took its toll, though Marina always knew she was the sort of person she speaks of in one of her poems whose enchanted visions 'cannot be weighed, in a world that deals only in weights and measures'. In a letter to Anna Teskova we see her analysing the problem of continuing to write in a situation where ordinary tasks consume most of her energy:

It's for feeling we need time, not thought. A simple example. When I'm rolling fish I can think — but feel? No. The smell stops me, the sticky hands, the splashing oil. The fish themselves stop me.

It is in this context we should attempt to understand her claim to almost supernatural grandeur in the poem 'An Attempt at Jealousy', which might otherwise be misunderstood as peculiarly female arrogance:

How is your life with the other one,
    simpler, isn't it? One   stroke of the oar
then a long coastline, and soon
    even the memory of me

will be a floating island
    (in the sky, not on the waters):
spirits, spirits, you will be
    sisters, and never lovers.

How is your life with an ordinary
    woman?   without godhead?
Now that your sovereign has
    been deposed (and you have stepped down).

How is your life? Are you fussing?
    flinching? How   do you get up?
The tax of deathless vulgarity
    can you cope with it, poor man?

— 'Scenes and hysterics   I've had
    enough! I'll rent my own house.'

How is your life with the other one
      now, you that I chose for my own?

More to your taste, more delicious
      is it, your food? Don't moan if you sicken.
How is your life with an *image*
      you, who walked on Sinai?

How is your life with a stranger
      from this world? Can you (be frank)
love her? Or do you   feel shame
      like Zeus' reins on your forehead?

How is your life? Are you
      healthy? How do you   sing?
How do you deal with the pain
      of an undying conscience, poor man?

How is your life with a piece of market
      stuff, at a steep price.
After Carrara marble,
      how is your life with the dust of

plaster now? (God was hewn from
      stone, but he is smashed to bits).
How do you live with one of a
      thousand women   after Lilith?

Sated with newness, are you?
      Now you are grown cold to magic,
how is your life with an
      earthly woman, without a sixth

sense? Tell me: are you happy?
      Not? In a shallow pit? How is
your life, my love? Is it as
      hard as mine with another man?

Tsvetayeva is usually spoken of, rightly, as someone who did not
believe that art could be made to serve politics. She did not believe it
could serve anything. Even though, talking about Rilke, she speaks of

poems as a form of *prayer*, she never made the mistake of blurring the distinction between poetry and religion. Poetry may be vitally important for her spiritual survival. Indeed, she says: 'If I were to be taken beyond the ocean into Paradise and forbidden to write I would refuse the ocean and Paradise.' Yet she does not make magniloquent claims for poetry. She knows that the 'doctor and the priest are humanly more important'. Marina Tsvetayeva's most passionate voice comes out of her great poem-cycle *Poem of the End*. This is a long narrative poem, but many Russians know it by heart. Perhaps every Russian writing now has felt its power. Two lovers meet and walk around the city of Prague. Gradually the man brings himself to explain that he wants their love affair to end. There follows lyric after lyric of naked, incredulous pain, in which Tsvetayeva seems to speak for every human being whose love has been rejected:

'Lyric 8' from *The Poem of the End*

Last   bridge   I won't
give up or take out my hand
this is the last bridge
the last bridging between

water   and firm land:
and I am saving these
coins for death
for Charon, the prince of Lethe

this   shadow money
from my dark hand I press
soundlessly into
the shadowy darkness of his

shadow money it is
no gleam and tinkle in it
coins for shadows:
the dead have enough poppies

This bridge

Lovers for the most
part are without hope: passion

also is just
a bridge, a means of connection.

It's warm: to nestle
close at your ribs, to move in
a visionary pause
towards nothing, beside nothing

no   arms no   legs
now, only the bone of my
side is alive where
it presses directly against you

life in that side
only, ear and echo is it: there
I stick like white to
egg yolk, or an eskimo to his fur

adhesive, pressing
joined to you: Siamese
twins are no nearer.
The woman you call mother

when she forgot
all things in motionless triumph
only to carry you:
she did not hold you closer.

Understand: we have
grown into one as we slept and
now I can't jump
because I can't let go your hand

and I won't be torn off
as I press close to you: this
bridge is no husband
but a lover: a just slipping past

our support: for the
river is fed with bodies!
I bite in like a tick
you must tear out my roots to be rid of me

like ivy   like a tick
inhuman   godless
to throw me away like a thing, when there is

no thing I ever prized
in this empty world of things.
Say this is only dream,
night still and afterwards morning

an express   to Rome?
Granada? I won't know myself
as I push off
the Himalayas of bedclothes.

But this dark is deep:
now I warm you with my blood, listen
to this flesh.
It is far truer than poems.

If you are warm, who
will you go to tomorrow for that?
This is delirium,
please say this bridge cannot

end
     as it ends.

Margarita Aliger, who is among the best-known poets of the generation born just after the Revolution, comes from a poor assimilated-
Jewish family in Odessa. Her father played the violin well, and knew
four languages; her mother read classics of Russian poetry to her. Aliger
found recognition as a poet early enough; but her life has been hard and
bitter. Her first husband was killed in the Second World War, her first
child died of meningitis at eight months. She is now a short, frail dark-
skinned woman of about sixty, who lives alone in a gracious flat
opposite the Tretyakov gallery. Recently Yevtushenko wrote a poem
about her called 'Poet in a Market', in which he described her going to
buy honey for her elder daughter who was in that year very ill, and has
since died. He saw in her frail figure standing among 'the cabbages and
the lard' unrecognised by other shoppers

the pure light
     and pride of
someone who was both Jewish woman
          and Russian poet.

Aliger has lived through, and understands at first hand, one of the most cruelly difficult periods of Soviet history. In 1976, she said to me that in spite of all the hardships she thought she had probably been happiest during the Second World War, because 'It was the time when all our people were together, and knew they were fighting an enemy *outside* that was evil'.

Aliger was on the same train as Akhmatova, travelling towards Chistopol in 1941. She remembers someone commenting on the beads Anna Akhmatova was wearing round her neck. 'That was a present from Marina,' Akhmatova said. And everyone fell silent, appalled by the knowledge of Tsvetayeva's suicide two months earlier. The question of guilt preoccupies Aliger. In her memoir of Akhmatova, she tells the story, and wonders whether, since it is impossible to say that anyone is innocent of Marina's neglect and loneliness, it makes any more sense to ask who is guilty. Aliger, with Tsvetayeva's daughter Alya, and Ilya Erenburg, has been among the most hard-working of the Commission set up to re-establish Tsvetayeva's reputation (and indeed publication) in Russia. Quite recently, Aliger's 35-year-long brooding over Tsvetayeva's suicide brought her to write one of her own finest poems, 'House in Meudon'. Meudon is the suburb of Paris in which Marina spent many years of poverty and exile.

The war was not only a time of horror and loss and the demands of courage for Aliger. It was also the time when she was closest to Fadaeev; and it is to their relationship so many of her best poems refer. Fadaeev was a novelist who acted as Secretary of the Writers' Union from 1939 to 1953. During the last years of his life, when he and Aliger were estranged, Fadaeev began drinking more and more heavily. In 1956 he killed himself. It was in the autumn of that year that Aliger wrote 'Two', a short sad lyric, which fixed (as Akhmatova might have done in her early period) on a single moment, like a perfect still:

Once again they've quarrelled on a tram
     shamelessly indifferent to strangers.
I can't hide how much I envy them.
     I can't take my eyes off their behaviour.

They don't even know their good fortune,
and not knowing is a part of their luck.
Think of it. They are together. Alive.
And have the time to sort things out and make up.

Regret sounds a stronger note than loneliness here, and there are other lyrics in which the main preoccupation is the unhappiness of being a survivor. It is a theme which has a peculiar poignancy whenever Aliger reflects on the gap between her own generation, and that of Yevtushenko and Akhmadulina, a gap she feels separates her even more strongly from the younger poets springing up after them whose lives have been so much easier and who cannot understand how it was in the thirties. 'It was not so simple as they think now,' she once said to me. In Aliger's poem to Lermontov (a poem I much admire) she is writing not only about the difference in fate between her life and that of the great poet who died young, but offering the apology of a survivor, who feels that the price of survival has been to live through more than any-one could be expected to endure:

Portrait of Lermontov

My twenty-six year old ensign,
please forgive me, please forgive
the twice as many years I've lived
in this bright world, where I still am.
Forgive me, please forgive me, for
every feast and every day, it's
been my fortune to have more,
twice as many more than you!
And yet if I've had twice your days
there has been room in them for twice
as many fears and injuries.
Who knows which century it was
easier to bear? Between us
who was luckier? What weighs more,
heavy blows the living feel, or
grass that's growing overhead?

You won't answer, since you're dead
And I won't answer . . . I'm alive.

The gap between generations can be felt as we move from Margarita Aliger to Yunna Moritz, who (like Akhmadulina) was only a child in the war that was the central experience of Aliger's life. Apart from Akhmadulina, Yunna Moritz is unquestionably the most widely praised of contemporary women poets. I was struck by the contrast between her and Akhmadulina, who is flamboyant, even reckless in manner, stylishly dressed, with a black-eyed, high-cheeked beauty. Yunna Moritz has a pale, long face, sad grey eyes and a gentle voice. She speaks quietly and slowly, as if she is thinking out her answers for the first time. When she reads, she avoids the rhetoric of public delivery, preferring to sound more like a person reading aloud to herself. She is also much more mysterious and difficult to reach as a person — not, I felt, out of a desire to *hide*, but out of a genuine hatred of the explicit. I knew before we met that she was a great favourite of Akhmatova, and that other poets have compared the quality of her nature poetry to Pasternak. But when I spoke to her she refused to see herself in terms of literary influences. She introduced herself to me with the sentence: 'I am a very strange poet.' She preferred to speak of the influence not so much of other writers but of whole cultures and periods, particularly the Baroque, which I took to mean the profusion of imagery, at once rich and homely, that fills her poems. She has a great love for the richness of the earth, and the people of the South with their exotic traditions of cookery. It seemed, however, that she meant rather more than this by the baroque impulse on her poem 'In Memory of François Rabelais'. This is a poem which brings together a belief in the immortality of the soul, the releasing power of laughter, and her own sense of an anthill existence, in which men and women live on the false expectation that things must be gradually improving. But I know enough about the circumstances of Yunna Moritz's own life to know that, when she claims in this poem that it is within the sacred power of laughter to make us find the most tragic facts of this world *comic*, it is a hard-won, tough and personal knowledge, which ignores nothing:

In Memory of François Rabelais

To lie at the edge of the forest
with your face in the earth is miraculous
for idleness is tender, and
can be possessed entirely
in vegetable joy just as
bees sing into clover.

Feel the space under the planet.
Hold on to grass and beetles.
Gulp down the smell of the zoo
on your own skin. We live among
fair booths, where time is short,
packed in together densely.

In Paradise no more idols!
People do what they like
joyfully, bathing and lazing,
with no thought of finicky manners.
The healthy spirit of Rabelais
rules the whole population there.

No better world to wait for!
laughter rises easily,
And stories – Pierrot can
dance on his drum as naked
as if he were in a bath-house.
The show is for everyone.

When laughter beats in your ears,
your soul knows it is immortal.
The freedom is like a mouthful
of wine   a breathing space
a forgetting of this life's brevity.
The saddest truth can be funny.

Now go back to your anthill,
put coffee on the stove there.
Chew at your greens for supper.
Enjoy the simplest flavour,
and as you do so   savour
the strangeness   of carrying on!

Once you can shout and laugh
like a monkey at death and fate
and how men and women act –
the pause is wholly blessed.
A laugh   is the outrageous sign
that your soul remains alive.

Unhealthy fevers shake us
in this stern world. Tormented,
by chasing after success,
we may lose all we possess.
Even our souls may leak away
then, and only return to us
with Hell and horned beasts!

I myself find Yunna Moritz at her best when she is most movingly
simple, as in these two poems for her sick mother which she read to me
in Moscow:

'Lyric 1'

Whiteness   the whiteness of these skies
heavily clamping down over our bodies;
when the time comes our souls will pass through you
only too easily. So here I am, Lord,
blocking my mother's entrance to paradise
ready to curse the light blue roof of it
however you harass me into the cracks
like a snake I won't give her up to you yet
Gnawing stones and howling here I sit.
And I refuse to let my mother past.

'Lyric 3'

Misfortune is as huge
    and heavy as this cold
I'm half-dead. Without home.
    Without a roof or wing
Alone under bare skies.
    A stump of birchwood chair
my table drowned by rain
    abandoned, covered in snow.

My pages rustled through
by icy winds. Mother!
Twig. Small bird.
Snow-girl. Don't touch the fire!

The bonfire. Lie quite still.
Like a water drop on sand
like a red tear on my cheek.
Don't touch! Lie quite still.
Don't touch the fire. Lie there.
Perhaps death will hold back.
And Spring will come. Spring!
with peas and beans returning
A star will fall in the well
Or a single drop of dew.
Spring birds   where are you flying?
A frail old woman can so easily
dwindle away to nothing
before you return. It's hard not to!
I wait in the hospital courtyard
and sitting, here make up my prayer.
Trees. Trees. Lake. Lake.
While there is time to spare
before my mother's small body is bruised
yellow and blue. Please. Give me
a small piece of Spring, whose
time will come anyway, spring always comes:
beans appear, peas come up,
and small prickly cucumbers.
I won't believe it, I won't believe it. No.
it is impossible mother should go
for ever   before the first strawberries.
And yet the stars are bright over the fields.
There is snow in the wind over the poplars.
Against the wall a snowdrift. Like a breast.
And we are children. Grant us a little Spring!

Bella Akhmadulina is probably the most gifted of the poets who rose
to fame alongside Yevtushenko and Vozhnozhensky. Born in Moscow
in 1937, with Italian and Tartar ancestors, she is a strikingly beautiful
woman with a warm, affectionate presence that hides febrile intensity.
It is, I believe, no accident that it is Bella Akhmadulina who has most
boldly taken upon herself the inheritance of her great women predecessors, Anna Akhmatova and Marina Tsvetayeva. Yevtushenko dates
her maturity as a poet from the moment she first acknowledged that
weight upon her, and singles out particularly her poem 'I Swear'. In

'I Swear' Akhmadulina personified the murderous forces of bureaucratic pettiness as a fairy-tale monster, to which she gives the name of Yela-buga, the town where Marina Tsvetayeva took her own life. When she spoke about the poem to me, she was at pains to point out that the inhabitants of that town were of course innocent. What she was vowing to destroy was the vicious small-mindedness which left Marina so alone and friendless in 1941, and still remains an enemy Bella can recognise in her own society:

I Swear

    by that summer snapshot taken
on someone else's porch, skewed to one
side, that looks so like a gibbet, and
points a way out of the house not into it;
where you are wearing some violent sateen dress that
cramps the muscles of your throat like armour;
and are simply sitting there, with the endurance of a
tired horse after the labour of
singing out to the end all your grief and hunger.
I swear: by that photo, and your delicate pointed
elbows, which are as child-like as the smile of surprise
that death uses to lure children to itself and leaves
as a mark upon their faces for evidence.
I swear: by the painful burden of remembering
how I gulped your airless grief from the
breathless rush of your lines, and had to
keep clearing my throat until it bled.
Yes, by your own presence, which I have stolen,
burgled, taken for myself, as if forgetting that
you belong to God, who cannot get enough of you;
and by that starved emaciation which
killed you at the end with its rat tooth.
I swear: by the blessed Motherland herself, even if
she grossly abandoned you like an orphan;
and your beloved African, that great genius of
kindness, whose own end was unkind, now
as a statue watching over small children.
By those children! And the Tversky Boulevard
And your own sad rest in Paradise, where
there is neither trade nor torment for you!

I swear: to kill that Yelabuga, your
Yelabuga, so that our grandchildren
can sleep soundly. Old women may still frighten
them at nights, not knowing the power of her
existence, thinking she doesn't exist, saying:
'Sleep little child, quietly, quietly, for
blind Yelabuga is coming to catch you.'
And with all her tangle of legs truly she will
hasten towards me crawling with horrible speed.
But I shall bring my boot down on her
tentacles without saying any more, and
put my weight on my heel, and my toe-cap into
the back of her neck, and keep it there.
Then the green juice of her young will burn
the soles of my feet with their poison, but I'll
hurl the egg that ripens in her tail
into the earth, that bottomless earth!
And not say a word of the porch in the photograph.
I will not speak of Marina's homeless death.
I swear it. Even while in
the dark, and in the stench of silt,
with the toads in the well about her, she
has one yellow eye fixed in my direction:
The Yelabuga
swears her own oath — to kill me!

At her finest, Akhmadulina combines a fierce, comic invention
with her most passionate utterance: she turns her wit upon herself (as
in 'Fever'), or upon the complacent materialism of the worldly (in *A
Fairy Tale of Rain*), with equal ferocity. Her voice often recalls the
voice of Tsvetayeva in 'Praise to the Rich'. In many of her poems the
figure of the poet is compelled to behave in ways that bring the contempt of more conventional people upon her. I asked Akhmadulina
whether she felt that her poetic gift was a kind of curse:

I am not sure it would be quite accurate to say that. What is more
important to me is the state I experience when I write . . . I think
whenever a gift is given to a human being it affects her fate, or her
gift is affected by her fate. Particularly a poet. Perhaps a poetic gift
does sentence whoever has it to some kind of grief or doom. Sometimes I do feel it is a heavy burden. And I say to myself, I don't

want to write, I won't write. But I have never been able to stop . . .
Sometimes when young people come to me for advice I tell them
. . . If you're able *not* to write, then stop. The only valid reason for
writing poetry is the total inability to live without doing so.

Nothing could be more like Tsvetayeva's own words, in her essay 'Art
in the Light of Conscience', where she describes poetry at its greatest as
a kind of possession 'to which the poet must abandon himself, as Blok
did when he wrote *The Twelve* in a single night and got up in complete
exhaustion, like one who has been driven upon'. In 'Fever' the poet
experiences her gift as a kind of delirium which isolates her from her
neighbours: it is a sharp, witty poem, as much self-mocking as self-
explaining, and the central image rises to an absurdity that is elegant as
well as surreal:

Fever

I must be ill, of course. I've been shivering
for three days now like a horse before the races.
Even the haughty man who lives on my landing
has said as much to me:
Bella, you're shaking!

Please control yourself, this strange disease of yours
is rocking the walls, it gets in everywhere.
My children are driven mad by it, and at night
it shatters all my cups and kitchenware.

I tried to answer him: Yes,
I do tremble,
more and more, though I mean no harm to anyone.
But tell everyone on the floor, in any case,
I've made up my mind to leave the house this evening.

However, I was then so jerked about by
fever, my words shook with it; my legs
wobbled; I couldn't even bring my
lips together into the shape of a smile.

My neighbour, leaning over the bannister,
observed me with disgust he didn't hide.

Which I encouraged.
— This is just
a beginning. What happens next, I wonder.

Because this is no ordinary illness. I'm sorry to
tell you, there are as many wild and
alien creatures flashing about in me
as in a drop of water under a microscope.

My fever lashed me harder and harder, and
drove its sharp nails under my skin. It was
something like the rain whipping an
aspen tree, and damaging every leaf.

I thought: I seem to be moving about rapidly
as I stand here, at least my muscles are moving.
My body is out of my control completely.
The thing is freely doing whatever it likes.

And it's getting away from me. I wonder if
it will suddenly and dangerously disappear?
Like a ball slipping out of a child's hand,
or a piece of string unreeling from a finger?

I didn't like any of it. To
the doctor
I said, (though I'm timid with him)
— You know, I'm a proud woman! I can't have my
body disobeying me for ever!

My doctor explained:
Yours is a simple disease,
perhaps even harmless, unfortunately
you are vibrating so fast I can't examine you.

You see, when anything vibrates, as you are,
and its movements are so very quick and small,
the object is reduced, visibly speaking
to — nothing. All I can see is: mist.

So my doctor put his golden instrument
against my indefinite body, and a sharp
electric wave chilled me at once
as if I had been flooded with green fire

and the needle and the scales registered horror.
The mercury began to seethe with violence.
The glass shattered, everything splashed about,
and a few splinters drew blood from my fingers.

— Be careful, doctor, I cried. But
he wasn't worried.
Instead, he proclaimed: Your
poor organism is
now functioning normally.

Which made me sad. I knew myself to belong
to another norm than he had ever intended.
One that floated above my own spirit only
because I was too narrow for such immensity.

And those many figures of my ordeals had
trained my nervous system so that now
my nerves were bursting through my skin, like old
springs through a mattress, screeching at me.

My wrist was still out of shape with its huge
and buzzing pulse, that always had insisted
on racing freely: Damn it, run free then, I cried
I'll choke with you, as Neva chokes St. Petersburg.

For at night my brain has become so sharp with
waiting, my ear opens to silence, if
a door squeaks or a book drops, then —
with an explosion — it's the end of me.

I have never learnt to tame those beasts
inside, the guzzle human blood.
In my presence, draughts blow under doors!
Candles flare - before I extinguish them!

And one enormous tear is always ready
to spill over the rim of my eyes.
My own spirit distorts everything.
I have a hell inside would corrupt heaven.

The doctor wrote me out a Latin scrip.
The sensible and healthy girl in
the chemist shop was able to read
the music in it from the punctuation.

And now my whole house has been softened by
the healing kiss of that valerian,
the medicine has licked into every
wound I have, with its minty tongue.

My neighbour is delighted, three times he
has congratulated me on my recovery,
(through his children). He has even
put a word in for me with the house management.

I have repaid a few visits and debts already,
answered some letters. I wander about
in some kind of profitable circles.
And no longer keep any wine in my cupboard.

Around me — not a sound, not a soul.
My table is dead, dust hides everything on it.
My blunt pencils like illiterate
snouts, are all lying in darkness.

And like a defeated horse, all my
steps are sluggish and hobbling now.
So all is well. But my nights are
disturbed with certain dangerous premonitions.

My doctor has not yet found me out. However
it will not long be possible to
fool him. He may have cured me once, but
soon I know I shall burn and freeze again.

A snail in its grave of bone, I am
for the moment saved by blindness and silence —
but still the horns of sick antennae itch
and will rise up once again from my forehead.

Star-fall of full stops and hyphens, I
summon your shower to me! I want to
die with the silvery goose-flesh of
water nymphs burning in my spine.

Fever! I am your tambourine, strike me
without pity! I shall dance, like
a ballerina to your music, or
live like a chilled puppy in your frost.

So far I haven't even begun to
shiver. No, let's not even discuss that. Ye
my observant neighbour is already
becoming rather cold to me when we meet.

Akhmadulina often works best within the context of an extended
metaphor, and clearly prefers to embody the evils of a materialistic
society in surprising and fantastic images. No one can ever be in doubt,
however, about the nature of what is under attack. At the centre of *A
Fairy Tale of Rain*, another heroine who feels herself to belong to a
world of values ignored in her society finds herself pursued by Rain,
which takes many shapes, but always suggests the playful fertility of
the human spirit. Whether Rain is the gift of poetry, or poetry itself, its
one determination is to prevent the heroine making a peaceful adjust-
ment to the arid materialism she feels on every side. She has an invitation to a party at a house of considerable splendour, where she knows
she will meet hidden disapproval, precisely because she cannot be
trusted to behave conventionally. She will be tolerated only because she
has a certain fashionable reputation. But the discomfort is mutual. The
heroine senses something sinister in the beauty of this house; a corruption in its very perfection of taste. When at last she rings the bell and
appears, soaked by rain, the guests try to bring her close to the fire to
dry out. Akhmadulina imagines in their invitation an echo of that
medieval hatred and fear of the strange that once had led people to
burn witches:

'Lyric 5' from *A Fairy Tale of Rain*

To put it mildly, the mistress of that house would
never have bothered to hide her dislike of me,
except for the fear of being thought old-fashioned.
That restrained her, which was perhaps a pity.

— How *are* you? (And how could
so haughty a slender throat hold back the thunder?)
— Thank you, I answered hastily: I feel
like a sow that's been wallowing in the mud.

(I don't know what came over me. I meant
to say, with some polite
gesture:
— Things are rather busy, but I'm fine
And much better for seeing you again).

But she began to speak at once:
You know, it's a disgrace, for someone like you, with
        so much talent
to walk so far. In all this rain!
Then everyone started to shout together.
— Bring her up to the fire! To the fire with her!

And once upon a time in another age
it could have happened to a beating drum
in the market place, with music perhaps and jeers
you would have cried:
To the fire, with her, to the fire!

Hello then, and leap up at me, Fire!
Brother, dog of many tongues, now lick
my hands in your great tenderness.
For you are the Rain also. Your burn is wet!

— Your monologue is rather peculiar,
    my host said tartly.
— But never mind, blessings on green shoots!
There's always charm in a new generation.

— Don't listen to me, I'm delirious, I said.
  It's all the fault of the Rain. All day it's
been pursuing me everywhere, like a devil.
It's only the Rain that's getting me into trouble.

Then, suddenly, through the window I saw
my faithful Rain, sitting alone and crying.
And two tears swam into my eyes, and they
were the last traces of water left in me.

Akhmadulina laid great stress on a section of the poem in which an apparently angelic group of children entertain the guests with a blood-chilling song. However, the climax of the poem comes when the heroine is no longer able to bear her denial of the spirit of Rain and summons it (now a pathetic creature, locked outside) towards her. At once, Rain floods into the house, destroying the order and beauty of it, and causing damage which Akhmadulina describes in a passage of superb comic inventive. The hostess and her guests, however, set upon the Rain ruthlessly, and soon destroy it (Akhmadulina was emphatic on this point). The heroine shrugs away the hostess's claim that she should put right the material damage, but she has to accept responsibility for allowing the murder of a rare source of tenderness and trust in a smart deadened world:

'Lyric 12' from *A Fairy Tale of Rain*

Then a shiver ran down every spine
and in quiet darkness the hostess screamed
as orange marks like rust suddenly
appeared in streaks upon that white ceiling.

And down poured the Rain. They caught at it
with tins, pushed it with brooms and brushes.
It escaped. And flew up in their cheeks
or formed like liquid cataracts in their eyes.

It danced a strange and surprising can-can,
and rang playfully on the restored crystal.
Then the house snapped its vicious jaws
over it. Like a man-trap, tearing muscle.

The rain with a look of love and longing even as it
soiled the floor, crawled to me on its belly;
even while men, lifting their trouser legs,
kicked at it, or jabbed it with their heels.

They captured it with a floor-cloth and then
squeamishly wrung it out in the lavatory.
Until in a voice made suddenly hoarse and wretched
I shouted out:
— Don't touch. It belongs to me.

It was alive, like a child or an animal.
Now may *your* children live in torment and misery.
Blind people, whose hands know nothing of mystery
why have you chosen to stain the Rain in blood?

The lady of the house whispered to me:
— Remember,
you will have to answer for all this.
I burst out laughing:
I know what I shall answer!
You are disgusting. Now please let me pass.

Although a psychological affinity with Tsvetayeva accords with
the speed and flow of Akhmadulina's poetry, and is clearly very much
stronger, Akhmadulina has always honoured Akhmatova deeply, as she
explained to me in Paris, before telling an extremely funny story about
one of their rare meetings. It seems Bella once offered to drive Akhmatova to her *dacha*. Unfortunately, Bella's car stalled at some traffic
lights; and the journey ended ignominiously with Akhmatova firmly
refusing even the offer of a lift in Bella's friend's car with the decisive
words: 'I never make the same mistake twice.' In spite of this irreverent
account, Akhmadulina explains the reason for the remoteness of her
acquaintance with Akhmatova in a very characteristic way:

I had immeasurable love and respect for Anna Andreevna but I am
so organized internally that I never try to meet the people I love so
much. It was the same with Pasternak. I loved Akhmatova's poetry
so much I could not think of any kind of relationship between us.
The distance between Akhmatova and Tsvetayeva and — myself —
is enormous. I love them both far more than I love myself.

She goes on to refuse the comparison between her poetry and theirs; but there must be many who share with me Yevtushenko's belief that she is the best poet of her generation, and very much in the tradition of the two great women poets who stand over her shoulder.

Acknowledgements

This is a version, condensed by the author, of three talks put out in 1978 on BBC Radio 3 (it has also appeared in *Bananas*). All translations © Elaine Feinstein except for Part II of the 'Epilogue' from *Requiem*, reprinted from *The Poems of Akhmatova*, trans. S. Kunitz and M. Hayward (Collins and Harvill Press, London, 1974); Elaine Feinstein's translations of Tsvetayeva were first published by Oxford University Press in 1971. The author would like to thank Simon Franklin, Angela Livingstone, Bernard Comrie and Richard Davis for literal versions of poems and prose passages.

Author's Note

This essay is based on several meetings and interviews with the poets concerned. I spoke informally to Margarita Aliger in 1974 in Moscow, and again in 1976 in Cambridge, and interviewed her on Moscow Radio in 1977. Yunna Moritz I spoke to formally in Moscow in 1977; Rimma Kazakova I spoke to informally in Moscow in 1974, and interviewed on Moscow Radio in 1977; Bella Akhmadulina I met in Moscow in 1974, in Paris and again in Cambridge in 1976.

8 WRITING AS A WOMAN

Anne Stevenson

Suppose we begin by calling to mind some scenes from Sylvia Plath's *The Bell Jar*. Esther Greenwood, a heroine who more obviously than most is a version of the author, has returned from a disillusioning experience as a student editor of a ladies' magazine in New York. The glamorous world of fashion writing and famous authors has proved to be a fraud. Her fellow students have been frivolous; the parties, tedious; the men, vain or sadistic, have failed to seduce or even interest her. At the climactic dinner, crabmeat and avocado salad, roasted in photographer's lights, have laid the whole company flat with ptomaine poisoning. Finally, at the end of her stay, Esther stands on the parapet of her hotel feeding piece after piece of her fashionable wardrobe to the night winds — a gesture of anger and defiance so total that she is forced to barter her dressing-gown for clothes to travel in the next day.

When Esther returns to her mother in suburban Westchester, the first thing she hears is that her application for a writers' course in Cambridge has been turned down. She has already seen through the shallow hypocrisy of her medical-student boy-friend, Buddy Willard and his 'clean-living' family. The summer has been a disaster in its first month, and Esther Greenwood, for the first time in the course of a stunningly successful adolescence, is forced to face up to what she is. What she is turns out to be a girl — a middle-class American girl, talented and ambitious, yes, but of whom things are expected that have nothing to do with her talents and ambitions. Poor Esther. Poor Sylvia.

Now, I want to disregard, temporarily, Sylvia Plath's own psychological troubles (they have been too much discussed in any case) and look instead at the predicament of Esther Greenwood. What are we to say of this account in *The Bell Jar* of a talented woman's first brush with — we must call it for lack of a better term — 'the real world'?

If we are truly bigoted we can dismiss Esther's suffering as the neurosis of an 'over-achievment-orientated school-girl'. But none of us would want to do that. More to the point, we can regard *The Bell Jar* as an honest, often brilliant account of a woman's confrontation with a society many of whose values are an insult to her integrity. However, there is more to *The Bell Jar* than this. For as a writer, Esther Greenwood, like Sylvia Plath, has a vested interest *in* her society. She craves its approval and she needs it for material. She also has instinctive 'womanly' feelings, and quite naturally she is curious about sex, babies, marriage and what her future as a woman will be.

The trouble in *The Bell Jar* seems to be this: throughout most of her life Esther has pulled herself to the top of her society – at school, at college – by native intelligence and stupendous will-power. Now, suddenly, she finds that she is a victim of forces beyond her control . . . forces that are also desires. She wants to be a complete woman, but in most womanly roles she can't excel. Why can she not cook, take short-hand, dance, play the piano, translate languages, do all the things in the world women are expected to do to help men? And why, on the other hand, do the things she *can* do (write, win academic prizes, win scholar-ships) seem not to matter to other people, particularly men – or, if they do matter, lead to disillusionment? The editing job was a fiasco; the writing course wouldn't accept her.

These two streams of (seemingly) personal failure undermine and finally paralyse her will. After a series of imaginary flights to other, quite impossible selves (she should marry a prison guard on Deer Island and have a parcel of kids; she should become a Catholic and confess to a priest; she should study shorthand, become a typist, be a waitress) – after these flights away from her own personality have come to nothing, Esther turns to the only refuge from her torment she can think of and attempts to kill herself in a corner under the house.

It is not my purpose to undertake an analysis of *The Bell Jar*, though I might point out that, as a piece of writing, the tough, amused bitter-ness of the first third of the book dissolves into jerky passages of con-fession and crude resentment once the breakdown has occurred. What is of interest to us, however, is that Sylvia Plath implies all the way through that the roles of 'writer' and 'woman' are in some way incom-patible. Yet, like so many of us, she was damned if she herself was going to forgo one to become the other. The tension between the two roles – the woman and the writer – is a source of energy in her poems, but it is also, I think, a source of their self-destructiveness. What seems most self-destructive in Plath's work is a haunting fear of failure. The emotional power she summons from her subconscious is a mixture of a fear of inadequacy and a knowledge of her superiority. She establishes her astringently defiant tone in a language of inventive complaint and embattled anger.

I hasten to add that this mixture of inadequacy and superiority is common in American writing. It is to be found all through Berryman and Lowell, and even in Whitman. Since we are talking of women, it is of interest to note that Emily Dickinson's letters — when she was exercising her ferocious wit — make use of the same defiant tone that Sylvia Plath perfected in parts of *The Bell Jar*. Let's compare two passages. Here is Emily Dickinson describing her family to Colonel Higginson:

> I have Brother & a Sister — My Mother does not care for thought — and Father, too busy with his Briefs — to notice what we do. He buys me many Books — but begs me not to read them — because he fears they joggle the Mind. They are all religious-except-me and address an Eclipse, every morning, — whom they call their 'Father.'[1]

Can you think of a more devastating attack on the male-dominated family than that? And yet, the wit is suspect. We know that Emily Dickinson adored her father, rather pitied as well as despised her mother, relied on her sister to make her way in the world possible. So her *real* attitude is defensive of the system she is attacking. What is wrong with her world is exactly what gives her advantages in it, as a woman and as a writer. She is superior in intelligence to everyone she knows, but inferior in ability to meet the world on *its* terms. She decides, therefore, quite early in her life that it will suit her better not to try. In her letters she makes fun of a state of affairs she could never have borne to change.

Sylvia Plath was, of course, temperamentally a different creature altogether. She wanted to be a good writer, but she also wanted to be an exceptionally efficient wife, mother and housekeeper; we know that from the recently published *Letters Home* (1975). Her attack on Dodo Conway, as Dodo pushes her creaking pram under Esther's window in the suburbs, is partly an attack on the general slovenliness of human beings when they allow themselves to go nature's way without the puritan constraints of self-control:

> A woman not five feet tall, with a grotesque protruding stomach, was wheeling an old black baby carriage down the street. Two or three small children of various sizes, all pale, with smudgy faces and bare smudgy knees, wobbled along in the shadow of her skirts.
> A serene, almost religious smile lit up the woman's face. Her head tilted happily back, like a sparrow egg perched on a duck egg, she smiled into the sun.[2]

But like Emily Dickinson, Sylvia Plath is not showing her full hand.

For (as Plath herself sees) Dodo Conway is a *happy* woman. She is far happier, with her babies and her protruding stomach, than Esther is, or Esther's mother whose efforts to bring up two children to be clean-living, responsible citizens are in some ways more threatening to Esther's creativeness than Dodo's untidy brood. Dodo presents Esther with an alternative which a part of her wants to accept.

Having no father, Sylvia Plath cannot fondly make fun of him, as Emily Dickinson could of hers. You remember how in *The Bell Jar*, Plath has Esther make a pilgrimage to her father's grave, not to honour him but to blame him. She can never forgive him for dying and leaving her to the mercies of her mother. The language of this passage is too double-edged to be accidental, and it is in some ways a key to the book: 'I had a great yearning, lately, to *pay my father back* for all the years of neglect, and start tending his grave' (my italics).[3] Literally, 'to pay back' means to pay back what she owes, to pay her debt to her father. But 'to pay back' also means to take revenge. Esther is revenging herself for *his* neglect of *her* at the same time as she is apologising for *her* neglect of *him*. Still, the relationship between daughter and dead father is more interesting and creative than that between daughter and living mother. The mother is presented in every instance as a despicable object; her goodness and devotion only annoy. There are moments when Esther wants to kill her:

> The room blued into view, and I wondered where the night had gone. My mother turned from a foggy log into a slumbering, middle-aged woman, her mouth slightly open and a snore ravelling from her throat. The piggish noise irritated me, and for a while it seemed to me that the only way to stop it would be to take the column of skin and sinew from which it rose and twist it to silence between my hands.[4]

We will go back to the question of fathers and mothers later, though we must take care not to fall into the swamp of amateur psychoanalysis. Half-way through *The Bell Jar*, nevertheless, we begin to form an idea of what this bell jar is of which Plath writes so frighteningly. It seems it is a kind of vacuum, a vacuum composed of self-cancelling values. Some of these values are social and shared with most middle-class Americans; some are domestic and relate to women in society; some are personal and attributable to Esther's ambitions as a writer and her high expectations of herself. Others, of course, have to do with her relationship with her mother and her dead father. But up to the moment of breakdown, all these values have been held together by a bullying will to succeed. When her will weakens, Esther's conflicting self-images collapse in upon each other, leaving a vacuum in which her mind is incapable of breathing. It is because her mind is stifling that she attempts to kill the body which sustains it.

Now, I'd be willing to bet anything that nothing like this ever happened to Emily Dickinson. Miss Dickinson's tortures were religious and personal. She was, to an extreme degree, passionate and shy. Personal relationships were too highly charged for intercourse, so she had to confine her social life to letters. But she accepted the crushing provincial society in which she lived because, as we have seen, it suited the peculiar nature of her genius. Had she been a man she would have had to find a way of life that gave her equal privacy – not easy in nineteenth-century New England where, if you went into the church, you had to preach to huge congregations, and if you went into literature you were meant to write for *The Atlantic Monthly*. Emerson and Whitman, at periods in their lives, had to work for their bread. Emily Dickinson was spared that indignity. It was no disgrace to be the family spinster. It was luck, and secretly Emily Dickinson knew it. That room with closed doors in the spacious house in Amherst saw terrible anguish, but it was not the cause of that anguish. It was a refuge from it. This was the principal difference between the bedroom in Amherst and the bedroom in Jamaica Plains.

Other women have known their luck. It is surprising how many spinster writers there have been: Jane Austen, Emily Brontë, Stevie Smith, Charlotte Mew, Marianne Moore, Elizabeth Bishop. These women may have suffered, but they suffered as women who attempted neither to fight male domination nor compromise themselves to suit it. Theirs was a narrow independence, even a selfish one, but it was real. It was bought at the price of what used to be called 'womanliness' – sex, marriage, children and the socially acceptable position of wife.

Sometimes I think a woman writer has to pay that price. In my own case, however, I've not been willing, any more than Sylvia Plath was willing, to sacrifice my life as a woman in order to have a life as a writer. Surely, in the twentieth century, when society allows so much, it ought to be possible to be a fulfilled woman and an independent writer without guilt – or without creating a bell jar vacuum in which it is impossible to breathe. As I look back over my own experience I see, however, that I have only *just* managed to survive. Writing poetry is not like most jobs; it can't be rushed or done well between household chores – at least not by me. The mood of efficiency, of checking things off the list as you tear through a day's shopping, washing, cleaning, mending and so forth is totally destructive of the slightly bored melancholy which nurtures my imagination. Even friends distract me, though I often make them an excuse not to write. It is possible that marriage, children, social obligations have always been ways for me of avoiding the hard work of making poems. But even if this were so, I can't now reverse my decision to have a family. I have to be a writer with a handicap.

One way out of the dilemma of the woman/writer is to write poems about the dilemma itself. Though I have never considered myself to be a specifically feminist poet, many of my poems are about being trapped in domestic surroundings. I dread, and have always dreaded, that marriage, a home and family would sap my creative energies, that they would devour my time and my personality, that they would, in a venomous way I can't easily explain, use me up. When I look at my early poems I am surprised that so many of them express what seems to me this particularly feminine dread.

The first poem I published in a magazine — when I was about twenty-three — was called 'The Women'. It was written in Yorkshire in 1956 when, although I didn't know it, I was going through a bell jar experience of my own. I was married to a young Englishman whom I assumed I adored. He was an athlete, a businessman who spent part of his time in the Territorial Army. Obviously his activities in these respects were not ones I could share. He and his friends, mostly just out of Cambridge, were the first men I had met who made me feel that being a girl made any difference to the way you were treated. In my coeducational American university women were, if anything, rather more in control of things than men. My poem, 'The Women', however, referred not to the *au pair* girls and débutantes our life in London perplexed me by including but to the wives of the officers in my husband's regiment.

We were 'billeted', I remember, with the Colonel and his wife. During the day the men went out on manoeuvres; if it was a weekend, they went shooting on the moors. The women stayed at home by the fire, surrounded by vases gorged with dahlias, gossiping, sighing, waiting for the men to come back so we could all broach the drinks cupboard. I spent the greater part of the mornings roaming the blustery streets of Halifax in hopes of bumping into the public library, but after lunch I was condemned to interminable cups of tea. One such afternoon I withdrew to my bedroom and wrote this poem:

Women, waiting for their husbands,
sit among dahlias all the afternoons,
while quiet processional seasons
drift and subside at the doors like dunes,
and echoes of ocean curl from the flowered wall.

The room is a murmuring shell of nothing at all.
As the fire dies under the dahlias, shifting embers
flake from the silence, thundering when they fall,
and wives who are faithful waken bathed in slumber;
the loud tide breaks and turns to bring them breath.

At five o'clock it flows about their death,
and then the dahlias, whirling
suddenly to catherine wheels of surf,
spin on their stems until the shallows sing,
and flower pools gleam like lamps on the lifeless tables.

Flung phosphoresence of dahlias tells
the women time. They wait to be,
prepared for the moment of inevitable
good evening when, back from the deep, from the mystery,
the tritons return and the women whirl in their sea.[5]

After the experience of 'The Women' I less frequently indulged my
childhood fantasy of becoming a heroine out of Jane Austen, and began
to wonder what I really wanted to do. Back in London I tried to write
a novel, but like Esther Greenwood, I found I had nothing to say. My
poems were better, but when I sent them to English magazines they
were turned down. I offered myself to the PEN club in Chelsea as a
typist, and they let me type some poems for them. But soon they discovered that I was too poor a typist even for their unpaid standards,
and they let me go. I began to feel I hadn't got it in me to be a writer.
The terrible parlours of 'The Women' yawned before me.

When I had a baby, things got not better but worse. I was determined
not to let such a natural event disturb my reading programme (I was
putting myself through James, Hardy and Proust) but of course it did,
even though I invented a way of breast-feeding and reading at the same
time, propping my book up on a music stand. The baby was unimpressed.
She howled every evening at dinner time, and since my husband dis-
approved of babies at our candle-lit dinners, meals were served to an

accompaniment of sobs — my own and the baby's in about equal proportions. I found, after a while, that I couldn't eat without vomiting, and soon I lost so much weight I had to go to hospital.

Shortly after I was released (no doctor could diagnose my ailment) we began moving, first to a village near Norwich, then to Grimsby, then to Belfast, then to New York, then to a Faulkner-like town called Corinth, Mississippi, and finally to Atlanta, Georgia, where we were divorced. All through this period — 1957 to 1969 — I was in a state of appalling numbness. My husband was puzzled, since he was having a difficult time establishing himself in his own business and wanted my support. In return he was prepared to provide me with a house, a maid and time. Why was I not writing the novels and poems I had promised him? When I grew more depressed and spent days and nights weeping, he decided he'd had enough. The terms of divorce taxed us both, since there was no third party except my bell jar. We had to concoct a separation on the grounds of mental cruelty — not mine to him, as so often had been the case, but his to me — which seemed, even to my foggy mind, unfair.

Now, I mention these facts of my biography, not because they are unique but because they are not. Thousands of educated women with small babies who have followed in the wake of an enterprising husband have undergone the same depressions, the same sense of failure, the same collapse into breakdown, if not divorce. Perhaps Emily Dickinson's father knew what he was talking about when he suggested that too many books joggle the mind. But I still wonder how much my depression had to do with my discontent with a woman's role in marriage and how much it had to do with my inability to write in uncongenial circumstances. The questions were distinct, though linked. Any writer has to keep his or her imagination alive, and that means he or she can't happily live a lie or write well in an alien role. On the other hand, it seems to me now that I blamed too much on the marriage and my role as a woman in it. I should have written in spite of everything that seemed against me. I should not have excused myself.

Luckily we are living in the middle of a century which, for all its drawbacks, allows people who have made a mistake in marriage to go back and try again. I returned to the University of Michigan with my daughter, wrote a book of poems, began a critical book and took an MA in English. Curiously, though, I have been unable to use the memory of those unhappy years directly in my poems. The reason for this may be the natural desire of human beings to suppress what is unpleasant. But I think there's a more important reason which has to do with the nature of writing itself. Unless you are setting out to write an autobiographical novel, like *The Bell Jar*, or a novel calculated to shock the public with its frankness, like *Fear of Flying*, it is better art to let your memory knit itself into your subconscious and twine around your imagination until you have found a way of transforming experience into fiction. 'Facts,' wrote Virginia Woolf, 'are a very inferior form of fiction.'

The facts of my experience, as I have said, were not interesting in themselves. They were familiar. It is because they were so familiar that they gave me an idea for a long poem that later became *Correspondences*. If I had suffered, in my ignorance of myself, from a sense of ignominy and numbness in marriage, other women must have suffered too. I began to think with troubled resentment of my mother. All through my childhood I'd seen her sacrifice herself and her interests for the sake of my father, myself and my sisters. She had wanted to be a novelist, and we all encouraged her. But, as in my own case, encouragement only made her feel guilty when she was not doing her 'duty' towards us. And when she did her 'duty' — and sighed afterwards — then *we* felt guilty for taking so much of her time. The process of 'wifing' and 'mothering' was steeped in guilt. By modelling myself on my mother, I had plunged unwittingly into the same guilt; but in my slow way, like swimming to the surface of water I was drowning in, I began to realise that guilt could also be an *excuse*. If I had really wanted to write I would have done so. So would my mother. Writing for us was, or could be, wishful thinking. There is always time. No amount of housework or baby-tending takes time from writing if you really want to write. Sylvia Plath wrote her great last poems in the early morning before her babies were awake. Wilfred Owen wrote his best poems in the trenches. Sweet are the uses of adversity.

In a burst of self-knowledge which was unsettling at first, I knew I had rigged that divorce — and all the unhappiness that preceded it — in order not to repeat the experience of my mother. After my mother's death from cancer in the early 1960s (when I married again) I was still unable to rid myself of her image — her ghost. Yet I was inexpressibly upset by her death. I felt I had to tell her something, that she had cheated herself and me by dying just as I was about to speak. It was this urgency to resurrect her and at the same time to kill her spirit (remember Virginia Woolf's struggles with The Angel in the House) that made it impossible for me not to write *Correspondences*. It was a book I couldn't avoid.

The first poem I wrote on this theme — the theme of mothers — was called 'Generations'. Probably it was the seed from which *Correspondences* grew. It was written when I was living in Glasgow with my second husband and two babies, four years after my mother's death. The bell jar threatened again, but this time I was determined to smash it. Even if I had to be cruel to my family; even if I had to leave them.

'Generations' is a bitter poem where 'The Women' is distanced and polite. The women in each stanza represent my grandmother, my mother and myself in that order ... three degrees of self-sacrifice:

> Know this mother by her three smiles.
> One grey one drawn over her mouth by frail hooks.
> One hurt smile under each eye.
>
> Know this mother by the frames she makes.
> By the silence in which she suffers each child
> to scratch out the aquatints in her mind.
>
> Know this mother by the way she says
> 'darling' with her teeth clenched.
> By the fabulous lies she cooks.[6]

With that poem I felt I had made a breakthrough. Shortly afterwards in 1970, we left Glasgow and lived for six months in Cambridge, Massachusetts, where my husband and I both had scholarships. Mine was at the Radcliffe Institute for Independent Women, and I found myself surrounded there by discontented contemporaries. America itself was in a profound state of discontent. The puritan values of honesty, loyalty, piety and self-sacrifice I'd been taught to respect in my childhood were everywhere being dismissed. Hippies, drug-takers, dropouts and failed intellectuals lined up for food and psychiatric treatment in the streets of Cambridge. Our flat in a racially mixed area was robbed five times; our four-year-old son was attacked by a gang of black children. All that time I was at Radcliffe, then, and writing *Correspondences* I was aware of living at a time of acute crisis. Excitement, despair, challenge, unhappiness and anger infected the New England air. I began to understand why Sylvia Plath and Anne Sexton had gone mad.

And yet I was determined not to go mad. It would have been too easy. All around me the world seemed mad. Lowell and Plath had set a fashion, and for a poet, madness (with blame on society and capitalist materialism) was all but obligatory. Two things saved me. In the first place, I had found an archive of letters from well-known American families in the Schlesinger Library, and reading them, I decided I could use them in a poem. The only way to fight the madness of the present was to gain some understanding of the past. I discovered a trunk of family letters in my sister's basement in New York, and these, too, profoundly moved me. In the second place, we had a weekly escape route from Harvard to Vermont. We drove up to my family's house in Wilmington nearly every weekend, and it was there I decided to set my poem in a mythical Clearfield, and make Vermont and the peace it stood for a symbol of the more solid America that had disappeared from the demented cities. I don't know when it occurred to me that my poem should take the form of letters. I think the family letters themselves suggested it; their language was already poetry, Victorian, distant. Why had no one thought of writing an epistolary poem before?

The central character in *Correspondences* is a woman like my mother — liberal, generous, self-sacrificing, devoted to good causes and prone to idealising her family. I called her Ruth after Ruth in the Bible, the daughter of Naomi (who, you may remember, calls herself 'Mara', meaning bitter). I turned Mara into the woman's name, Maura, and created both Maura and Ruth in the image of the self-sacrificing mother. Maura sacrifices her independent life as a writer to marry an idealistic but impractical reformer. Ruth sacrifices a lover to devote herself to her kindly but unexciting husband. In both cases I suspect these women took the *happiest* course open to them. That is to say, I doubt that Maura in 1900 would ever have become more than a mediocre writer; and Ruth, in 1940, was certainly better off with her unpretentious American husband. None the less, neither one of these women was willing to take risks, and their happiness was bordered with wistfulness, with a longing for knowledge beyond their experience.

It is Ruth's children who are given the opportunity of risk, and two of them take it. Kay marries a fashionable psychiatrist in New York, has a baby, becomes very unhappy and leaves her husband after a nervous breakdown. Nick, her younger brother, leaves New England after his mother's funeral and heads west, deserting his career at college. Only Eden, Kay's younger sister, stays at home in Vermont, trying to preserve the family's values.

The title, *Correspondences*, refers partly to the letters of the two sisters, Eden and Kay, each of whom confronts a disintegrating world which, after their mother's death, is impossible to hold together. Eden, in Vermont, discovers a box of family letters, dating from the 1830s, and in Part One these letters make up the *Correspondences* within the correspondence of the sisters. Part Two is entitled 'Women in Marriage' and concerns three generations of women, Maura, Ruth and Kay — the grandmother, mother and daughter of 'Generations'. Each of these women makes a different compromise in her marriage. Part Three is composed of journals written by Ruth's husband, Neil Arbeiter, and her son Nick. The entire poem ends with a letter from Kay to her father in which she explains her reasons for not being able to return to New England from London, to which she has made a partially satisfactory escape:

'In the floodtides of *Civitas Mundi*
New England is dissolving like a green chemical.
Old England bleeds out to meet it in mid-ocean.
    Nowhere is safe.'

It is a poem I can't continue.
It is America I can't contain.

Dear Father, I love but can't know you.
    I've given you all that I can.
    Can these pages make amends for what was not said?
    Do justice to the living, to the dead?[7]

You can see, even from the little I've said, that *Correspondences* is about more than women's predicament in American history. It was intended to be a study of puritan values in New England — of their strengths, their weaknesses, their corruption by ambition and greed, and their final overthrow in the world of Vietnam and Watergate. Yet, as I wrote I could not help but be aware of the amount of my own experience that was going into it. In each generation there is misunderstanding between the women and the men. In 1830, for instance, Elizabeth Boyd is all but crushed by her Calvinist father for not accepting the judgement of God when her husband is drowned. In 1840, Marianne Chandler, who loves parties but hates sex, suffers from the sexual blundering of her puritanical husband. Later he divorces her with contemptuous blame:

Of the causes of strife between us —
your selfishness, your vanity, your whims, wife,
your insistent and querulous disobedience,
no more.
It is enough for you to live with your naked conscience

upon which must lie the death of our infant daughter
as her innocent body lies, unfulfilled in its grave.
Farewell.
Find peace if you can with your sister,
her friends and fashions.
Frivolity is an armor of lace
against the mind's inner vengeance and poisons.[8]

In later generations of Chandlers, pompous Jacob tells his daughter off for wasting her time 'scribbling' in college when she should be taking care of her mother at home:

Maura! Maura! Those kisses were never gifts.
Bestowed as they were with the charity of Our Lord Himself,
those kisses were loans! Loans upon interest these many
long years! Now it is time to repay them graciously,
selflessly, with little acts of kindness and understanding.[9]

In 1900, Maura, chastened at last, determines to give up her dream of becoming a writer and vows to devote her life to her impractical, idealist husband, Ethan Boyd:

What does Nature
ask of Woman?
Give to him that needeth.
Employ the hour that passeth.
Be resolute in submission.
Love thy husband.
Bear children.[10]

Ruth, Maura's daughter, tries to follow in her mother's footsteps, but falls in love with an English novelist — a plummy, selfish fellow whose pseudo-sophistication impresses her. She lives a secret, divided life with her husband until she dies of cancer, publicly virtuous but privately horrified and undermined by a devouring sense of guilt. In a letter to her lover in 1945, she writes of this guilt:

And what are these terrible things
they are taking for granted? Air and grass,
houses and beds, laundry and things to eat —
so little clarity, so little space between them;

a crowd of distractions to be
bought and done and arranged for,
drugs for the surely incurable pain of
living misunderstood among many who love you.[11]

Finally, for Kay, Ruth's daughter, the fibre of a repressive society breaks down just as she herself does. In 1954 she finds she can no longer tolerate her life in Westchester County and runs away to New York. But in an asylum she discovers there is no escape in madness either. Having rejected her mother, Kay at last turns to her for help. And yet she knows there is no way back to her mother's beliefs; any compromise with a former life will be forced. The hysteria at the end of this poem is one many of us felt in the fifties and sixties; Sylvia Plath was spokesman for a whole generation of Kays:

Come when you can, or when
the whitecoats let you.
But they may not let you, of course.
They think you're to blame.
Good God, mother, I'm not insane!
How can I get out of here?
Can't you get me out of here?

I'll try, I'll try, really,
I'll try again. The marriage.
The baby. The house. The whole damn bore!

Because for me, what the hell else is there?
Mother, what more? What more?[12]

Naturally, when I was writing that poem I realised Kay was a version of myself. All that I had suffered in my first marriage, all that I had felt about my child, my husband, my mother, came together in it. It was a poem I found painful to write. And yet, Kay is not me, either. She is a sort of Esther Greenwood. I have never had a breakdown in a museum or lived in Westchester County or been married to a fashionable psychiatrist. Kay's *feelings*, her mixed love and hatred for her child, her sense of imprisonment in her house, her impulse to fly, to escape to drink or to an anonymous city — these feelings *have* been mine. They can be found in other poems . . . in one called 'In the House', for instance, which I wrote long before any of the poems of *Correspondences*:

... Whatever it is, it's clear it has claims on me.
its surface establishes itself
outside and around me,
drawing me through or into
what I take to be my proper dominion.

These keys are my keys, this door my door.
The interior is entirely familiar . . .

Again, these interminable stairs, bristling with children.
'Mother, mother', they wail. They bleat with desire.
They quarrel and hold up their wounds to be kissed.
And yet when I bend to them
It is like kissing a photograph.
I taste chemicals.
My lips meet unexpectedly a flatness . . .[12]

But in Kay's poem from *Correspondences* I learned how to put experience into poetry without 'confessing' it. I should add, too, that the 'facts' pertaining to the Chandler family in my poem differ from those pertaining to my own family in history. The nearer I came to my time and to people I knew, the more imperative it seemed to me to get feelings right but to invent 'facts'. Apart from the embarrassment of taking family skeletons out of cupboards before the flesh is off, so to speak, fiction has to be more obvious than life. A reader has to see reasons for feelings in behaviour.

But I see I have left the subject of women and women writers and got on to a theory of literature. I still haven't answered the question I asked at the beginning of this essay. Is it possible for a woman to be an adult, married, sexual person and a poet as well?

In one sense, poems like those I have quoted answer the question by writing about it. If — as women — our theme is woman's survival and self-discovery, then we have found a subject that meets the requirements of experience both as women and as writers. In the 1970s, too, we can say what we please. We no longer need to be embarrassed by social taboos. The problem, however, does not really concern itself with sexual explicitness. For a woman it goes deeper. I encountered it when I had finished *Correspondences*, for I realised then that I had written a woman's book — that is to say, the experiences of my characters were experiences I understood through having lived my life as a woman. The two world wars are scarcely mentioned. The Civil War is recognised only as it divides the family into allegiances North and South. Now, there are many people these days who would say that women's books are just what women should be writing. The American poet, Adrienne Rich, for example, believes that women are awakening into a shared, powerful consciousness of what it means to be female. The 'drive to self-knowledge,' she says, 'is more than a search for identity; it is part of her refusal of the self-destructiveness of male-dominated society.' We must find, she thinks, a language of our own to express 'a whole new psychic geography' of female emotion.[14]

For my part, despite *Correspondences*, I am inclined to disagree with Adrienne Rich. I am not convinced that women need a specifically female language to describe female experience. The question of language is in any case an especially thorny one. For even if we agree that women have a less aggressive, more instinctive, more 'creative' nature than men (and I'm not sure that's true) language is difficult to divide into sexes. A good writer's imagination should be bisexual or trans-sexual. The only society I know of in which men and women traditionally have spoken different languages – and accepted roles accordingly – is in Japan. At the risk of digression, let me remind you that in tenth-century Japan women wrote poetry and fiction in the vernacular (the language of society, love, grace, beauty) while men did business, politics and went about extending their territorial rights in Classical Chinese. The result of this sexual differentiation in language was a vast and marvellous literature created almost exclusively by women (high-class, aristocratic women, mind you) of which Lady Murasaki's *Tale of Genji* is perhaps the most famous example.[15]

A flight of fancy prompts me to imagine a woman's language which appoints itself guardian of the traditional beauties of English as opposed to the speed-read efficiencies of American. Imagine a woman's language which preserves the dignity of the *King James Bible* and the *Prayer Book*, which forbids the use of technological jargon in any work of literature not intended for the laboratory or classroom. But such a dream is, of course, impossible. In our democratic society, such an exclusive language would be hooted down as 'irrelevant' – not least by women who ask for equality at the same time as asking for an independent consciousness and a language of their own in which to express it.

For better or worse, women and men writers in the West, in the later twentieth century, share a common consciousness. Their language is a reflection, or even a definition, of that consciousness. If anything we want *more* communication, *more* understanding between the sexes.

We are beginning to see that though our physical functions differ (necessarily) our psychic needs are alike. If there is to be a new creative consciousness — one that is not based on phallic values of conquest, power, ambition, greed, murder and so forth — then this consciousness must have room for both male and female; a consciousness the greatest literature has, in fact, been defining for a long time.

What has all this to do with *Correspondences* and the writing of women's books? Well, now that *Correspondences* has been written, I'm proud of it. Through it I crossed a bridge — or rather built a bridge — into the twentieth century. All the anger, the confusion, the misery and the doubt I experienced during the fifties and sixties went into it, and because they were a woman's angers and miseries, they exposed part of the general consciousness of the age — a part that in the past had been suppressed.

But now I want to stand on the shoulders of *Correspondences*, as it were, and look at a wider world. For both sexes it is important that we understand each other and the world we have to share. There must be no suppression and no play-acting either. For me it is as fraudulent to adopt the role of a 'new' woman as that of an 'old' one; being a writer proscribes role-playing. In both cases the role that is offered substitutes a public stance for particular perceptions. And a writer must leave herself free for particular perceptions.

Of course, choosing what often feels like a selfish independence means that one pays a price — a high price — in human terms. I don't think you can write truthfully and be entirely comfortable. Tension is a mainspring of the imagination. And something has to be sacrificed — the satisfaction of a role, the satisfaction of a cause, the satisfaction, even, of a sense of guilt. This is why I should like to conclude with a poem I wrote last year called 'The Price'. What I hope I am saying in this poem is that a price is asked for every engagement with the truth — but it need not be a price that destroys affection. It is also the price *of* affection, since what is most valuable in human understanding is so often what is least definable as politics or even as right or wrong:

The fear of loneliness, the wish
to be alone;
love grown rank as seeding grass
in every room,
and anger at it, raging at it
storming it down.

Also that four-walled chrysalis
and impediment, home;
that lamp and hearth, that easy fit
of bed to bone;
those children, too, sharp witnesses
of all I've done.

My dear, the ropes that bind us
are safe to hold;
the walls the crush us keep us
from the cold.
I know the price and still I pay it, pay it —
words, their furtive kiss,
illicit gold.[16]

Notes

Anne Stevenson's poems are reprinted by permission of Oxford University Press.

1. T.H. Johnson (ed.), *The Letters of Emily Dickinson*, 3 vols. (Cambridge, Mass., 1958), vol. ii, p. 261.
2. *The Bell Jar* (London, 1966), p. 122.
3. Ibid., p. 175.
4. Ibid., pp. 129-30.
5. *Travelling Behind Glass* (London, 1974), p. 1.
6. Ibid., p. 50.
7. *Correspondences* (London, 1974), pp. 87-8.
8. Ibid., p. 30.
9. Ibid., p. 41.
10. Ibid., p. 44.
11. Ibid., p. 63.
12. Ibid., p. 70.
13. *Reversals* (Middletown, Conn., 1969), pp. 15-16.
14. 'When We Dead Awaken', *College English*, vol. xxiv (October 1972), pp. 18-25; reprinted in B.C. and A. Gelpi (eds.), *Adrienne Rich's Poetry* (New York, 1975).
15. See Arthur Waley in the introduction to his translation of Lady Murasaki's *The Tale of Genji* (London, 1973), pp. vii-xvi.
16. *Enough of Green* (London, 1977), p. 31.

9 FEMINISM, FILM AND THE *AVANT-GARDE*

Laura Mulvey

This essay should act simultaneously as introduction and as conclusion. It is the last in a series on women and literature and the only one on cinema. It should build bridges and forge links between women working in different disciplines. I have, however, felt the differences crowding in: aesthetic differences, but also economic and historical. In the short history of cinema (it is only eighty years old) its industrial base has overwhelmingly determined its development and 'independent' cinema only sporadically becomes something other than very strictly marginal. The relationship between the two sides has always been ambivalent. Popular entertainment cinema, essentially the product of the Hollywood studio system, has exerted an important influence on art and experimental cinema (from Eisenstein through to Godard), and the strivings of Hollywood directors to create an aesthetic despite limitations characteristic of commercial cinema have produced some of the best films ever made. Cinema is a technology and changes in technology affect its cultural orientation. Recently, independent film-making has begun to emerge (not replacing the commercial product but quite separately, alongside it). And, furthermore, technological developments have allowed experimental film to grow out of a tiny trickle into something approaching a considerable rivulet – a cinema in which the economic base is not primarily that of the commodity expected to pay off with a return on capital invested. This is clearly not the case in literature, where any original investment is infinitely smaller.

It is not until recently that any conjuncture has been possible between feminism and film. Women's political consciousness, under the impetus of the Women's Movement, has turned critically towards cinema, and in spite of its brief time span, cinema now has a history that can be analysed from a feminist point of view. For the first time, the consciousness is there, and the body of work is sufficient. The heterogeneity of the cinema is reflected in its first encounter with feminism, which includes campaigns against sexism within the industry, analyses of sexism in representation, use of film for propaganda purposes, and debates about culture and politics. To me, this essay acts as an introduction on two levels. First, the background, the peculiar history of film, is unlike that of literature and needs particular

177

definition. Second, woman and film or woman in film have only existed as critical concepts for roughly a decade. A first phase of thought has, it seems, been surpassed. It is now possible to make some tentative assessments of feminist film criticism, achieve some perspective on the past and discuss directions for the future.

The collision between feminism and film is part of a wider explosive meeting between feminism and patriarchal culture. Early on, the Women's Movement called attention to the political significance of culture; women's absence from creating dominant art and literature is an integral aspect of oppression. From this point, debates on politics and aesthetics acquired new life. It was (not exclusively, but to an important extent) feminism that gave a new urgency to the politics of culture, exemplified the contradictions inherent in a desire to build a counter-culture, and focused on connections between oppression and command of language. Largely excluded from creative traditions, largely exploited and subjected to patriarchal ideology within literature, popular arts and visual representation, women had to formulate a feminist opposition to sexism within culture, and come to terms with the extent to which traditional or dominant forms were inextricably associated with the exclusion of women from their creation. What would women's cultural practice be like? What would art and literature within an ideology that did not oppress women be like? Debate has swirled and spiralled around these questions: on the one hand, desire to explore the suppressed, the meaning of femininity, to assert a woman's language as a slap in the face for patriarchy; simultaneously a polemic and pleasure in self-discovery. On the other hand, a drive to forge an aesthetic that attacks language and representation not as naturally linked with male or female but rather as soaking up dominant ideology, as a sponge soaks up water.

It is at this point that the crucial problem has to be faced: whether the new can be discovered, like a gold-mine in a garden; or whether it consists only of the work of confrontation that is done, the act of opposing traditional forms, questioning the way that male-dominated language conceals assumptions about sexual difference and oppression of women, laying open contradictions implicit in all ideological and cultural activity. And it is at this point that feminists have recently come to see that the arguments developed by the modernist *avant-garde* are relevant to their own struggle to develop a radical aesthetic. At the moment this is still a wary approach, given the limitations feminists necessarily feel towards any aspect of male-dominated culture. But the questions posed by the *avant-garde*, consciously confronting traditional practice, often with a political motivation, working on ways in which aesthetic challenges alter relations both with modes of representation and with expectations in consumption — all these questions arise similarly for women, motivated by a history of oppression and longing for change. However, the path leading even to this point is twisted, and in this essay I want to trace the main stages, moments of assessment and outside influences, using debates about women and film to show how feminist film practice has come to be interested in — almost to have an objective alliance with — the radical *avant-garde*.

As a preamble, before dealing specifically with cinema, I want to outline the main arguments about women's place in past culture, all of which have had a complicated but concrete effect on women artists and film-makers. Behind all these arguments, however contradictory, lies a fascination with the unspoken history of women, turned into something mysterious because unrecorded by male chroniclers and overlooked by male historians. There is also an impetus to fantasise a tradition — a desire on the part of women, as they search for a form of expression, to place themselves in a line of work, a feminine cultural context, however tenuous, as a homage to the anomalies endured by women in the past.

First of all, particularly in the early days of the women's movement, but still present, is a recurring hope that women have, in fact, produced more in mainstream culture than has ever been recognised. The research that has come out of this has rediscovered at least some handfuls of women artists and writers whose work had been overlooked and under-valued. Secondly, in contrast to this rediscovered presence, is the emphasis on absence, the insistence on the part of some feminists that the few outstanding, exceptional women could not properly alleviate the overall picture of discrimination. In proportion to women's exclusion from cultural participation, their image has been exploited. Finally, there has been an important revival of interest in minor arts and crafts, where, allocated their place in the division of labour, women could 'embroider' their daily work. This orientation also tends to emphasise the way that women have worked together, without claims to authorship or genius. A tension arises here between celebration of the past and taking it as a guide-line for the future. There is a difference between an interest in women's traditions — the individual or group achievements which women have to their credit despite the hostile environment of patriarchal culture — and a belief in a feminine sensibility, tied to the domestic and then freed only into a corresponding orientation in art.

These general issues have all found their place in debates between women about film. I want to trace the way in which these debates developed and how each line of argument raised problems that seemed to block the natural growth of feminist film culture. Out of these dilemmas feminists have been forced to become more ambitious, more demanding; and it is these results that I will discuss in the second part of my essay as 'The Search for a Theory' and 'The Search for a Practice', describing the alliances and influences which have worked together to produce an aesthetic that is still only in its early infancy.

History and Problems

In 1972 *Women and Film*, the first journal of feminist film criticism, came out in California, and the first two women's film festivals were organised (in New York and in Edinburgh). These events were a response in film terms to the early attention paid by the Women's Movement to the politics of representation. A rough history of women in the cinema soon started to emerge.

The Work of Research

These early days of research into women's place in film history quickly established the fact that women had been excluded from the production and making of films, possibly in proportion to their notorious exploitation as sexual objects on the screen. The women's film festivals showed the results of painstaking research, surprise finds and lost women directors whose names could be counted on the fingers of very few hands. Overall, the history of the cinema presented a particularly depressing picture of discrimination and marginalisation of women. In the very early days of one-reelers, before the film industry attracted big money, some women did direct films in Hollywood. The coming of the studio system, and, even more so, the economic reorganisation with the introduction of sound which involved large-scale investment from banks and the electronics industry, closed the ranks so completely that Dorothy Arzner and Ida Lupino were literally the only women to direct films in Hollywood until the 1970s. Dorothy Arzner is probably the outstanding rediscovery of the women's film festivals. Both found their way up through acceptable women's jobs: Arzner was an editor, Lupino an actress. They are the exceptions that prove the rule. The work of women directors in the pioneering days has been largely lost. There is nothing left but a few fragments of the films of Lois Weber, the outstanding woman director of the pre-World War I period. Leni Riefenstahl, as the maker of Fascist documentaries in the thirties, is ironically the only woman director whose name is a household word. Leontine Sagan, the brilliant director of *Mädchen in Uniform* (Germany 1931) is still forgotten, in spite of the interest her film aroused in the women's festivals. In Europe in the fifties, in film industries impoverished and disorganised by the war and overshadowed by American imports, a few women began to make films: Mai Zetterling, once again actress turned director; Agnes Varda, photographer, married to new-wave director Jacques Demy; and, in Eastern Europe, Marta Meszaros and Vera Chytilova. And then there was the *avant-garde* tradition. Here, outside the distrust of women endemic in commercial cinema, marginalised within a marginal sphere of cinema, women had more impact. At least they were recorded and remembered. Germaine Dulac's *La Souriante Mme. Beudet* had an immediate appeal for feminists. Maya Deren's pioneering work in the United States during the forties had earned her the condescending title 'mother of the *avant-garde*', but her balletic dream/fantasy films still have an immense impact. And it was this tradition that appeared to feed most dynamically into women's contemporary work.

Behind the work of research that went into these festivals, there lay a desire or an inspiration that, once rediscovered, films made by women would reveal a coherent aesthetic. The experience of oppression, awareness of women's exploitation in image, would act as a unifying element for women directors, however different their origins, and careful analysis would show the struggles associated with being female under male domination coming through to challenge the complacency towards women that had been the norm in cinema. Certainly, the films made by women were predominantly about women, whether through choice or as another aspect of marginalisation. But the question of whether a unified tradition emerged became increasingly in doubt, except on the superficial level of women as content. However, Claire Johnston and Pam Cook in their study of Dorothy Arzner took the question further, arguing that Arzner managed to throw the male assumptions and codes dominant in Hollywood into crisis, subverting them and opening up their contradictions:

In general the woman in Arzner's films determines her own identity through transgression and desire. Unlike most other Hollywood directors . . . in Arzner's work the discourse of the woman . . . is what gives the system of the text its structural coherence, while at the same time rendering the discourse of the male fragmented and incoherent. The central female protagonists react against and thus transgress the male discourse which entraps them. These women do not sweep aside the existing order and found a new female order of language. Rather, they assert their own discourse in the face of the male one, by breaking it up, subverting it, and in a sense, re-writing it.[1]

This argument took the debate beyond a simple hope for a unified tradition into a careful, detailed analysis of the language and codes used by a woman director alone in an otherwise exclusively male world. Such work became a crucial advance in feminist film criticism, the first bricks towards building a theory. Claire Johnston points out in her Arzner| article: 'the need for oppressed people to write their own history cannot be overstressed. Memory, an understanding of struggles of the past and a sense of one's own history constitute a vital dynamic in any struggle.'

The Attack on Sexism

Traditional narrative film evolved within certain stylistic conventions: the language of form should not intrude or overshadow the free flow of the story and must allow content to come to the fore. The first steps of feminist film criticism mirrored these conventions, concentrating on the sexist content of cinematic narrative and exploitation of women as images. This was indeed a necessary polemic (similar politically to campaigns against sexism in advertising or role indoctrination in children's books), exposing and protesting against the way in which active and passive roles in film narrative are divided along sex lines. At this point (the early issues of *Woman and Film*, the special woman's issue of *The Velvet Light Trap*), the main demand was to replace one female role model by another, stronger and more independent, or, alternatively, for images of women that were realistic and relevant to women's real-life experience. Both these demands assume that identification is the fundamental problem for women in cinema, and that feminist films would offer alternatives – the optimistic without relation to reality, or the pessimistic reflecting the problems women know – lived out through the protagonist on the screen.

The importance of denouncing sexism is undoubted; but, as these demands are directed primarily at commercial and popular cinema, they involve a confrontation with the sexist nature of the industry itself and its discrimination against women. Hollywood's immediate response to the Women's Movement was a retreat into what Molly Haskell in *From Reverence to Rape* describes as 'the buddy movie', showing how far these campaigns would still need to travel from the late sixties and early seventies.[2] The commercial cinema was not going to change overnight in either of its fundamental attitudes to women. Furthermore, this argument raised the issue of reversals. A change in content alone, based on a reversal of sex roles, could do no more than reproduce the conventions established by male-dominated exploitative production with a new twist, and this twist could itself easily degenerate into a fetishistic male fantasy about the fascinating, phallic woman. It is, however, the tradition of the melodrama, the old Hollywood genre of women's problems and family traumas, that has re-emerged, providing vehicles for the women stars — always a necessary precondition for a Hollywood film concerned with women to become a bankable commodity.

First Feminist Films

The conditions in which feminists first made films arose through economic and technical changes. These developments not only affected women but allowed a cinema to develop with an alternative economic base to the 35mm commercial product. So far as women were affected, these changes allowed them to enter the world of cinema as a little more than the previous drop in the ocean. Looking at the history of women in the production side of cinema, there seems to be a rough correlation between the size of the investment and the (non)participation of women. The larger the amount, the less likely was a woman to be trusted with it. Shirley Clarke describes her experience in Hollywood in an interview in *Take One*:

> I didn't have any means of getting any money. It may have to do with the fact that people with money do not talk about money to women. That's one of the things that showed up in my Hollywood dealings. Everyone said 'Fantastic. Do something for us. But don't expect much. Being a woman it's going to be difficult.' So when I got out there, they had a man who was going to be my producer. And he was going to tell me how to make my film. Men just don't like to talk to women about money — that's all.[3]

The firm glimmer of an alternative world came, hardly noticed, in the 1940s. Maya Deren made *Meshes in the Afternoon* in 1941 with 16mm equipment and no sound. After the war, the 16mm equipment that had been used for wartime newsreels came on to the second-hand market in the United States and provided the basis for what came to be called the Underground Cinema. These 16mm cameras and film opened up film-making to people outside the industry, and made, not one, but several new kinds of cinematic developments possible. The equipment is smaller, cheaper in itself, in stock and laboratory costs, but it was not until the early sixties, with the invention of Coutant's Eclair Camera in France, that synchronised sound could be recorded with ease while shooting. In cultural terms these developments produced two distinct cross-fertilisations. Film became available as a medium for artists, both in the visual arts and dance. In the sixties film could be used by political activists for propaganda and campaign films. The particular association of 16mm with *cinéma-verité* allowed it to appear the instrument of truth itself, grasping the real unmediated by ideology. Film seemed to be freed from its historic enslavement to the commercial product.

Looking back at feminist film criticism and festivals in the early seventies, it is obvious that the first unified wave of films produced by women came directly out of the Women's Movement, characterised by a mixture of consciousness-raising and propaganda. Film was used to record women talking and then to direct discussions around particular crucial issues, so that the women on film could interact with the experiences and ideas of women at a meeting. There was a particular heady excitement to these films. For the first time ever, films were being made exclusively by women, controlling the equipment, about women and feminist politics, for other women. Susan Rice in the first issue of *Woman and Film* comments on Kate Millett's film *Three Lives*:

> *Three Lives* is a Women's Liberation Cinema Production, and it is the only feature film I know of that not only takes women as its subject-matter, but was produced, directed, shot, recorded, lit, and edited by women. What makes this more than a stunt is the intimacy that this female crew seems to have elicited from its subjects. The element I find most compelling about the film is that it captures the tone and quality of relationships and significant conversation between women. If the film were to fail on every other level, this would stand as a note-worthy achievement.[4]

Or Dora Kaplan in the next issue writes of 'This new movement of women making political films politically' that:

> This commitment to educate, change consciousness, and sensibility showed itself to be unalienated; that is, carried over to the process of film-making itself; a film crew working collectively without hierarchy and specialization; a film crew working on an equal basis

with the 'subject' in decision making and production; and a film
crew recognizing the distribution of the product to be an integral
part of the process.[5]

Although it is hard to overestimate the vigour and immediacy of some
of these films, they are closely tied to the ideology of consciousness-
raising and agitation around particular feminist issues. This is their
strength; their weakness lies in limitations of the *cinema-verité* tradition. While as documents they can have an immediate political use,
their aesthetics are bound by a concept of film as a transparent medium,
reproducing rather than questioning — a project which reduces the
camera to a magical instrument. There lies behind this a further
assumption, that the camera, by its very nature and the good intentions
of its operator, can grasp essential truths and by registering typical
shared experiences can create political unity through the process of
identification. The politics are thus restricted to emotion and the
cinema stays trapped in the old endless search for the other self on the
screen.

Summary

Up to this point, I have used feminist film criticism as it was around
1972 to mark a particular stage of conscious development and to
express particular problems that clearly showed a need for a theoretical leap forward. But no leap forward could be conceived without this
first springboard: insistence on the conditions of sexist exploitation
and cultural oppression, and resurrection of women's struggles to
make movies and their achievements in the past. However, the way
forward seemed blocked; the answers offered in this period did not
match the needs of a feminist film culture. Demands for identification, for women's films that played on identification processes, still
stayed subservient to pre-existing cinematic formal traditions redolent
of sexual exploitation, and to the cinema of male domination. Any
changes within the industry could only result from long-term agitation
and activity on the part of women wanting to work within it (still now
a long-term measure), and gradual erosion through shifts in ideology.
As a 16mm cinema gradually evolved and discrimination still prevailed in the industry, it became obvious that the independent sector
would provide an area for first growth of a feminist film-making
practice. What would this cinema be like?

Desire to break with the past is simultaneously both rational and
passionate. It is an instinctual retreat from forms associated with the

past combined with a polemical drive to build a feminine aesthetic on uncontaminated ground. But the break is also an inevitable consequence of the aesthetic and theoretic questions posed by what this new ground could be. These questions start to revolve around the insufficiency of a break with sexist content alone, and thus begin to foreground the language of representation as a major problem. The dominant cinematic tradition has been characterised by primacy of content, whether narrative fiction or documentary, inevitably involving a tendency to subordinate the formal side, the cinematic process itself. This balance is sealed by using play on identification between spectator and screen-protagonist to close up remaining or necessary gaps between form and content. (For instance, Hitchcock reconciles his extravagant and un-usual use of cinema with the demands of convention, involving the spectator through suspense.) In order to construct a new language of cinema, therefore, a break in this all-pervasive artistic unity appeared to be a priority. At the same time a predigested, fully grown, alterna-tive cinematic language could not be expected to fall neatly from the sky at the moment of need. Such an expectation assumes that women's cinema had a developed tradition winding through the overt history of cinema like an unseen thread, or that the very fact of being a feminist and making a film would in itself answer all problems. Neither proposi-tion could hold up. The first ignores the extent of past oppression, the second asserts that individual intention transcends the language and aesthetics of cinema. To communicate, a common form is needed; or else either the pre-existing forms will survive willy-nilly or an intuitive, mystical rapport is proposed between spectator and creator, at best a matter of hit or miss.

Thus the first constructive steps towards feminist film culture have begun to turn in the direction of the matter of film language itself, probing dislocation between cinematic form and represented material, and investigating various means of splitting the established rapport between screen and spectator. One could say that, as woman's place in past cinematic representation has been mystified, made at once a linchpin of visual pleasure and an affirmation of male dominance, so feminists now — struggling to alter these apparent norms and demanding that woman's image should no longer be used in such ways — have become fascinated with the mysteries of cinematic representation itself, hitherto rendered invisible by means of the sexualised female fantasy form. A tearing of the veil, but no ready-made answers lie behind it. The absence of answers, combined with fascination with the cinematic process, act together to point towards the development of a feminist formalism with political, aesthetic and theoretical implications. Politically, a feminist formalism is based on rejection of the past and on giving priority to challenging the spectator's place in cinema, symptomatic of and integral to any ideology of representation. Aesthetically unified space and time, realist or illusionist aesthetics, have immense limitations; they cannot satisfy the complex shifts a feminist aesthetics desires. Splits in the cinematic sign allow ideas to interact with fiction, and thought with fantasy. At the same time a pleasure in *tabula rasa*, structure within deconstruction, is discernible, in which once again the bare bones of cinematic processes force themselves forward. Finally, from a theoretical point of view, it is essential to analyse and understand the workings of cinematic language – how the present reacts against the past, what shifts in meaning are associated with what shifts in form – before any further advances can be made and before claims can be set up for a new language of cinema.

At the end of May 1978, three women from the collective of the only English-language journal of feminist film theory – *Camera Obscura* (published in Berkeley, California) – presented their work at the London Film-makers' Co-op, for discussion with English film-makers (men and women) and feminists interested in the cinema. The three had been associate editors of *Women and Film*, the pioneering magazine of feminist film criticism. They broke with *Women and Film* on the grounds that feminism had to move beyond the first springboard, the basic critique of sexism and the affirmation of women's lost tradition and new images (outlined above). The new journal, *Camera Obscura*, is conceived on two linked fronts. First, the need for 'investigation and theoretical reflection on the mechanisms by which meaning is produced in film':

It is important to know where to locate ideology and patriarchy within the mode of representation in order to intervene and transform society, to define a praxis for change. Crucial to the feminist struggle is an awareness that any theory of how to change consciousness requires a notion of how consciousness is formed, of what change is and how it occurs.[6]

On the other hand, the journal takes particular texts, so far only films made by women, as 'contributing to the development of a feminist counter-cinema, both by having as their central concern a feminist problematic, and by operating specific challenges to cinematic codes and narrative conventions of illusionist cinema'. A new theory and a new practice. I was struck at the Co-op weekend by the similarity between the *Camera Obscura* assessment of needs and the assessment I was developing for this essay. I was also struck by the historic conjuncture between feminist film theory, the *Camera Obscura* presentation, and the Co-op, home of *avant-gardist* film practice – a meeting, one felt, that could not until recently have taken place. It seemed to be a concrete indication, or mutual recognition, of a growing two-way traffic: on the part of feminist theorists, use of and interest in the aesthetic principles and terms of reference provided by the *avant-garde* tradition; and on the part of the *avant-garde*, among both men and women film-makers, a sense of the relevance of the feminist challenge to representation for their work and ideas.

The Search for a Theory

Both film theory and feminism, united by a common interest in the politics of images and problems of aesthetic language, have been influenced by recent intellectual debates around the split nature of the sign (semiotics) and the eruption of the unconscious in representation (psychoanalysis). There has also been a definite influence from Louis Althusser's Marxist philosophy, especially his essay 'Ideology and Ideological State Apparatuses'.[7]

Ideology

The importance for the workings of bourgeois ideology which Althusser attributes to identification processes, imaginary representation of the subject, and illusion of reality, gave a new sense of political seriousness to aesthetic debates among *avant-garde* film-makers and film theorists. His arguments gave weight in particular to attacks on a realist aesthetic tradition, on the grounds that aesthetic unity and identification processes used means to entrap the spectator similar to those of bourgeois ideology itself. One could not, therefore, confront the other. Pam Cook, in her essay on Dorothy Arzner, makes the point that 'the system of representations generated by the classic Hollywood cinema fixed the spectator in a specific closed relationship to it, obliterating for the spectator the possibility of experiencing contradiction.'[8] This kind of argument fed into and reinforced anti-realism, providing the ground for theoretical links between *avant-gardists* opposing illusionism and political film-makers opposing bourgeois ideology. Furthermore, the debate continued around the nature of the cinematic apparatus; whether the destiny of the photographic process is simply to reproduce what it records in keeping with the natural perspective vision of the human eye, thus remaining inescapably bound to an aesthetic of realism. The answer clearly led towards formalism: foregrounding the process itself, privileging the signifier, necessarily disrupts aesthetic unity and forces the spectator's attention on to the means of production of meaning. *Camera Obscura* (in their first editorial) pointed out that:

> Like the Camera Obscura, the cinematic apparatus is not ideologically neutral, but reproduces specific ideological predispositions: codes of movement, of iconic representation and perspective. The notion that 'reality' can be reflected in film negates any awareness of the intervention, the mediation of the cinematic apparatus. The impression of reality in the cinema is not due to its capacity for verisimilitude, its ability to reproduce faithfully a copy of an object, but rather to the complex process of the basic cinematic apparatus itself, which in its totality includes the spectator.[9]

From a feminist point of view, one crucial area of struggle is with or in ideology. Patriarchal ideology is made up of assumptions, 'truths' about the meaning of sexual difference, women's place in society, the mystery of femininity, and so on. From this political point of view, feminist film theory followed the debate with interest. However, ideology — whether bourgeois or patriarchal — is rarely a blanket-like or eternal totality, and it is crucial for feminists to be aware of contrafictions within it.

Semiotics

The twentieth century has seen the growth of oppositional aesthetics, under various *avant-garde* banners and movements. Although here too women have played only a marginal part, a search for theory cannot overlook the kind of questioning and confrontations that underlie other radical aesthetic movements. I want to mention only two aspects of relations between semiotics and the *avant-garde*, both affecting women. Julia Kristeva in her work on modernist poetics has built a connection between the crisis that produced the language of modernism and 'the feminine'.[10] She sees femininity as the repressed in the patriarchal order and as standing in a problematic relation to it. Tradition is transgressed by an eruption of linguistic excess, involving pleasure and 'the feminine' directly opposed to the logical language and repression endemic to patriarchy. A problem remains: woman, in these terms, only stands for what has been repressed, and it is the male poet's relation to femininity that erupts in his use of poetic language. The next step would, from a feminist point of view, have to move beyond woman as symbolic and unspeaking to a point where women can speak themselves; beyond a definition of 'femininity' assigned by patriarchy to a language made also by women. But Kristeva's important point is this: transgression is played out through language itself. The break with the past, its connotations of masculinity unable to face the feminine, has to work through the means of meaning – making itself, subverting its norms and refusing its otherwise imperturbable totality. Here, by extension of the argument, the importance of the independent film-making sector appears fully: it is outside the constraints of commercial cinema, through reference to and in debate with the language of counter-cinema, that necessary feminist experimentation can take place. Semiotics foregrounds language and emphasises both the crucial, integral importance of the signifier (for a long time overlooked and subordinated to the signified) and the dual nature of the sign, thus suggesting the aesthetic mileage that can be gained by play on separation between its two aspects. For feminists this split, the possibility of foregrounding the signifier, has a triple attraction: aesthetic fascination with discontinuities; pleasure from disrupting the traditional unity of the sign; and theoretical advance from investigating language and the production of meaning.

Psychoanalysis

From a feminist point of view, one of the most crucial contributions made by Freudian psychoanalysis is a pinpointing of femininity as problematic for society ordered by masculine dominance. Female sexuality, and also the feminine in male sexuality, hover as difficult and potentially uncontainable elements, repressed or erupting into neurotic symptoms. Here again, there is a split, insisted on by Freud, between an appearance (whether a symptom, a habit, or a slip) and the meaning behind it. In positing an unconscious the workings of which could not find direct conscious expression, resulting as they did from initial repression, Freud showed how, psychoanalytically, things can seldom be what they seem. Thus the image of woman in patriarchal representation refers more readily to its connotations within the male unconscious, to its fears and fantasies, than to the working-through of the female Oedipus complex, confrontation with castration and sexual difference. As Claire Johnston says in her study of women in the films of Raoul Walsh:

> For the male hero the female protagonist becomes an agent within the text of the film whereby his hidden secret can be brought to light, for it is in woman that his lack is located. She represents at one and the same time, the distant memory of maternal plenitude and the fetishized object of his fantasy of castration — a phallic replacement and thus a threat.[11]

I have argued elsewhere ('Visual Pleasure and Narrative Cinema') that psychoanalysis can be used to reveal the way in which conventions of narrative cinema are tailored to dominant masculine desire — that voyeuristic pleasure is built into the way a spectator reads film.

> It is the place of the look that defines cinema, the possibility of varying it and exposing it. This is what makes cinema quite different from, say, strip-tease, theatre, shows, etc. Going far beyond highlighting a woman's to-be-looked-at-ness, the cinema builds the way she is to be looked at into the spectacle itself.[12]

Polemically, this proposition leads on to the necessity, for counter-cinema, of exposing the force of pleasure inherent in the cinematic experience in so far as it is organised around male erotic privilege and built on an imbalance between male/female, active/passive.

The Search for a Practice

The disparate elements which I have drawn together under the heading *The Search for a Theory* do not add up to a coherent whole. I have concentrated, furthermore, on those influences on feminist film theory that have implications for film-making practice — influences which all point towards both the desire and the necessity for rupture with closed, homogeneous forms of representation. Psychoanalysis dissolves the veneer of surface meanings; semiotics focuses on language itself as the point for change; confrontation with ideology brings up the issue of how a text places a spectator in relation to it. Now I want to outline influences from the *avant-garde* tradition and the ways in which feminist film-making practice has taken a position in relation to them.

Throughout this essay, I have referred to the persistent difficulty of formulating the means by which an aesthetic break can find expression; how does an independent aesthetic evolve out of confrontation with a dominant one? An important aspect of *avant-garde* aesthetics is negation: a work is formed, or driven to adopt a particular position, by the very code itself of the dominant tradition that is being opposed. These works have then to be read, achieve meaning, in the reflected light of the aesthetics they negate. One aspect of the problems implicit in formulating a new aesthetic from scratch is thus circumvented. Traditional forms are known and recognised, and the spectator can recognise and read their negation. In cinematic terms traditional illusionist aesthetics have privileged the signified, organising a text so that its mechanics would attract minimal notice. A crucial and influential response within *avant-garde* aesthetics has been pioneered by the New American Cinema of the 1960s, which stresses the place of the signifier, illuminating the complexity of the cinematic process (as Annette Michelson puts it in the introduction to *New Forms in Film*, 'the assertion of the still photographic frame composing the strip, the assertion through the flicker of the medium as projection of light, the assertion of the nature of projection through the use of sound . . .').[13] This emphasis on the importance of the signifier has thrown the place of the signified into crisis. For instance, Peter Gidal, a leading *avant-garde* film-maker in England, has rejected all content and narrative, both in his own work and as an aesthetic principle. In the introduction to *Structural Film Anthology*, he writes: 'The Structuralist/Materialist film must minimize the content in its overpowering, imagistically seductive sense, in an attempt to get through this miasmic area of "experience" and proceed with film as film.'[14]

For feminist film-makers, the way these arguments elevate the signifier is important. There is a link with those elements in feminist film theory that demand a return to *tabula rasa* and question how meaning is made as necessary steps towards revolutionising woman's image in patriarchal representation. But women cannot be satisfied with an aesthetic that restricts counter-cinema to work on form alone. Feminism is bound to its politics; its experimentation cannot exclude work on content, and it has, in this way, more in common with the *avant-garde* tradition that has attempted to radicalise the signified. Peter Wollen (in his article *The Two Avant-Gardes*) traces a line of development where the demand for a new politics inseparably links problems of form and content. Going back to Eisenstein and Vertov, influenced by Brecht, re-emerging with the late work of Godard, this tradition has broken down rigid demarcations between fact and fiction and laid a foundation for experimentation with narrative.[15]

It is hard, as yet, to speak of a feminist film-making practice. Women film-makers are still few and far between, and influences on them, arising though they do out of the aesthetic and theoretical climates I have described, are not coherent. Rather than generalising, it is preferable to exemplify tendencies and movements among women film-makers. For instance, Annabel Nicholson (a long-standing member of the London Film-Makers' Co-op) has brought together the old tradition of women's applied arts, and experiment with film as material. In her expanded piece *Reel Time*, she brings out the relationship between the projector and a sewing-machine, running loops of film of herself sewing film through the sewing-machine, then the projector, until the film tears and starts to slip. Joyce Wieland, in her first film *Handtinting* (made in New York in the 1960s) carried over her previous experiments with quilting from her art works into film, puncturing the strip with needles and dyeing the celluloid. There is also an aspect of her work which is miniature, home-movie scale: she describes *Rat Life and Diet in North America* as 'a film made at my kitchen table', and, using her pet gerbils as characters, she creates a film version of a domestic still-life.[16]

Yvonne Rainer turned to film-making from an established position as an experimental dancer (Maya Deren and Shirley Clarke also started their careers as dancers – one role in the arts where women are less likely to suffer discrimination and oppression). Rainer has done crucially important work with narrative, reinstating the possibilities of its radical use so firmly rejected by some. She describes her way of working:

> A novelist might well laugh at my makeshift dallying with story-telling. For me the story is an empty frame on which to hang images and thoughts which need support. I feel no obligation to flesh out this armature with credible details of time and place . . . I was much more concerned with interweaving psychological and formal content, i.e., with images being filled up or emptied by readings or their absence, with text and image being illustrated to various degrees . . . This made for a situation where the story came and went, sometimes disappearing altogether as the extreme prolongation of certain soundless images . . . I accumulate stuff from my own writing, paragraphs, sentences, scraps of paper, stills from previous films, photos. Ultimately the process of sorting out forces me to organize it and make the parts cohere in some kind of fashion.[17]

Rainer shifts her story-telling and gives an ironic commentary on its development by means of written titles, interrupting the flow of images, using cliché in words and in situations, dwelling on emotion and performance and women's relation to them as traditional modes of expression. As a logical result of this combination of interests, melodrama becomes a point of reference; but also, other forms of communication considered special to women — diaries, letters, intimate conversation and confidences — all distanced by an ironic handling of familiar self-doubts and self-questioning.

In my own films (co-directed with Peter Wollen) *Penthesilea* (1974) and *Riddles of the Sphinx* (1977), and also in Chantal Akerman's films, there is a meeting between the melodramatic tradition and psychoanalysis. Akerman's *Jeanne Dielman*, for example, shows the life of a woman over three days, dwelling minutely on daily repetition and domestic details. Once her routine is thrown off course, slight slips accumulate, leading almost imperceptibly to cataclysmic eruption at the end. And then Akerman's *News from Home* uses letters from an anxious mother to her daughter read as sound track over long formalist shots of New York as image track, separating sound and image to create two difference spaces with a dramatic emotional interaction. *Riddles of the Sphinx* deals with dilemmas of motherhood lived out within patriarchal society; the story of a woman (first married, in the home, then separated and working) with a two-year-old daughter is embedded in the centre of other approaches to the subject, direct or visual or poetic. The form of the film works around different kinds of heterogeneity — separations between form and content, division of the text itself into seven sections, use of single circular (360 degrees) camera movements for single scenes to build up the woman's story as a series of tableaux; and throughout, a mixture of theory and fiction, purely visual elements and exposition of ideas. What recurs overall is a constant return to woman, not indeed as a visual image, but as a subject of inquiry, a content which cannot be considered within the aesthetic lines laid down by traditional cinematic practice. Pleasure and involvement are not the result of identification, narrative tension or eroticised femininity, but arise from surprising and excessive use of camera, unfamiliar framing of scenes and the human body, the demands made on the spectator to put together disparate elements; from reading the story, the visual themes, and the ideas in conjunction with one another — a reading which is not laid down by the text but opened up as part of developing relations between feminism and experimental film and psychoanalysis.

I began by pointing out how, in the brief history of film, feminism has only recently had any impact at all. Even now, the sphere in which this impact has been felt is extremely restricted; it is a recent technological development allowing the growth of film outside the industry, but without solid, even small-scale economic foundations. The future directions of 16mm and of experimental film are uncertain, but the conjuncture between their growth and the historic eruption of feminist politics is unprecedented in the history of the arts. Here, at least, the demands of women can have a determining affect on aesthetics, as the work of feminist film theorists and film-makers gains strength and influence within the experimental sphere.

Notes

1. 'Dorothy Arzner: Critical Strategies' in Claire Johnston (ed.), *Dorothy Arzner. Towards a Feminist Cinema* (British Film Institute, London, 1975), p. 4.

2. *From Reverence to Rape: The Treatment of Women in the Movies* (London, 1974), p. 362.

3. 'Shirley Clarke: Image and Images', *Take One*, vol. iii, no. 2 (Montreal, 1972), p. 22.

4. 'Three Lives', *Women and Film*, vol. i, no. 1 (Berkeley, Calif., 1972), p. 66.

5. 'Selected Short Subjects', ibid., vol. i, no. 2 (1972), p. 38.

6. 'Feminism and Film: Critical Approaches', *Camera Obscura*, no. 1 (Berkeley, Calif., 1976), p. 3.

7. Althusser, 'Ideology and Ideological State Apparatuses', *Lenin and Philosophy and Other Essays* (London, 1971).

8. Claire Johnston paraphrasing Pam Cook, 'Approaching the Work of Dorothy Arzner' in Johnston (ed.), *Dorothy Arzner. Towards a Feminist Cinema*, p. 2.

9. 'Feminism and Film: Critical Approaches', *Camera Obscura*, no. 1 (1976), p. 10.

10. 'Signifying Practice and Means of Production', *Edinburgh '76 Magazine: Psychoanalysis, Cinema and Avant-Garde* (Edinburgh, 1976).

11. 'The Place of Women in the Cinema of Raoul Walsh' in P. Hardy (ed.), *Raoul Walsh* (Edinburgh, 1974), p. 95.

12. Laura Mulvey, 'Visual Pleasure and Narrative Cinema', *Screen*, vol. xvi, no. 3 (Autumn 1975), p. 17.

13. 'Film and the Radical Aspiration', *New Forms in Film* (Monteux, 1974), p. 15.

14. 'Theory and Definition of the Structural/Materialist Film', *Structural Film Anthology* (British Film Institute, London, 1976), p. 4.

15. 'The Two Avant-Gardes', *Studio International*, vol. cxc, no. 978 (November/December 1975).

16. 'Kay Armatage interviews Joyce Wieland', *Take One*, vol. xiii, no. 2 (1972), p. 23.

17. 'Yvonne Rainer: Interview', *Camera Obscura*, no. 1 (1976), p. 89.

NOTES ON CONTRIBUTORS

Gillian Beer is a Fellow of Girton College, Cambridge, and a University Lecturer. She is the author of *Meredith: A Change of Masks* (London, 1970), *The Romance* (London, 1970), and a number of essays on the novel. She is at present working on a book about evolutionary theory and fiction, and is one of the editors of the Clarendon George Eliot.

Inga-Stina Ewbank is Professor of English at Bedford College, London University. She is the author of *Their Proper Sphere: A Study of the Brontë Sisters as Early-Victorian Female Novelists* (London, 1966) and (with Peter Hall) *John Gabriel Borkman. English Version* (London, 1975). As well as working with Peter Hall on the National Theatre production of *John Gabriel Borkman* (1975 and 1976), she translated Ibsen's *Pillars of the Community* for John Barton's Royal Shakespeare Company production (1977), and prepared the literal translation for the National Theatre production of Geoffrey Hill's version of *Brand* (1978). She is at present working on books about Ibsen and Strindberg; a study of Shakespeare's dramatic language; and an edition of the plays of John Webster.

Elaine Feinstein is a novelist and poet who lives in Cambridge. She has written six novels including *The Crystal Garden* (London, 1973) and *Children of the Rose* (London, 1975), of which the most recent is *The Shadow Master* (London, 1978), and four volumes of poetry of which the most recent is *Some Unease and Angels: Selected Poems* (London, 1977). She is the translator of *Marina Tsvetayeva: Selected Poems* (London, 1971) and of Aliger, Moritz and Akhmadulina (Manchester, 1979), and is at present working on a biography of Marina Tsvetayeva.

John Goode is Reader in English Literature at Warwick University. He has edited (with John Lucas and David Howard) *Tradition and Tolerance in Nineteenth Century Fiction* (London, 1966) and *The Air of Reality: New Essays on Henry James* (London, 1972), as well as contributing to John Lucas (ed.), *Literature and Politics in the Nineteenth Century* (London, 1971) and an essay on 'Woman and the Literary Text' to Juliet Mitchell and Anne Oakley (eds.), *The Rights and Wrongs of Women* (London, 1976). He has recently published *George Gissing: Ideology and Fiction* (London, 1979) and is working on a study of Thomas Hardy.

Mary Jacobus is a Fellow of Lady Margaret Hall, Oxford, and a University Lecturer. She is the author of *Tradition and Experiment in Wordsworth's Lyrical Ballads, 1798* (Oxford, 1976), as well as a number of essays on Thomas Hardy and Wordsworth, and contributed to a recent collection, edited by Susan Lipshitz, *Tearing the Veil: Essays on Femininity* (London, 1978). She is at present working on a study of Thomas Hardy.

Cora Kaplan is a Lecturer in the School of English and American Studies at Sussex University. She is the editor of an anthology of women's poetry, *Salt and Bitter and Good: Three Centuries of English and American Women Poets* (New York and London, 1975), and of Elizabeth Barrett Browning's *Aurora Leigh and Other Poems* (London, 1978). She is at present working on a book on Elizabeth Barrett Browning, Emily Dickinson and Christina Rossetti.

Laura Mulvey is a free-lance writer and film-maker. Her films include *Penthesilea* (1975) and *Riddles of the Sphinx* (1977, distributed in America by the Museum of Modern Art, New York), codirected with Peter Wollen. She has taught at the Royal College of Art and at the Slade School of Art, London University, and has written for *Screen*. She is at present working on a new film script.

Elaine Showalter is Professor of English at Douglas College, Rutgers University, New Jersey. She is the author of *A Literature of Their Own: British Women Novelists from Brontë to Lessing* (Princeton, New Jersey, 1977), and is at present working on a study of madness and the Victorian imagination.

Anne Stevenson is a poet and critic who lives in Oxford. Her volumes of poetry include *Reversals* (Middletown, Conn., 1969), *Travelling Behind Glass* (London, 1974), *Correspondences* (London, 1974), and *Enough of Green* (Oxford, 1977), as well as a critical study, *Elizabeth Bishop* (New York, 1966). She is at present working on a sequence of poems in dialogue, provisionally entitled *Conversations*, and a study of puritan strains in American literature.

INDEX

198